CONTENTS

Introduction

CHARLES A. KELBLEY

Fordham University

I

THE SUBJECT OF THIS VOLUME is the incredibly complex concept of justice. No doubt, Plato's *Republic* remains the best relevant evidence for proving that this can be so. But whether justice needs to be as complex as the *Republic* makes it is another question entirely, one which, fortunately, need not be settled in this volume. For whatever the answer may be, reading that classical work, as well as most other treatises on justice, is usually enough to persuade the questioning reader that we may never be able to determine precisely where the boundaries of justice lie or just what ingredients compose its definitive nature. Perhaps, after all, justice is complex by its very nature, something which is necessarily true, it will be said, of any broad concept with endless ramifications. Although this may or may not be true, it is, importantly, true that not a few people now regard justice as hopelessly beyond rational analysis, and this is a much more troubling proposition. Accordingly, it is hoped that this volume will help to throw light on this issue. In particular, this volume aims to make a modest contribution to the seemingly perennial task of restoring faith in the value of justice as an attainable, rational value to be highly prized.

We must assume that complexity or the associated skepticism regarding the nature of justice is surely not a result intended by philosophers. Indeed, the attempts to define a conception of justice continue for very good reasons. Yet there is room for improvement. While philosophers continue to debate the correct philosophical context in which to situate justice, many non-philosophers, who are equally concerned with justice, do not even pretend to be familiar with philosophical theories of justice. Politics and economics, for example, may often be the point of departure for thinking about justice. As we shall see, there is much merit in such approaches. But philosophers, and many non-philosophers as well, are apt to suspect that wherever an economist or lawyer prizes justice without explicit reference to the underlying *value* of justice, there is likely to be a philosophical void.

The foregoing suggests three interrelated issues: *complexity*, the *interdisciplinary* approach to justice, and the *value* issue. In the course of this introduction I hope to suggest the basis for the following propositions. The complexity of

justice arises from its nature as a moral value. Moral values are relational concepts, which means that their contents depend on other values which in turn
depend on the various sources of values and concepts. All disciplines, both the
natural and the social, are at bottom systematic attempts to define values. (In
this sense, we may speak even of the *value* of nature, not merely of the *facts*
of nature.) Justice, as one of the highest values, interprets and determines the
nature of lower level values (the value of nature, for example). For this reason
it is one of the most complex of values. For this reason, also, it draws upon all
the other disciplines. This explains the relation between justice on the one hand,
and complexity, value, and interdisciplinary method, on the other.

The essays included in this volume will certainly tend to demonstrate the
complexity of justice and, at least initially, engender a certain perplexity in the
reader who surveys the various attempts herein to define and apply it. Fortunately, it seems that the more we multiply our approaches to justice, consciously avoiding an exclusive reliance upon the formal discipline of philosophy
(which is the natural home of justice conceived as a moral virtue), and the
more we employ, in addition to philosophy, the vantage points of disciplines
such as sociology, jurisprudence, constitutional law, political science, and even
natural science, the more we will come to look upon this complexity as inevitable. The frank recognition of this complexity is probably a healthy sign
of a realistic approach to justice and, perhaps paradoxically, the best way to
begin to reduce our initial perplexity. By its nature, then, justice is a subject
which requires the cooperative effort of many disciplines. This may help to
take care of the "complexity" and "interdisciplinary" issues, at least in a preliminary way.

Importantly, it follows from the above that philosophers are not necessarily
delinquent (unable or unwilling to define an intelligible and comprehensive
theory of justice). Nor have other disciplines simply become more powerful
or bolder in the tasks which they set themselves (so that justice would now
become one of their concerns too). Rather, a comprehensive approach to
justice, one which faithfully represents its many-sided nature, has always required input, both factual and theoretical, from disciplines other than philosophy. That this requirement has not always been recognized can, of course, be
accounted for in several ways. The philosopher may, for example, be narrow
or simply limited (understandably) in terms of knowledge or theoretical approach. By philosopher I do not necessarily exclude political scientists or
sociologists, etc., since anyone who philosophizes about justice, whether lawyer
or scientist, qualifies as a philosopher in some sense.

The point is that the limitations of philosophers cannot be attributed to
philosophy itself, since philosophy is not, and indeed cannot, be indifferent to
information or theory which has a bearing upon a conception of justice. Philosophers, unfortunately, can be and often are indifferent. Yet it is fundamental
to see that the theory and practice of social virtue requires contributions from

virtually every discipline, but especially from those which have a special ability to enlighten us about the structure and meaning of our social and moral nature. Even natural science, as the last essay herein demonstrates, has this ability.

In an age when the various special sciences were undeveloped, or, indeed, not even thought of, it was necessary for philosophy to proceed without benefit of the theory and information which is now available in these disciplines. But to say that sociology or political science can contribute significantly to our understanding of justice is not really to say anything very new. For even Plato's theory of justice, or, for that matter, virtually any of the historical conceptions of justice, relied upon some understanding, however primitive, of sociological, political, and economic ideas. Theories of justice have always depended upon values and other visions. This may help us to appreciate that what is sometimes said of law, that there is, contrary to popular conceptions, no "black letter" law, no law, that is, which is so fixed that it cannot be improved, changed, or even controverted, is also true of justice. In this spirit, it must be recognized, I think, that philosophy cannot and does not start anything independently. It relies upon various givens of the world and upon a constantly developing appreciation of human nature. On this basis, it perennially struggles to present a coherent basis for the theory of justice. In turn, the theory of justice will imply a theory of law as well as a set of social policies for social institutions. Whence the circularity in our approach to justice. On the one hand, the theory of justice, in its dependent position, buys, as it were, its raw materials from foreign territories. On the other hand, it comes back to these territories with directive guidance which helps to determine what will thenceforth be produced in those territories. Philosophy still learns, and doubtlessly always will, from other disciplines. Indeed, so large and diverse are the data which are available to the philosopher of justice that it becomes questionable whether any single person can master and profitably use them all as a basis for a conception of justice.

It is understandable that, by their willingness to be represented herein, and thus to assume the contingencies and vicissitudes of their work in relation to others, the contributors to this volume necessarily pass on to students of justice, not so much a set of fixed conclusions about this subject, as a set of problems (many of which the contributors could not have been aware of) which need to be seen in relation to each other. Ultimately, these problems need to be resolved in terms of a higher synthesis which will move us one step closer to that harmonious idea of justice which we are all seeking.

II

This volume is not an interdisciplinary approach to the subject of justice, in spite of the fact that several disciplines are represented by the various contributors. A truly interdisciplinary approach is quite difficult to achieve, so much so that I doubt that it has ever been accomplished, at least not in terms of what I understand this to entail. By "interdisciplinary" I mean, of course, an approach by authors from several disciplines. But in a genuinely interdisciplinary work all authors would thoroughly understand at least the basic ideas (the assumptions, methods, and conclusions) of each of the other approaches and, in some substantive way, take these other approaches into account within their own reflections on justice. It is regrettable that this is seldom achieved, even within the confines of one discipline. The philosophers who contribute to this volume, for example, will not be found doing this; nor will the authors representing other disciplines be found "interdisciplinizing" in this sense. Yet there is a commitment on the part of all the contributors to add their perspectives to the others and a tacit belief, I think, that other perspectives are relevant. From one point of view, this ignorance of each other's perspectives is in fact benign; each author writes and thinks more purely, undisturbed by the way his approach relates to or contrasts with another's. There is a value, then, in having a distinct approach speak only for itself, but with the faith that this distinction contributes to a larger view which is projected in the distance, thanks to these various perspectives.

Given the nature of these essays, it seemed appropriate to divide them into three parts. Part I contains essays which form part of what I will call the "pure theory of justice." By pure theory I mean largely the conceptual analysis of justice. For example, Robert Johann leads off with an examination of the critical relationship between "dominant ends" and the concept of justice, and how these relate to the notion of rationality. In many ways his essay is concerned more with the topic of "goodness" than it is with justice. But the appropriateness of this emphasis becomes evidently crucial in light of the fact that the very theory of justice which he criticizes, John Rawls's, is itself heavily dependent on the way in which the right (or justice) is structured in relation to the concept of the good. Without Rawls's criticism of "dominant ends," his theory of justice would be quite different. Thus, Johann's essay takes a position on what is certainly one of the most important decisions in any theory of justice: how to relate the concept of justice to the "good" and to "ends." The careful reader will want to compare Johann's position very carefully with the relevant sections of Rawls's work which Johann is criticizing.

Speaking of Rawls, the reader will find that, in addition to Johann's study, other essays (in Parts II and III in this volume) are indebted to John Rawls's *A Theory of Justice*. David Richards' analysis of the moral and constitutional issues involved in reverse discrimination and compensatory justice demonstrates the power of the Rawlsian theory of "justice as fairness." James Kelly's analysis of justice uses a sociological framework to approach the topic, but he also relies heavily on insights and principles from Rawls's work. And in my own contribution frequent use is likewise made of Rawls's theory. Today it is a commonplace to note that Rawls's work has provoked and stimulated so much thought in philosophical circles. But his work has also been fruitful in debates on justice from legal-constitutional, political, and social scientific points of view. Not only is Rawls's work, it may be said, the most provocative theory of justice in recent times, but it also exemplifies the model of a philosophy of justice which other disciplines can both profit from and, importantly, contribute to.

The second essay in Part I is concerned with the "relativity" or variability of conceptions of justice. Whereas Johann sees the concept of justice threatened for want of a "final end," Vincent Cooke sees the philosophic danger to a viable conception of justice in the "arbitrariness" often thought to be consequent upon the "relativity" of our thoughts on justice. If there are many conceptions of justice co-existing in the world, then (the observer of this scene may conclude) justice is based on an ultimate arbitrariness. But Cooke believes it is possible to accept the relativity of our conceptions of justice while still rejecting the inevitability of arbitrariness. Here Cooke approaches justice in such a way that it is not dependent on something else, such as Johann's "final end," but remains at most dependent on certain moral notions and ideals. In this connection, it is helpful to keep in mind Rawls's fruitful distinction between the *concept* of justice and *conceptions* of justice.[1] The former defines an unchanging notion (justice being the lack of arbitrary distinctions between persons and the achievement of a proper balance between competing claims); the latter (the varying conceptions of justice) interpret in different ways what it means to make an arbitrary distinction or to achieve a proper balance between competing claims. In this sense, conceptions of justice are all relative, depending on how well they interpret the concept of justice. Importantly, they would all be relative to the invariant concept of justice.

James Loughran's essay returns us to the theme of justice's dependent status. In the course of reviewing several works on ethics in the British analytic tradition, Loughran emphasizes the dependence of ethical beliefs on anthropological beliefs, on what we believe it is for people to "flourish," and in this way questions the independence of moral theory. For reliance on the "good" and on "anthropological beliefs," he argues, is a fundamental premiss for a theory of justice. This raises a problem, and readers will have to make some decisions on their own. For everything which Johann and Loughran say about the dependency of justice cannot harmoniously co-exist with what, in later essays, is defended by Richards, Kelbley, and Kelly regarding the independence of justice within the tradition of the social contract theory of morality.

Finally, Leonard Feldstein's essay departs from the more standard of the contemporary philosophical approaches to justice (Johann, Cooke, and Loughran). Nevertheless, his contextualizing of justice within an overall philosophy of the person as "harmony" is certainly an important and dominant classical theme going back to Plato. But contrary to Plato's emphasis on justice as being more or less a state of the person's (and society's) orderly arrangement, Feldstein sees justice as a "search for human being," an ongoing process of search and research in both the individual and society. The relevance of Feldstein's approach to my earlier point concerning justice as one of the highest values should be obvious: justice seeks a *balance* between competing claims, not merely of claims of citizens against citizens, but of "claims" in the more inclusive sense, including, for example, claims within myself against myself, made in the name of "personal justice." Obviously, Feldstein's combined experience as philosopher and psychoanalytic psychiatrist is a considerable enrichment of our understanding of justice. His essay is one example of the way our approach to social justice can benefit from an analysis which makes its point of departure the person.

Part I thus introduces several major themes which have traditionally been discussed in the philosophical literature treating the more purely theoretical and conceptual questions regarding justice: the relation of a "final end" to justice (Johann); the possibility of the objectivity of justice in face of the obvious plurality of conceptions of it (Cooke); the relation between anthropological beliefs and the rationale for being just (Loughran); and, finally, the conceptual puzzle of situating justice within an overall understanding of the nature of the person (Feldstein). Naturally, as has already been indicated, these essays are not free of controversy—which, incidentally, is true of each of the essays in this volume.

III

The essays in Part II are certainly not distinct from those of Part I by reason of an absence of philosophical issues and theory. Indeed, there is a great deal of philosophical argument at work in these essays, too. Yet each of the three essays is concerned in one way or another with the philosophy of law, and they thus seem to constitute by themselves an almost natural division of the book. Unlike the essays of Part I, they are concerned, especially Dolan's and Richards', with another discipline, the law.

Both Joseph Dolan's "Relocating Justice" and David Richards' essay on "reverse discrimination" are incisive critiques of the tradition in the philosophy of law known as legal positivism. Dolan and Richards reject the positivist's attempt to deprive law and justice of a basis in morality. In differing but complementary ways, both contributors use a natural law model as their foundations for locating justice and law, not, as the legal positivist would have it, in a contingent or gratuitous relationship, but in a way which makes justice, or principles thereof, the seedbed of valid law. Despite this basic agreement between Dolan and Richards, the reader will have no easy task in harmonizing their essays in other fundamental ways on the relations between law and justice.

Richards, following the Rawlsian model, plainly accepts a social contract theory of justice, whereas Dolan just as plainly rejects such a model (although without referring at all to John Rawls's recent version of the social contract theory of justice). This is clearly one of the problems which is left for the reader to adjudicate. But more important than their differences, perhaps, is their agreement that justice is based on human moral dignity, which is prior to and normative for all political arrangements.

Dolan and Richards are, then, jointly opposed to the separation of the juridical and moral orders, a thesis which is affirmed variously in all the essays in this volume. The fact that Richards sees a particular moral theory underlying constitutional values and uses this theory to support a position on compensatory justice in contemporary debates on admissions' criteria for professional schools, and the fact that Dolan does not and, instead, relies upon an Aristotelian-Thomistic framework of natural law, are perhaps less important than the fact that Richards and Dolan jointly oppose legal positivism and that their essays contribute to the resurgence of interest in a "fusion" of law and philosophy.

IV

The three essays in Part III bring various perspectives from the sciences to bear upon our reflections on justice. They take us one additional step away from the "pure theory" of Part I. Here it is not philosophy alone, or philosophy and another discipline, but science alone which begins to lead into moral theory. James Kelly's essay focuses mainly on the way in which sociologists think about justice in terms of "legitimacy," often employing, tacitly or explicitly, a moral theory to support the doctrine of legitimacy. Kelly would like to see sociologists, and social scientists in general, make their moral theories explicit and give arguments in defense of them. The legitimacy which the sociologist seeks to embody in social institutions is not unlike the justice sought by philosophers and legal scholars. In particular, Kelly argues that the aspirations of sociologists for the legitimacy of social policies can best be supported by John Rawls's theory of justice as "fairness." Once again, it is noteworthy that both Richards, a legal-constitutional scholar, and Kelly, a sociologist, have found Rawls's theory so very useful in their separate treatments of justice in the context of different disciplines.

Martin Fergus' essay approaches justice from an international perspective. Significantly, his contribution to this volume is unique in this respect. In using world hunger as the particular problem which generates the need for moral notions, Fergus reveals, at the same time, the urgency for a conception of justice which transcends national boundaries. But whereas Richards' discussion of the particular American civil rights issue of "reverse discrimination" was illumined by the moral theory of the social contract tradition, Fergus' particular problem does not immediately lend itself to resolution in the precise framework of an explicit and extant moral theory. Instead, his analysis of the hunger problem may be said to generate questions about values and the need for a moral theory to deal comprehensively with them.[2] Yet it might be profitable, as a thought experiment, to extend the "original position" device, used so well by Kelly and Richards for the social and moral problems internal to one society, to problems such as world hunger which involve relations between many societies. In principle, there would seem to be no reason why the moral critique of "arbitrariness," as applied to the social and natural endowments of individuals and groups within one society, should not be vigorously applied to the arbitrarily conferred social and natural endowments of entire countries or continents.[3] Unfortunately, this is a gargantuan task, the achievement of which depends upon many things—chiefly, the development and enrichment of the moral sense of individual countries and of international political and legal theory.

Finally, Richard Rozett, whose field is chemistry, explores a number of problematic relations between man and the natural world, mediated through and engendered by the various technologies built upon science. The difficult choices, which modern science and technology force us to make, reveal what is probably the most neglected area in the theory of justice: man's relations with the natural world. It is unfortunate that the theory of justice has traditionally been concerned almost exclusively with human or, better, interhuman relations. Even property law, where, within the traditional, substantive fields of law, one would most expect to find a treatment of man's relations with the natural world, not so much treats of the rightful relations between man and world as "deals with the relationship between persons with respect to things."[4] Thus, the importance of things and the natural world is derivative, depending upon relationships between persons. As Rozett's essay demonstrates, we are only now beginning to be acutely aware of the unfortunate effects of this anthropocentric view of justice. Beyond the current interest in environmental law, we desperately need development of that part of the theory of justice concerned with our relations with the natural world.

NOTES

1. *A Theory of Justice* (Cambridge: Harvard University Press, 1971), pp. 8–10.
2. For several competing approaches to the moral issues involved in the hunger problem, see *World Hunger and Moral Obligation*, edd. William Aiken and Hugh La Follette (Englewood Cliffs, N.J.: Prentice-Hall, 1977).
3. See Brian Barry, *The Liberal Theory of Justice* (Oxford: Clarendon, 1973).
4. Charles Donahue, Jr., Thomas E. Kauper, and Peter W. Martin, *Property: An Introduction to the Concept and the Institution* (St. Paul: West, 1974), p. xv.

I
PHILOSOPHICAL ISSUES
IN THE
THEORY OF JUSTICE

1

Rationality, Justice, and Dominant Ends

ROBERT O. JOHANN
Fordham University

IN *A Theory of Justice*, John Rawls makes the statement: "It seems indisputable, then, that there is no dominant end the pursuit of which accords with our considered judgments of value" (p. 558).[1] Indeed, underlying any claim that there is such an end lurks a streak, so Rawls contends, of fanaticism and inhumanity. If this is not always immediately manifest, it is because of "the vagueness and ambiguity of the end proposed" (p. 554). Here Rawls alludes to the Ignatian ideal of seeking always to do what is "most for the glory of God" (p. 553), and to Aquinas' view that "the vision of God is the last end of all human knowledge and endeavor" (p. 554). Yet, although less manifestly extreme, such conceptions are nonetheless disfigurements of the self. So "to subordinate all our aims to one end . . . strikes us as irrational, or more likely as mad" (p. 554). For it means putting the self "in the service of one of its ends for the sake of system" (p. 554). But, as surely everyone knows, or at least ought to know, "Human good is heterogeneous because the aims of the self are heterogeneous" (p. 554).

I have quoted Rawls at some length because in these passages he so clearly exemplifies the kind of passionate opposition—all the more remarkable in a book otherwise noteworthy for its balance and moderation—which mention of a final end can be counted on to provoke in some contemporary circles. Final end, *summum bonum*, normative human nature—these and all such notions are ruled out of court as basically inimical to man's essential dignity and freedom, which is taken to consist in forming his individual conception of the good life and, as long as it allows others to do likewise, living accordingly. This stance is regrettable. There is no quarrel here with the idea that freedom is our most precious possession. But I do contend that liberal hostility to the notion of final end is founded on a misconception. Indeed, I maintain that Rawls's view that there is no dominant end the pursuit of which accords with our considered judgments of value is simply false. What I plan to do in this essay, therefore, is first to sketch out a conception of the function of the final end (one different from that assigned to it by Rawls) and then to indicate why the notion is indispensable. Next I shall suggest a candidate for the role of final end which would seem immune to Rawls's criticism. Finally, I shall indicate the essential shortcoming of any moral theory (including that of *A Theory of Justice*) which rejects the idea of final end.

I

In order to clarify the precise function which the final end is called on to fulfill, it will be necessary to make a pair of preliminary distinctions. The first is that between the self as subject and the self as object.[2] This distinction is not meant to point to anything very abstruse. It is founded, rather, on two quite ordinary ways of viewing or considering a human being, the personal and the impersonal way, respectively. To view a human being impersonally is to attend only to that about him which is or can be known by observation and manipulation. This approach corresponds to the object-self. It is that dimension of the self which is disclosed when the self, without being engaged in communication, is made the object or term of various investigative operations. To consider a human being personally, on the other hand, is to view him precisely as an intentional source (*intentio intendens*). This, the subject-self, is what one is aware of about oneself in the very exercise of one's intentional life. It is the self of which one is conscious, not as something attended to, but in the very act *of attending to* anything whatever. Also, the subject-self is what one knows of the other when the other is engaged *in person*, as co-source of a dialogue. It is the self as free initiative, a being meaningful to us, not only as a *what*, a quiddity, one of a kind, but also as a *who*, as uniquely existing, a being whose act is self-position. The subject-self, therefore, is the self as continually defining itself, taking personal stands, giving or withholding its allegiance, saying "I will" or "I will not," "I do" or "I do not." It is the inquiring, judging, deciding, choosing, intentionally active self. The object-self, on the other hand, is everything about oneself which is or can be known independently of one's intentional life, i.e., which is what it is regardless of the way in which one is aiming oneself.

This distinction should not be misunderstood. The subject-self and the object-self are not two selves, but two dimensions of one and the same self. Moreover, the two dimensions are not simply different aspects of the self, each extrinsic to and exclusive of the other. They are related to one another as the concrete to the abstract, the inclusive to that which is included but able to be attended to apart from its context. Thus one cannot consider or deal with someone as subject without also being aware of him as an object in the world. For it is the object-self which mediates the presence of the subject-self. But one can prescind from the personal and subjective dimension of the self and attend to it only as an object in the world.

The first distinction between the self as simply given and the self as intentional source leads us to the second and correlative one. It is a distinction between two ways of viewing a human choice, which again we can term the *objective* way and the *subjective* way. To view a choice objectively is to view it in terms of what is chosen, a specific change of the inclusive situation in which the object-self is located, and one undertaken by the self because of its presumed connection with some intended state of affairs (end) to which it leads. The choice, objectively considered, is thus the *becoming* of an end and will make sense insofar as it is taken to lead to the end aimed at.

To view a choice subjectively, on the other hand, is to consider it precisely as an intentional act, a determinate self-positing of the subject-self. From this angle, choice is the commitment of the chooser to the end for which the specific change is being undertaken. It is thus a matter of *being* rather than of *becoming*, a determinate way of being for the subject and something which will have to be justified, not in terms of what it leads to, but in terms of what it is.

As with the earlier distinction, this is a matter, not of two realities, but of two dimensions or aspects of one and the same reality, one and the same choice. And again they are related to one another as the inclusive and the included. Thus choice as a realization of the subject can make sense only if choice as a specific objective change makes sense. The way the subject exists as a result of the choice, after all, is precisely as one who is intentionally transforming the objective situation in a specific way because of the end to which he is committed. But to approve of choice as a specific change of the objective situation —i.e., to accept it as making sense in view of a given end—is not necessarily to approve of it, or even to be able to approve of it, as a determinate realization of the subject-self. The state of affairs (end) to which the objective choice leads may be one which the chooser happens to want but not one which he can approve of his wanting. In other words, if he wants such and such an end, then a certain course of action commends itself as the one to be followed, i.e., as making the most sense. But whether or not what he thus finds himself wanting is really worth pursuing or even worthy of his allegiance is an altogether different question.

This brings us to the first point which I should like to make, the one concerning the function of a final end. This function has been interpreted as one of eliminating or narrowing the scope of purely preferential choice in determining the good. Its primary role has been seen as providing grounds for deciding which of the ends we happen to desire it would be most rational to pursue. This is the job assigned to it, for example, by Rawls. He notes that in teleological theories, where the idea of the right depends on a prior definition of the good, any vagueness or ambiguity in the conception of the good is transferred to that of the right. Hence if the good of individuals is something that, so to speak, is just up to them to decide as individuals, so likewise within certain limits is that which is right. But it is natural to think that what is right is not a matter of mere preference, and therefore one tries to find a definite conception of the good [p. 559].

And the way to do this is to appeal to a final end in relation to which everything else which we may want is a mere means. What our good would be in a particular situation, then, would not be what we just happen to prefer, but what most promotes this final end:

> For if there exists such an end to which all other ends are subordinate . . . the procedure for making a rational choice, and the conception of such a choice, would then be perfectly clear: deliberation would always concern means to ends, all lesser ends in turn being ordered as means to one single dominant end. The many finite chains of reasons eventually converge and meet at the same point. Hence a rational decision is always in principle possible . . . [p. 552].

It is clear from these quotations that the dimension of choice which is being considered here and for which a final end is supposed to provide a rational basis is what I have called the objective dimension. The "final end" is being taken as some final, factual state of affairs, progressively achievable by action, toward which all our choices can be seen as so many steps. And these choices themselves (the value of which as means depends, not on their being intended, but on their being of certain kinds) are being viewed, not as intentional acts, but as specific transformations of the situation. Thus every choice results in a state of affairs which more or less approximates the final state, and it will be justified to the extent that, among the alternatives available, what it accomplishes is the closest approximation.

All well and good. But it is equally clear that no basis at all is being provided in this scheme for choices subjectively viewed. Given this final end, whatever most promotes it is what I should do. But is my pursuit of this end itself justifiable? If its status as an end comes simply from the fact that I find myself most drawn to it, the question of its real worth is left unanswered, as is the question of whether I really ought to pursue it. On the other hand, since it is the final end, the ultimate state of affairs, there would seem to be nothing beyond it in the light of which its own worth could be appraised. If, therefore, it is had as worthy of the subject's allegiance, this cannot be a matter of judgment (for evaluative judgments require standards of appraisal), but must be something immediately self-evident. But no determinate state of affairs, for reasons which I shall indicate shortly, is self-evidently beyond criticism or possessed of a *de jure* final quality.

It would seem clear, therefore, that this first interpretation of the nature and function of a final end in theories of choice bears on only one aspect of choice:

its objective dimension. If it should turn out that a "final end" so conceived does not really help matters—and I think Rawls's criticism of it more than exposes its futility—this would not necessarily mean that the notion of a final end can therefore be set aside. For it might be the case—and I shall, I hope, show that it is—that the role of final end is tied not to choice viewed objectively, but to choice precisely as a realization of the subject. Instead of its being a matter of reducing the need for relying on individual preference in determining the good, the primary function of a final end is to enable the chooser to discern whether whatever he turns out to want most really deserves to be brought into existence. Given the fact that he wants it, can he also approve of his, or of anyone else's for that matter, wanting it? In other words, the function of a final end is to enable the chooser reflectively to ratify his choices when these are viewed subjectively. Unless there is a final end—but one which, as we shall see in a moment, necessarily transcends the determinate states of affairs which our actions effect—then, however rational it may be for me to do this or that, given my inclinations, there is absolutely no basis for approving of my having such inclinations, much less of my going along with them.

Let us at this point, then, examine in more detail just how the final end must be conceived if it is to serve the function being assigned to it here. When that is done, I shall provide further arguments showing the necessity of this function.

What we are looking for is an end which is normative for the subject's intentional life. It must be something in relation to which his various intentions, precisely as actualizations of his subject-self, can be appraised as worthy or unworthy. This means that no end which is an end for the subject only by choice, i.e., only insofar as he happens to intend it, can serve this function. For what depends on one's intentional life cannot be normative for it. The end in question, therefore, must be one to which the subject-self is ordered by its very nature and antecedent to its particular intentions. Without at this point saying positively what this might be, we can rule out the kind of "final end" we have been dealing with so far. That is to say, the subject-self cannot be ordered by nature to any matter-of-fact, determinate state of affairs as final end. For the final end of the subject must be something to the nature of which his own being and activity as a subject are inherently relevant. It must be something which somehow includes him in his subjectivity and is a function of his life as subject. But this the empirically determinate does not and is not. The empirical order involves the subject only insofar as it involves his actions, but these are involved, not as intentional, i.e., not as aimed by the subject at an end, but only as specific changes in a wider process of becoming. In other words, the intentional character of the changes by which an objective state of affairs is brought about has no bearing on what that state turns out to be. This is a function of the objective nature of those changes, not of whether or how they were meant. But a reality in relation to the existence and nature of which the subject and his intentions as such are irrelevant cannot be that to which the subject is ordered by his own nature. It may be something more or less congenial to himself as object, something the subject finds his object-self more or less drawn to. But it is not an end for him precisely as subject until he adopts it. Thus when Rawls remarks (see p. 560) that the self is prior to the ends which it affirms and that even a dominant end must be chosen, what he says is true of the subject-self in relation to any empirical state of affairs intended as final end. But all this means is that no empirical state of affairs, including, it should be noted, the satisfaction of the felt needs of the object-self, can by itself justify a subject's intending it. (This, by the way, is what is wrong with any theory which limits the practical thrust of reason and inquiry, i.e., rational deliberation, to investigating the ways and means of most effectively, reliably, and comprehensively reaching the goals which have been set by nature independent of reason. No given inclination of the object-self nor any set of such inclinations, however harmoniously they may be organized into a "rational plan," can be judged as worth following simply because they are given. And if they cannot be judged as worth following, then the subject cannot approve of his doing so. More will be said about the practical thrust of reason in the final part of this paper.) The final end which we are seeking, therefore, cannot be conceived as some final state of affairs to be empirically effected, and in relation to which everything else accomplished is to be appraised as means. How then is it to be conceived?

The first thing to be said (and this follows from the points just made) is that the final end must be conceived as essentially a matter of intention. If the subject's intentional life is essentially relevant to it, then it must be something the reality of which depends on its continually being intended by the subject. This does not mean that the order of empirical fact has no bearing on it. As we saw earlier, the subject-self is inclusive of the (empirical) object-self. The subject's intentions are real only as embodied in empirical change. So here, this final matter of intention will be inclusive of the order of empirical change, and the latter will be necessary to its constitution. But the import of these changes will be primarily as mediating the subject's intentions, and only secondarily as bringing about a determinate state of affairs.

The final end, therefore, is not the end of a process of becoming, but the end of an intentional orientation. And, as *final end*, it is the term of an *original* orientation, a kind of operative intentionality which is antecedent to and underlies all the particular intentions of the subject. This operative intentionality is indeed identical with the subject's very nature as subject. He is, therefore, precisely as subject, an interest in an end. Since this interest underlies all his intentional activities, it is by its very nature a standard for appraising any standards which the subject may subsequently adopt, e.g., any of the inclinations of the object-self. And since the end in which the subject is thus interested is what he is really about in all that he does, it is indeed a final end in the light of which all other ends can be evaluated. But, *pace* Rawls, here is an end which, since it underlies choosing, is not an end only as chosen. Nor is the self prior to it, since the self as subject is constituted only in relation to it.

Finally, as that in the light of which all judgments of appraisal are ultimately made, this end is present to us as having an ultimate and unconditional worth. Unlike some determinate state of affairs toward which I find myself inclined, it is not something the connection of which with me is just another fact about me. Neither, however, since it is final, is its worth grasped in a judgment of appraisal—there being nothing beyond it in the light of which it might be appraised. Rather, its worth is grasped implicitly in the appraisal of anything else, since only as somehow contributing to this end will anything at all be seen to have objective worth. The final end we are talking about, therefore, is not simply the ultimate reality toward which I am, as a matter of fact, ordered. It has a *de jure* quality. It is present as having rightful authority in the direction of conduct, an ultimate claim on the allegiance of the rational subject.

II

I said earlier that I would suggest a candidate for this role of final end. But before I do so, let me expound a little on the reasons why a final end is necessary. The role, once again, is to provide a ground or basis for choice as determinate actualization of the subject-self. The need for this conception stems from some of our most ordinary and basic convictions, it being a necessary idea if our theory is to do justice to these convictions. Interestingly enough, Rawls shares these convictions but, because of his denial of a final end, is unable, I contend, to account for them.

One such conviction is that it is possible for a person to fail simply as a person. This is a matter, be it noted, not of failing to reach the goals which one has set for oneself, but of setting the wrong goals. Rawls, as we saw, speaks of a disfigurement of the self. The disfigurement which he has in mind is, to be sure, the one resulting from the pursuit of any goal as a dominant or final end. It is not that one is bound to fail in such an effort. The point is that one should not try. To subordinate all one's concerns to the achievement of any empirically determinate objective, no matter what it may be, is already to be wrong. Now, I think that this is true. But the interesting thing is that what is wrong here is not, as Rawls believes, the self's commitment to a final end, but the mis-identification of that end with some determinate objective to which the object-self happens to be drawn. Indeed, I maintain that the only thing which *can* be wrong with pursuing an empirical goal as final end is that such a pursuit is at odds with one's essential vocation as a person. That is, the pursuit of such an end as final conflicts with the subject-self's final end. Moreover, without the latter final end as a standard, it is impossible even to judge, much less to condemn, the pursuit in question. Let me explain.

If we take the view of the self which I have presented, the way in which a person might fail as a person or the self become disfigured is clear and straightforward. Since the subject-self is, by its nature, the operative intention of a reality which includes it in its very subjectivity, to orient itself ultimately toward a goal which interests and involves only the object-self is to be at odds with itself, "disfigured," if you like. Moreover, since this constitutive interest of the subject-self is present as having an ultimate claim on its allegiance, no orientation at odds with it will be rationally defensible. Indeed, any such orientation will be *objectively* wrong—wrong for anyone.

But now let us take Rawls's view of the self. Rawls, to be sure, does not distinguish between the subject-self and the object-self, but some such distinction is necessary, I think, to make sense of what he says. Thus he remarks in one place (as we have seen): "For the self is prior to the ends which are affirmed by it; even a dominant end must be chosen from among numerous possibilities" (p. 560). Just a little earlier, however, he says (as we have also seen): "Human good is heterogeneous because the aims of the self are heterogeneous" (p. 554). And what disfigures the self is its being "put in the service of *one of its ends* for the sake of system" (p. 554; emphasis added). Now, I contend that, as they stand, these two sets of remarks do not fit together. To say that the self is prior to the ends which it affirms and that even a dominant end must be chosen is to be talking about ends which are not ends until the self adopts them. To speak, on the other hand, of a heterogeneity of aims or ends which the self must respect if it is not to disfigure itself is to be talking about ends which are ends, not by adoption, but by nature. Only in this way can they be in any way normative for the self. This, we may remark, is no insignificant slip-up. It manifests a confusion at the very heart of Rawls's understanding of man and it is crucial to his theory.

Now, we can begin to make sense of this if we distinguish the subject and object dimensions of the self. Although the subject-self is not prior to the final end but is constituted in relation to it, it is prior to any empirical state of affairs taken as end. The object-self may be naturally inclined toward various such states of affairs, i.e., they may be ends for it in the sense that it has native or acquired tendencies toward them. But they are ends for the subject only if the subject adopts them. Or, perhaps more exactly, they become *actual* ends for the subject only when the subject adopts them; before that, they are *possible* ends. Thus when Rawls asserts that the self is prior to the ends affirmed by it, he would, from our point of view, be speaking of the subject-self in relation to these possible empirical ends. And when he speaks of the heterogeneous aims of the self, he would be understood as referring to the multiple inclinations and tendencies of the object-self. The ends by nature of the object-self are only possible ends for the subject and must await its decisions for confirmation.

This, I think, removes part of the incoherence of the remarks cited (it shows how the same ends of the self can both be and not be ends by choice, both be and not be ends by nature). But the basic contradiction remains. For in asserting the priority of the self over its ends, Rawls is denying any original intentionality underlying all the self's activities or any final end in the light of which all its adopted ends can be appraised. Prior to its actual choices, the choosing self has no task to accomplish, no goals to reach. These arise only when, consulting its given inclinations, the self adopts some plan of life. But, if this is the case, then failure as a person and self-disfigurement become impossible. If the person has no end simply as a person, he cannot fail as a person. And if there is no form or figure which the self as such is supposed to realize or maintain, then the self cannot by its choices disfigure itself. And this is true, no matter what the self does and no matter what the reason, whether it be "for the sake of system" or whatever. For this type of failure and disfigurement imply an evaluation of choice, not as objective change, but as actualization of a self. But, as we have seen, there is no basis for evaluating a choice so viewed other than in the light of a final end conceived as we have conceived it.

There is another related conviction which Rawls shares—indeed, he places great emphasis on it—but which his theory cannot do justice to, and precisely because of his rejection of the notion of final end. This conviction has to do with the fundamental importance of self-respect in human life. Rawls indeed considers it the most important of the primary goods: "Without it nothing may seem worth doing, or if some things have value for us, we lack the will to strive for them. All desire and activity becomes [sic] empty and vain" (p. 440). For self-respect, as Rawls defines it (and I have no problem in following him here), has two aspects: "First of all . . . it includes a person's sense of his own value, his secure conviction that his conception of his good, his plan of life, is worth carrying out. And second, self-respect implies a confidence in one's ability . . . to fulfill one's intentions" (p. 440). Without these, one cannot devote oneself energetically to anything.

Now, what interests me here is the first aspect of self-respect, the secure conviction that one's plan of life is worth carrying out. It is my contention that in the context of Rawls's theory, and more specifically in view of his denial of a final end, a conviction of any kind, secure or otherwise, about the worth of one's plan of life is not only impossible, but meaningless. For, presumably, what Rawls is talking about is not just a matter of feeling but a matter of judgment. A conviction about the worth of my plan of life is more than a liking for it; it is a case of reflective approval. It presupposes a question in the form: Is what I find myself doing and perhaps even liking to do really worth doing? And the judgment of approval is an answer in the affirmative. Unless such a question is possible, no such judgment is possible, and if the question is meaningless, the judgment is all the more so. What then is required for a question about the worth of an action to be possible? As a step toward an answer, it should be noted first of all that such a question can be asked in two senses. I may be asking about the worth of an action, relative to an individual's actual aims and purposes. Given someone committed to such and such an objective, is the action contemplated one which can claim his rational allegiance? Or more simply: Is the action one which it is rational for him to do? Thus, in Rawls's theory, the worth of particular actions is judged in the light of the rational plan which a person has adopted. In our language, it is the evaluation of a possible choice, considered objectively. However, I may also be asking about the worth of an action absolutely, i.e., regardless of one's previous commitments. Again in our language, this is evaluating the action, not as a specific transformation of the objective situation, but as a determinate realization of the subject.

Now, it is clear that when the action under consideration is one of adopting and carrying out a rational plan, the question about its worth is necessarily being asked in this second sense, i.e., absolutely. If I am asking about the worth of my plan of life, I am asking, not about what is worth doing, given my commitments, but precisely about the worth of those commitments. But such a question makes sense only if there is an original interest underlying all the subject's actions in the light of which they can be appraised. For to ask about the worth of anything is to ask whether choosing it is consistent with some antecedent orientation. Apart from an antecedent orientation, no question of worth can arise; indeed, none would be meaningful. When, however, that whose worth is being questioned is one's very plan of life, i.e., one's overall commitment, the antecedent orientation has to be a natural orientation of the subject as such, one intrinsic, that is, to the very process of rational inquiry and judgment. For only as underlying inquiry and judgment could it be present as rationally normative for the subject. To deny such a natural orientation, then, is to make the question about the worth of one's rational plan, not only impossible, but meaningless. It is to negate one of the question's essential presuppositions. But this is precisely what anyone does who rules out of court the very idea of final end. For, as we have seen, the final end is nothing other than the term of the natural orientation of the subject-self.

III

So much for our first two points—the function of the final end and the need for it. What I want to do now is to suggest a candidate which can fulfill that function and still be immune to Rawls's criticisms. The candidate which I have in mind is the reality of shared experience, our participation in a common life. What I am saying is that the subject is essentially involved in a communicative process. I do not mean by this that he is always and inevitably engaging others (in person) in a dialogue. What I mean, rather, is that his life is essentially a shared undertaking in a shared world; it is a life in response to meanings which arise through communication and articulate the desires and expectations of others in his regard. It is this common life which alone provides the context in which the self-disposition implied in any deliberate act first becomes meaningful. And it is the maintenance of that life which he necessarily intends, whatever else he intends. For, on the one hand, involvement in the communicative process (or common life) can only be intentional—one cannot be so involved without meaning to be so. On the other hand, since this involvement is essential to his being as a subject, his intending it is logically antecedent to any of his particular intentions and is presupposed in all of them. Let us look at this more closely.

Our common life is essentially a matter of intention—it exists only as continually meant. And each of us as subjects—i.e., as intentional agents, forever aiming ourselves now at this goal, now at that—each of us exists only as intending, whatever else each intends, his involvement in that life and its maintenance and development. As term of this intending, our common life is thus an end. And since this intending is original and essential, constitutive of us as subjects and presupposed in all our intentions, its term is the End presupposed by all our ends.

To intend an end is to be subject to its requirements, i.e., to be obligated to the means necessary to attain it. Since the end in question is not an objective state of affairs, but the transobjective reality of our common life, the means necessary to it are not specific changes of the objective environment, but determinate ways of comporting and regulating ourselves in relation to one another. Moreover, since the End as all inclusive presents itself as having a final and total claim on our allegiance, the means to it, these ways of comporting and regulating ourselves in relation to another, present themselves as obliging us absolutely and unconditionally.

What this means is that in forming my aims and purposes, I, the subject, am unqualifiedly obliged to do so in a way consistent with the requirements of our common life. These come down essentially to a certain respect for, and responsiveness to, the other as you, i.e., as an equal partner with me in the joint enterprise which is our common life. Not to do so, to pursue my objectives without regard for you, and in ways, therefore, which are inconsistent with the requirements of the communicative process, is not only to be at odds with myself (with my essential reality as subject), but, also insofar as it means subordinating the comprehensive reality of our common life to something which ultimately has meaning only in terms of it, to be doing something which is rationally indefensible.

Our common life thus becomes the supreme goal and the final standard of objective worth. Only in the measure to which it somehow contributes to this inclusive good can any action or object be judged to have objective worth or to be objectively good. But (and this is worth noting in connection with Rawls's theory) this supreme good cannot be defined or understood in complete independence of the right, i.e., of what is morally required. (Rawls suggests that a theory which does not specify the good independently from the right [p. 30] is deontological. It would seem that the theory being defended here, despite its insistence on the notion of "final end," fits that definition.) Indeed, as we have seen, the order of right is intrinsic to it and necessary to its constitution. For "the right" is that order of regulative meanings which spell out the requirements of the communicative relation and to which our actions must conform if communication and fellowship are to be maintained. Morality in general and justice in particular are precisely a matter of regulating our lives individually and collectively in the light of those meanings. And since not to do so is, as we saw above, rationally indefensible, morality in general and justice in particular refer simply to what it is rational to do without further qualification. As essentially ordered to our common life, the rational subject is already confronted with rational exigencies independent of his particular intentions. The device of the original position is thus no longer necessary (see pp. 17–21). The just (or moral) arrangement is not the one which it would be rational for one to choose in the original position, i.e., as a person committed to a certain objective and under certain limiting conditions. The just (or moral) arrangement is, rather, that which accords with my rational nature prior to any of my commitments. It is that arrangement which it is categorically, and not merely hypothetically (as inevitably in Rawls's theory),[3] rational to adopt.

Now, it seems to me that this view of man's final end is not inspired by some lurking streak of inhumanity or fanaticism. If one recognizes that essential to our humanity is our capacity to appraise the worth of what we contemplate doing and to act accordingly, then the position adopted here would seem the only one which preserves the humanity of our basic commitments. By providing a standard in the light of which such commitments can be appraised, it enables these fundamental acts of self-definition to be human acts. Ultimate stands can be taken rationally, i.e., not because the subject simply finds himself powerfully attracted to one or another, but because he can grasp their objective worth. This, we have seen, is the basic function of the final end. It is meant, not to eliminate pure preferential choice, but to allow the subject to determine whether what he happens to prefer is worth pursuing. If it turns out that different possible courses are equally consistent with the requirements of this End, then it is perfectly proper for the subject to consult his inclinations. As in basic accord with the communicative relation and as a way to embody it, whatever in this case the subject happens to prefer will also be rationally justified. If, however, one or another possible course presents itself as more consistent with the End than the remaining ones, then that is the course which it will be rational to follow. But if what one is inclined to do is utterly irrelevant to the End, then it has to be judged as objectively worthless and a waste of time. One thinks here of Rawls's example (see p. 432) of the man with the passion for counting blades of grass.

The alleged "vagueness" of the less extreme final end theories can now be understood. It results from the recognition that man's final end, that in the light of which his very commitments are to be appraised, is necessarily a matter of intention. As the transobjective reality of fellowship, it transcends the determinate and matter of fact and is able to be realized with infinite variety. The fact that having such an End leaves the question about the most appropriate way of realizing it one which subjects must deliberate afresh in each new situation is no argument against it. Or rather, it will be seen to be an argument only if one has misconceived the function of the final end.

Something similar must be said in connection with Rawls's contention that there is no dominant end the pursuit of which accords with our considered judgments of value. This would clearly be the case if the dominant end were identified with some determinate state of affairs—that is to say, if the dominant end were misconceived. Indeed, how could it be otherwise? But not only is it not true of the dominant end which I have proposed, but my proposal would seem to provide an explanation for how our considered judgments of value, both in general and specifically, get to be that way. The general account we have already considered. It is because the subject is essentially an intention of the communicative relation that he finds himself in the very exercise of his intentional life categorically subject to its requirements. If he ignores them and acts in ways at odds with them, he inevitably experiences himself at odds with his own being as well as with all rational beings. He is aware of himself as deserving condemnation. This is how we come to have considered judgments of value prior to our theorizing about them.

But our proposal would seem to account for our specific convictions as well. Without going into any detail, let me briefly indicate how the very principles of justice which Rawls affirms to be in accord with our considered convictions in this area are at least *prima facie* rooted in the subject's nature. His two principles are the principles of equal liberty and the difference principle, or more generally the principle of freedom and the principle of equality. As for freedom, it is clear that the communicative relation presupposes the autonomy of the parties to it. For communication is essentially a matter of intention, and to intend something is not simply *to be aimed in* a certain direction; it is to aim oneself. It is a matter of self-disposition or self-regulation. I cannot effectively intend the communicative relation, therefore, without intending the other's independence of me. To coerce him or to interfere with his capacity to make up his own mind is to deal with him, not as a subject and partner, but as an object subordinate to my ends. As noted earlier, respect for the other's integrity as subject and responsiveness to him on that basis are essential requirements of a common life. To be essentially involved in such a life is to be categorically subject to those requirements.

In this connection, we may note in passing that, unlike what is commonly imagined by those who reject the notion of a final end, it does not, when adequately conceived, prevent or restrict the individual from forming his own conception of the good life. Quite the contrary. For since the final end is our union *as subjects* in a common life, our integrity as subjects must, as I remarked above, be strictly safeguarded. This means that no one has the right to impose on another his own judgments about what should be done. Each must be free to direct his life as he sees fit, as long as doing so does not interfere with the right of others to do likewise. And as for setting up specific priorities, this must be a matter, not of unilateral dictation, but of genuine communication, i.e., a continual process of coming to mutually acceptable terms. The final end thus provides a basis for individual judgment; it does not eliminate it.

Something similar can be said about the principle of equality. As Macmurray observes, "equality . . . is an aspect of the mutuality of the (personal) relation,"[4] and is implied by it. To intend the communicative relation is to intend the other as co-source *with* me of our common life. To intend him other than as equal is to intend him, not as subject, but in some sense as a means to my ends. The principle of equality does not imply a *de facto* equality, therefore. It does not mean that the parties have, as a matter of actual fact, equal powers or abilities. Like the reality of which it is an aspect, the equality is intentional. On the other hand, if I really intend the other to function equally with me in determining our common life, I cannot be indifferent to the actual inequities under which he may labor as a result of what Rawls has called the natural and social lotteries, and which inevitably limit his effective contribution. For our functioning as subjects is mediated by, and dependent upon, objective factors. Disparity with respect to the latter will mean disparity in the former. An effective intention of the communicative relation implies, therefore, an effort to equalize the conditions under which the parties to it function. And this, I would suggest, comes tolerably close to Rawls's second principle.

IV

This brings me to my final point. So far I have been at pains to show how it is possible to conceive of a final end in a way which not only accords with our considered judgments of value but actually grounds them. Now I want to go a step further. This final step, which, with all that has preceded, can be briefly sketched, is the counterclaim that no theory dispensing with the notion of final end can really do justice to our considered moral judgments.

In order to support this claim, let me first make explicit two distinct conceptions of reason which underlie the contrasting views which we have been examining. According to one conception—and this is the one presupposed by Rawls—reason is primarily and essentially theoretical, and only secondarily and accidentally practical. This means that the basic function of reason is not to do, but to know; not to accomplish anything in the order of existence, but to translate what exists into an order of ideas. This is not to say that reason has no practical relevance. Given a being with aims and desires, reason can explore the way in which these are interconnected and the conditions on which their realization depends. Having no practical aims of its own, it has no way of appraising the aims with which it is confronted; yet it can determine cognitively what is required for their accomplishment.

According to the second conception—and this is the one implicit in the position which I am defending—reason is primarily and essentially practical, and only secondarily and derivatively theoretical. This means that the basic function of reason is not to know (however much knowing may be involved in fulfilling its function) but to do, to bring into being what cannot exist without it. Reason seeks to accomplish the rational good—to do what it makes sense to do, to bring about a world in which the rational subject is at home. Reason is thus originally a practical intention of a world in accord with its own nature, a world which makes sense. It is, moreover, an unrestricted intention of sense. By that I mean reason's thrust is not restricted to what can be had as making sense from some limited point of view or perspective. It is not restricted, for example, to determining what it makes sense to do given one's commitment to this or that objective. For since such commitments themselves are "doings" of the subject, the question inevitably arises whether or not they make sense. The practical thrust of reason, therefore, extends to what makes unconditional or unquestionable sense, i.e., to what makes sense for the rational subject as such. What this is we have already seen. It is the maintenance and development of our common life, that inclusive context within which the rational subject is essentially situated. Reason, in its original nature, therefore, is the practical intention of the communicative relation as alone making unconditional sense, and the requirements of this relation inevitably present themselves as having an unconditional claim on its allegiance.

This distinction between two conceptions of reason is apparently lost sight of by Rawls when he asserts flatly that: "The concept of rationality by itself is not an adequate basis for the concept of right" (p. 404). What he says is perfectly true if reason is understood as essentially theoretical. If reason's practical aims are all accidental to it, then clearly no course of action can be more than conditionally rational or good. That is to say, something will be the rational thing to do and so a good course for someone to adopt, given his aims and interests. But the rectitude of these aims and interests is left up in the air. As Rawls puts it, "there is nothing necessarily right, or morally correct, about the point of view [these contingent purposes] from which things are judged to be good or bad" (p. 403). But the case is otherwise if reason is essentially practical, i.e., is itself a practical intention. For then it will be possible for a course of action to be unconditionally rational (or good). This will be any course which is consistent with reason's essential aim. It will be that which it is rational to do, not just from the standpoint of a person already committed to this or that objective, but for anyone insofar as he is rational, i.e., for the rational subject as such. But nothing can be unconditionally rational or good without being right or morally good. In fact, this is just the way moral goodness has been traditionally tied in with rationality. The moral good is precisely that which is in accord with the subject's rational nature; that which presents itself as what it is unconditionally (or categorically) rational to do.

There is more. Not only is it possible to derive the concept of right from the concept of rationality if the latter is properly understood. There is, I will suggest, really no other way. Or, perhaps more exactly, only an understanding of reason as essentially practical can do justice to our experience of moral obligation. Since the final end is the term of this original practical orientation, this last contention comes down to one made earlier. No theory rejecting the notion of final end can do justice to our moral judgments. For if there is no final end, the practical aims of the rational subject are all contingent matters. They are interests which he happens to have appropriated from his empirical nature but which he need not have as a condition of being a rational subject. This being the case, however, then no principles of conduct—whether they are principles of justice or whatever—apply to him simply as a subject or, as Rawls puts it, simply "in virtue of his nature as a free and equal rational being" (p. 253). The idea of moral exigencies—i.e., practical exigencies which confront a person regardless of his empirical needs or desires—is deprived of any possible referent. And the moral question, the question about what I unconditionally (or categorically) ought or ought not to do, cannot even arise.[5]

It would seem, therefore, that the notion of final end is not something to be lightly discarded. As one might expect with an idea which has had such a long and venerable tradition, its proponents, however variously they may have interpreted it and however much some of their interpretations deserved criticism, were on to an essential element in ethical theory. Indeed, if what I have proposed is at all adequate, our moral experience is simply inexplicable without it.

NOTES

1. The page references for this and subsequent quotations and citations from John Rawls's *A Theory of Justice* (Cambridge: Harvard University Press, 1971) are given in parentheses in the text.

2. Although he uses different terms, I am indebted to John Macmurray for the basic thrust of this distinction. See "The Field of the Personal" in his *Persons in Relation* (London: Faber & Faber, 1961), esp. pp. 27–43.

3. See Thomas Nagel's criticism of Rawls's attempt to give his view a Kantian interpretation in "Rawls on Justice," *Philosophical Review*, 82 (1973), 220–34, esp. 223.

4. See *Persons in Relation*, p. 158.

5. Rawls, to be sure, tries to interpret his principles of justice as categorical imperatives. However, as Thomas Nagel points out ("Rawls on Justice," 223n3),

the details of this interpretation are not altogether convincing. For Rawls admits that the argument for adopting the two principles presupposes that the parties desire certain primary goods: "These are things which it is rational to want whatever else one wants" (p. 253). In other words, given the fact that one has other wants and given the further fact that one has committed oneself to fulfilling them, then, since such fulfillment presupposes a measure of the so-called primary goods, it is rational to want these. Obviously, the rationality here is conditional (or hypothetical). And since the claim of the principles of justice rests upon a desire which is thus only hypothetically (or conditionally) rational, that claim itself can be only conditional, not categorical.

2

Justice in a World of Conceptual Relativism

VINCENT M. COOKE, S.J.

ONE WAY OF CHARACTERIZING THE MODERN AGE is to say that we are conscious, perhaps excessively so, of the importance of history, context, and social and cultural structure—in short, that we are aware of the relativity of our beliefs and judgments, of our norms and institutions. Cultural relativism is a cliché of anthropology and sociology. Almost every schoolboy at one time or another proudly points out that Eskimos have seven or ten different words for snow, and are thus capable of making judgments unavailable to members of the boy's own culture. Morals vary from place to place, and institutions and practices which are revered and honored in one society are condemned as heartless barbarisms in another. Relativity, specified by examples such as these, seems to be simply a fact of life.

Our awareness of relativity, however, sometimes has an unwelcome effect on the judgments which we make and the claims which we press in the name of justice. To be sure, we continue to make these judgments, but talk about justice seems increasingly to take on the tone of simply a public rhetoric. It is the category we employ when we wish to appear most solemn and to be taken most seriously. But it is not a category which we feel very much at home in using. This is shown by the very quick and easy way in which argument begun in the name of justice shifts to the more manageable arenas of legality, tradition, or self-interest. It is as if we feared to go beyond the surface of our justice claims lest we reveal a hidden inability to articulate a case in reason for their defense. If I am not mistaken, it is precisely the specter of relativity which suggests to us a kind of ultimate arbitrariness about what we judge to be just or unjust.

It is my conviction that the belief that relativity implies a kind of ultimate arbitrariness is fundamentally mistaken. It is a belief which can thrive only in an atmosphere of conceptual confusion. In this essay I shall argue that the rightful claims of relativity are perfectly compatible with those of moral objectivity; indeed, that they demand moral objectivity if we are to do full justice to the moral phenomenon. Further, I shall suggest that the major obstacle to our confident employment of the categories of justice is, not relativity, but a mistaken view of what constitutes human rationality.

I

The first thing which should be said about justice is that it is one of our concepts, and, as such, shares the general characteristics of human concepts. To be sure, it is a very complicated concept; some might prefer to adopt the convention of calling it a set of concepts and distinguishing the members of the set in any of a variety of ways. For instance, one might speak of justice in a sense in which it is practically the equivalent of morality in general, and then go on to distinguish a variety of moralities according to a particular time or place. Alternatively, one could start with an intuitive consciousness of a more restricted notion of justice which "we," or some specified linguistic community, seem to share, and then proceed further to divide that concept into notions such as commutative, distributive, retributive, or social justice, and so on. The possibilities of classification and analysis are very great. For my purposes, it is unimportant that we settle any of these questions. Whether one prefers to speak of one concept of justice or many concepts, and whatever analysis of justice is finally judged satisfactory, the point which I want to make is that whatever is true of concepts is also true of justice.

Concepts are rules which members of communities possess for doing things. Wherever there is a doing, and in *this* sense an action, there is a rule which is the criterion for whether the action is performed or not performed, performed well or performed poorly. The rule need not be something explicitly formulated. It may be simply what someone knows when he knows how to perform the particular action. Put another way: it is what someone understands when he understands how to do something; it is the point into which someone gets insight when he grasps what is going on.

Examples of concepts are easy to give. Human beings do many things, but one of the most significant things which they do is to talk and make judgments. In fact it seems to be part of our notion of a concept that we restrict its application to the possession of those rules or sets of rules which involve at least in part the ability to perform some linguistic or, more generally, some symbolic task. In this sense, we say concepts pertain to our "mental" performances. Thus, the normal criteria for someone having the concept of writing are that he be able to write and be able verbally or in some symbolic way to identify instances of writing, and so on. We do not know quite what to say about the conceptual apparatus of the person who cannot write but can talk quite properly about writing, except perhaps to say something such as "He has the verbal concept but still has failed to get the point of how to do it." We readily grant, however, that someone who could write and speak about writing, and who subsequently suffers paralysis in his hands, still has the concept of writing even though he now cannot write. This perhaps reflects the heavy weight which we place on the "mental" criterion for what we call the possession of concepts.

Consider a simple example: the concept of *red*. We say that someone possesses the concept of red if he can do such things as distinguish red things from things of another color, and also use the word "red" in locutions such as "Red is a color," "Stop lights are red," and so on. The possession of the concept enables the possessor to do something (pick out red objects) and to say something ("Red is a color"). The saying is, of course, simply a special kind of doing. It is the possession of the concept which guides (or regulates) both the linguistic and the non-linguistic performance. The concept in turn (as distinguished from the possession of the concept) is the criterion for whether what is done can correctly be said to be an instance of being guided by the concept. Individuals possess the concept of red, but what any particular individual does cannot be said to be the criterion for whether the concept is employed, or correctly employed. The concept, precisely insofar as it is a rule, is something embedded in a public practice or institution. It is the public practice which serves as the norm for the individual performance.

Wittgenstein made some of these points in the following way. He said: "If language is to be a means of communication there must be agreement not only in definitions but also (queer as this may sound) in judgments."[1] Concepts (institutions, practices) constitute that agreement in definition, judgment, and performance in general which makes human action possible. It is *actions* which we perform or do not perform, perform well or perform badly.

Finally, it should be noted that radical deficiency (that is, deficiency in ability, not merely a particular mistake) in definition, judgment, or performance in general is precisely what we mean by a conceptual deficiency. A person who can talk about dogs as "four-legged animals and man's best friend," but who cannot distinguish a dog from a hippopotamus when he sees one, does not have our concept of a dog—or, at any rate, does not have it in its entirety.

In this section I have made some observations about concepts in general. In the next section I want to apply these observations to our concept or concepts of justice. In what follows I shall adopt the convention of speaking about the concept (singular) of justice, while leaving it to the reader to make the appropriate modifications if he thinks it more accurate to speak of our concepts (plural) of justice.

II

We ask the question: "What is justice?" The beginning of an answer is to say that justice is a concept. It is a set of rules for doing and saying a variety of things. Someone possesses the concept of justice if he can identify just actions, institutions, and so on; if he can properly press claims in the name of justice; if he can say things such as "Justice involves treating equals equally, and unequals unequally"; and, finally, if he can treat equals equally, that is, if he has the radical capacity to be just. The above is an attempt at an elucidation of the concept of justice. It is not, of course, what analytic philosophers call necessary and sufficient conditions.

It should be noted that possessing the concept of justice involves not merely the ability to say certain things—what Wittgenstein called agreement in definitions—but also the ability to make judgments. As long ago as Kant, it was seen that concepts and judgments are internally related to one another. For this reason Kant was able in the Metaphysical Deduction of the Categories to use the kinds of judgments which we make as the criteria for the kinds of categories which we possess.[2] Wittgenstein developed this idea by noting that rules (concepts) and empirical propositions tend to merge into one another,[3] that certain empirical propositions share in the necessary character of conceptual truths. The point is that a person does not have the concept of justice if he is merely able to define the term and relate it to other linguistic symbols. He must also be able to pick out clear cases of justice and injustice. This ability is a conceptual ability; someone who does not have this ability does not simply disagree with us about what is just; he does not mean what we do by "justice."

If we are right in making the ability to make a certain set of existential judgments constitutive of our possession of a concept, and if in the case of certain concepts it is simply a matter of fact that cultures and societies differ on the judgments which make up that set, then it would seem to follow that concepts such as these can best be described as what Wittgenstein called family resemblance concepts. That is, there is no one set of univocal rules for judgments and actions which constitute the employment of the concept. Rather, there are sets of rules which resemble one another in various respects and differ in other respects.[4]

It seems to me that justice is such a family resemblance concept. In one society it may be a conceptual truth that an institution such as slavery is just; in another society it may be a conceptual truth that slavery is unjust. There is, of course, also the intermediate situation where judgments about slavery are taken to be "merely empirical" ones, i.e., our attitude toward the proposition is such that we conceptualize it as one capable of being either true or false. The totality of the conceptual and empirical truths which we are radically capable of formulating at any particular time constitutes what I want to call our conceptual scheme or world-picture.

Our conceptual schemes change in the course of time and in varying circumstances. Wittgenstein said that the propositions which describe our conceptual schemes might be described as a kind of mythology. "And their role is like that of rules of a game; and the game can be learned purely practically, without learning any explicit rules." Referring to what we have called those empirical propositions which share the characteristics of necessary truths, Wittgenstein suggested that they be considered as propositions which look like empirical propositions but which have been hardened and function "as channels for such empirical propositions as were not hardened but fluid; and that this relation altered with time, in that fluid propositions hardened, and hard ones became fluid."

Wittgenstein went on to compare our hardened empirical propositions with the banks and bed of a river, and the non-hardened propositions with the flow of the water. In the course of time the waters flow and the river bed and banks shift. There is a distinction between the two kinds of change but not a sharp division.

> But if someone were to say "So logic is an empirical science" he would be wrong. Yet this is right: the same proposition may get treated at one time as something to test by experience, at another as a rule for testing.
> And the bank of that river consists partly of hard rock, subject to no alteration or only to an imperceptible one, partly of sand, which now in one place now in another gets washed away, or deposited.[5]

The point which I want to make is that our concept of justice, like most of our concepts, varies with particular times and places and also with the attitudes (interests, wants, needs) which particular kinds of human beings bring to a situation. If there were no scarcity of goods and resources in our world, our concept of justice would, at the very least, be different from what it as a matter of fact is. Hume has even argued that "Justice, in that case, being totally useless, would be an idle ceremonial, and could never possibly have place in the catalogue of virtues."[6] Likewise, were human attitudes such that we could be governed entirely by friendship and generosity there would be no need for the rules which we have for pressing claims in the name of justice. Justice is one of our variable concepts, and in this way it differs from those which are so basic to our conceptual scheme or world-picture that they seem scarcely ever to have varied at all. Concepts of this latter invariable sort are those which Strawson studied and which he claimed constitute the body of a general metaphysics.[7]

It is because justice is a concept and the variable family resemblance type concept which it is that judgments about justice are relative. They are relative to particular times and situations as well as to the particular kinds of societies which give birth to the kinds of individuals who make the judgments. All this seems almost trivially true. There is nothing surprising about the relativity of judgments concerning justice. What remains is to consider the proper consequences of this relativity.

III

Let us recapitulate the argument so far. Concepts, we have seen, are rules for human judgments, actions, and institutions. It is concepts which guide or regulate these human performances or sets of performances. One of our concepts is justice. The rules which constitute our concept of justice vary with particular time, place, and culture. In this sense, our concept of justice is relative.

There is, however, one further peculiarity of our concept of justice which must be attended to. It is part of our concept of justice that we do not simply identify justice with any particular set of rules which are said to constitute just performances in a particular society. We distinguish the "just action" (appropriately placed in scare quotes) as that which any particular society calls just, from the really just action, or that which is worthy of our ultimate approval. Sidgwick made a similar distinction in terms of what he called "Conservative Justice" and "Ideal Justice."[8] This means that, although our concept of justice may well be acquired and sustained by ritualization in the received tradition of a particular society, there is an element in the concept which already places us in a perspective which transcends and calls into question the content of any tradition.

This seems to me to be so because the concept of justice is not simply a concept which we acquire and use, but also one which we are called upon to approve or disapprove by a further and distinct human performance. This further human performance, precisely as a human action, must in turn be concept directed. But the content of the concept must be something given prior to the content of any tradition; otherwise it would not allow us to stand in judgment of the tradition. As that which guides the performance of our approval or disapproval of the material content of our culturally acquired concept of justice, it is a kind of prior knowledge which, I suggest, can be identified with the agent's grasp (understanding) of his own nature as a responsible human agent ontologically prior to any particular performance.

This prior knowledge is a kind of "knowing how" which makes it radically possible for the subject to be in performance what he is in nature, i.e., a responsible human agent. When we stand in judgment over the content of any received tradition of justice, we do so only insofar as we employ what I want to call the canons of responsible human agency which we are implicitly aware of when we are aware of ourselves as responsible human agents. These canons of responsible human agency are the ultimate formal norms which enable us to attain objectivity even when we are inevitably operating within a notion of justice which is relative to a particular time, place, or culture. They can also be called "transcendental" in the sense that they are constitutive of what it is to be an agent, and thus cannot be the product of experience which itself is already a human performance and thus presupposes the canons of agency as the conditions of its possibility.

What, then, are the canons of responsible human agency? The answer to this question can only be briefly sketched here, since a completely adequate answer would involve the elaboration of a total Philosophy of Man. What follows, however, is enough of a sketch to enable the reader to grasp the main thrust of my position.[9]

Human agents are material beings, and therefore spatio-temporal beings. They are necessarily involved in a system of interaction with other spatio-temporal beings. When this interaction is on the conscious level we call it experience. Human beings attend to one another and to the world around them. As they grow and develop, they gradually gain insight into the happenings and actions about them. They draw inferences beyond their immediate environment about spatially and temporally remote happenings and actions. It is by growing up in a community of interacting human beings that they acquire the conceptual apparatus, language, and culture which make their individual human performances the kind of performances which they are.

Yet human beings do not live merely externalized in their environment and communities. They have a degree of interiority—what I want to call spirituality—which enables them to grasp themselves as beings which transcend the confines of any particular space, time, or culture. It is this understanding of themselves which enables them to recognize the limitations, inadequacies, and relative character of any particular conceptual scheme.

From man's knowledge of himself as a material–spiritual agent we can derive, by a kind of transcendental deduction, the canons of responsible human agency. Insofar as man is necessarily involved in that conscious interaction with his environment which we call experience, he must be attentive to that experience. He must be intelligent and imaginative in the questions which he asks and in the hypotheses which he frames. He must be reasonable in the inferences he draws. Insofar as man is aware of his own interiority and the limitations of any cultural situation, he must accept the responsibility of transforming any situation which does not meet the genuine needs of human agents.

All this, surely, requires much more argumentation than can be provided here. I have merely painted the metaphysical picture in broad strokes. The point I want to make, however, is that the problem of the relativity of conceptual schemes involving the notion of justice can be adequately resolved only by being confronted with a metaphysical philosophy of man which neither denies the facts of relativity nor presents a picture of man which deprives our perplexity of its moral pathos. A purely materialistic view of man has no difficulty accounting for the facts of relativity, but it fails to provide any convincing reason why we should then continue to engage in the moral enterprise. It is because man is material that his elaborated concepts are inevitably relative; it is because man is also spiritual that he has enough knowledge of what it is to be a responsible human agent to enable him to employ his resources in the never-ending task of attentive, intelligent, reasonable, and responsible efforts to understand and instantiate justice in this world.

IV

Four objections should now be considered. These will serve as vehicles for further clarifying and explaining my position. First, one might object that all that has been accomplished is a bit of legerdemain. Appeal has been made to the concept of responsible human agency in order to find a way of mediating the relativity of particular concepts of justice. But is not the concept of responsible human agency, from which we derived the canons of responsible human action, equally relative and culturally conditioned? Why, then, does not the same problematic arise in the case of this concept as arose in the original case of the concept of justice?

My answer is twofold. First, the concept of responsible human agency is a formal or heuristic concept rather than a material concept. It does not tell us what in a particular cultural situation is the responsible thing to do, but tells us rather how to go about discovering what the responsible thing might be. Second, I grant that the concept of responsible human agency is relative and culturally conditioned. It is the concept which defines responsible human agents. It is also the concept within which they live and act. It is the rule which determines the kind of beings which they are. It is surely a contingent matter of fact that responsible human agents exist. If there are no such beings, then my argument is not wrong; it is superfluous, as, indeed, would be all talk about justice or morality in general. The argument is offered to responsible human agents for their reflection. Every transcendental argument requires some *point de départ*. The existence of responsible human agents in the sense defined seems to me justified and relatively non-controversial. If someone denies that he is a responsible human agent, then, to be sure, he avoids my *point de départ*, but he also makes any attempt at rational discourse pointless.

A second objection arises from a misunderstanding about the nature of concepts. One might grant that the argument follows from an analysis of the concept of responsible human agency, but ask why this concept should be normative for human beings. This objection usually arises from a misconstrual of concepts as mental pictures or images. The problem then arises whether the picture "corresponds to reality." But concepts are not pictures or images; concepts are rules. Further, they are not simply rules for judgments but rules for actions in general. When we give a transcendental deduction of what is involved in the concept of responsible human agency, we are elucidating the rules which responsible human agents follow, not only in judgment but in performance. Such rules are of their nature normative and need no further justification.

Thirdly, one might object that a purely formal or heuristic norm of morality is insufficient. Concrete ethical decisions could never be deduced from such a norm. What the objection states is correct. Concrete ethical decisions require not simply a formal norm, which is sufficient to provide objectivity, but also material norms which are embedded in the values of particular societies and individuals. By accepting the fact of relativity, we are committed to the indispensability of such material norms. The formal norm, however, provides us with a way of employing, correcting, and thus transcending any particular set of material norms by calling us to the burden of attention, intelligence, rationality, and ultimate responsibility. The canons of responsible human agency call upon us to evaluate any set of material norms in terms of their purpose—what one might call the ultimate material norm—which, it seems to me, can only be to satisfy authentic human needs and wants. Once again we see the importance of an adequate philosophy of man. It is only in this way that concrete moral problems can be adequately resolved.

A final objection argues that, even if everything which has been said so far is correct, there is no way of rationally determining authentic human needs and wants, so the whole program is ultimately fruitless. It seems to me correct to say that authentic human needs and wants cannot be strictly rationally demonstrated. But strict demonstration should not be equated with the total scope of human rationality. There are many things which we know about authentic human interests from our personal and collective experience, from the work of social scientists, psychologists, novelists, dramatists, and poets. It is only when we irrationally restrict the kind of knowledge which we will countenance to that which can be strictly demonstrated that we are left without an ultimate material norm for our judgments about justice or morality in general.

V

In this essay I have attempted to answer the charge that the relativity of judgments about justice argues to an ultimate arbitrariness, and thus undermines the whole moral form of life. It should now be clear that relativity of judgments about justice should be exactly what we would expect in a world of varied situations, times, needs, and people. We grow into mature moral agents in a particular time, place, family, and culture. This, however, does not condemn us to simply repeating the ritualized rules and practices of the received tradition. As responsible human moral agents we stand in judgment of the tradition, and, in this sense, transcend it. We perform as responsible human moral agents when we employ the canons of responsible human agency in our reflections upon the way any particular concept of justice serves the authentic interests of man. Objectivity is not the antithesis of relativity. It is the authentic human way of coming to terms with relativity.

NOTES

1. *Philosophical Investigations* (Oxford: Blackwell, 1967), par. 242. References to Wittgenstein's works are to paragraph numbers.

2. See Kant, *Critique of Pure Reason*, A67–A83, B92–B116.

3. *On Certainty* (New York & Evanston: Harper & Row, 1969), par. 309.

4. Whether this is exactly Wittgenstein's understanding of the term "Family Resemblance" is unimportant for our purposes. See *Philosophical Investigations*, par. 67.

5. *On Certainty*, pars. 95–99.

6. *An Enquiry Concerning the Principles of Morals*, ed. L. A. Selby-Bigge (Oxford: Clarendon, 1894), p. 184.

7. P. F. Strawson, *Individuals* (Garden City, N.Y.: Doubleday, 1963).

8. Henry Sidgwick, *The Methods of Ethics*, 7th ed. (Chicago: The University of Chicago Press, 1907; reissued 1962), pp. 290–94.

9. My views have been influenced very much by Bernard Lonergan, S.J., *Insight* (New York: Philosophical Library, 1957) and by Malcolm Clark, *Perplexity and Knowledge* (The Hague: Nijhoff, 1972).

3

Reasons for Being Just

JAMES N. LOUGHRAN, S.J.

Fordham University

IN THIS ESSAY I shall argue four points. (*a*) A wide gap separates much of contemporary moral theory from the ordinary experience of moral life. (*b*) This is the case because philosophers have ignored the connections between ethical beliefs and beliefs about man and human flourishing. (*c*) Morality presumes a background of anthropological beliefs—beliefs which, admittedly, are paradoxical. (*d*) If the preceding three points are correct, they suggest the meaning and importance of the "Why be moral?" question, the way in which it should be approached, and the kind of answer which one might give.

INADEQUACIES OF CONTEMPORARY MORAL THEORY

When the history of twentieth-century moral philosophy in the English-language, analytic tradition is related, it is customary to mark off the last twenty years or so as chiefly concerned with the questions: What is good moral reasoning? What are good moral reasons? Moreover, it is generally held that considerable progress has been made during this period. In order to illustrate these remarks and to provide a context for the discussion and criticism in this essay, I shall focus on four philosophers who have been concerned with the so-called prescriptivist–descriptivist debate on the nature of moral judgments.

Among the prescriptivists, R. M. Hare[1] has attempted to provide an alternative to the intuitionism of G. E. Moore and the emotivism of C. L. Stevenson. Hare is no doubt correct in stressing that moral judgments must be universalizable and logically consistent with one another. He is credited, moreover, with having said much of value about moral reasoning and its peculiar logic. Philippa Foot[2] and G. J. Warnock,[3] spokesmen for the descriptivist side, are noted for their insistence that moral judgments relate to human wants and needs. Moral terms do indeed have an action-guiding function, as Hare stresses, but only because they are in some way expressive of the real interests of human beings. Finally, D. W. Beardsmore,[4] who in seeking a resolution of the pre-scriptivist–descriptivist dilemma, is noted for his contention that a set of moral concepts, reasons, and even arguments is already contained in the very language we speak, the "way of life" into which we have been inducted.

One can readily agree that the participants in this debate, despite major disagreements, have made valuable contributions toward an understanding of the nature and justification of moral judgments. Yet all four philosophers come to a halt prematurely in their analyses of the moral point of view. At the very least, their descriptions and accounts neglect, or equivalently rule out as illusory, important dimensions of moral experience. To put it another way: their theories fail to explain satisfactorily certain presuppositions concerning morality, presuppositions which underlie our everyday usage of moral terms. These remarks call for extended discussion.

In ordinary language, "moral" and "immoral" are highly charged words. When someone says of a choice, action, policy, etc., "That's immoral!" we take notice. We recognize immediately that the person making the claim is doing more than simply voicing disapproval. There are, I think, three main reasons why this outcry interests and consequently intrigues us.

First, and obviously, a disagreement, a dispute, is taking shape. Someone puts forth a challenge and claims to have the answer concerning what is right. Most significantly, he proclaims not merely how he personally would assess the situation and decide to act, but how we all *should* evaluate and choose in the given circumstances.

Secondly, we expect that he can give *reasons* for his position and show us why his opponent is wrong. We expect not only that he can demonstrate the reasonableness of his own approach, but that he can present it as *the* rational solution to the problem at hand. By the judgment "That's immoral!" he alerts us to his discovery of something evil. He has spotted something which contradicts the human, violates man's nature, or blocks the achievement of his destiny —something which is, in short, irrational.

Thirdly, "That's immoral!" requires us to consider the matter in question from an identifiable point of view. Indeed, in making our own judgment, we are asked to look at things from a perspective which takes precedence over all other perspectives. The implication is that the moral point of view is, to use a phrase of Warnock's, "uniquely authoritative in practical matters." It is from the moral point of view that we discern our obligations as human beings, and we see that those obligations are categorical.

These sorts of considerations account for our ordinary reactions when something is called moral or immoral. Our normal use of these terms[5] is thus built on three latent assumptions concerning morality: (*a*) Moral disputes or personal moral problems, whatever their peculiar character and complexity, are in principle open to resolution; there is a good and a bad way to be, decide, or act, and it is always worthwhile and required that one try to find the right solution, for disagreement on moral issues is never really tolerable. (*b*) We need reasons to back up our judgments that things are moral or immoral; these reasons will relate to what is held to be truly human or inhuman; for to be moral is, in some way, to be rational, and to be immoral is to be irrational. (*c*) The most important thing in life is to be moral; men are "bound" to be moral; there are no exceptions or exemptions in this area.

Now, the extraordinary thing is that Hare, Foot, Warnock, and Beardsmore seem not to be very impressed by these common presuppositions concerning morality. In fact, all four deny, or at best give very weak support to, what I have called the three "latent assumptions" of ordinary moral discourse. I propose now to gather together their objections and contrary positions to each of these assumptions, and to assess the basis of their claims.

(*a*) *Moral Disputes.* None of the four philosophers, it should be noted, holds that moral arguments necessarily end in deadlock. It is always worth discussing the issues, and agreement might well be reached, although such an outcome would stem from contingent factors. All four, however, labor to show why moral stalemate will frequently be inevitable and urge that we reconcile ourselves to this state of affairs.

All that Hare requires for a proper moral judgment or stance is that it be prescribed universally. You and I might recommend with absolute consistency two contradictory courses of action: "Never abort a human fetus" *vs.* "Abort all fetuses carried by women who contract measles." Both satisfy Hare's formal rules for morality; there is no reason to presume that one is wrong.

In her earlier articles Foot tended to embrace a position according to which strict descriptive rules controlled the correct use of moral words; by implication, in a moral conflict, at least one of the disputants would be using such words improperly. But more recently she would seem more inclined to stress a theme which runs, somewhat discordantly, through all her writings: to understand or justify a moral judgment it must be seen against a "background," from within the point of view of the one making the judgment, as flowing from a particular outlook (might not one also say "way of life"?).[6] Naturally, unless divergent "backgrounds" can somehow be evaluated or reconciled, such an emphasis will never get us beyond moral diversity.

Warnock, in his turn, stresses the distance between his general moral principles—non-maleficence, beneficence, fairness, and honesty—and the concrete situations and choices which confront men. More to the point, he allows that his four principles may well generate conflicting moral reasons. Faced with opposing opinions about a question such as "Should one lie to save a life?" one may as well flip a coin to decide—at least as far as strictly moral considerations can throw light on the situation.

Finally, Beardsmore contends that the only possible explanation or justification of one's moral opinions is the connection which they have with the accepted standards of the community and the traditions in which one has been raised. Where communities and standards vary, so too will the moral judgments of individuals. Different ways of life mean different moralities, and there is no way to judge among them.

(b) *Reasons, Rationality, and Morality.* All four philosophers emphasize that reasons play an important role in their moral theories. None wishes morality to be confused with whim. Hare goes to great lengths to show that moral choices can be seen as justified by syllogisms, in which both one's guiding principles and pertinent facts serve as premises, that is, reasons. Foot, of course, argues that factual considerations are what justify moral judgments. Warnock's four principles function as reasons and, by throwing light on particular situations, make the facts of the case relevant for moral decisions. Beardsmore's view is that one's way of life includes moral concepts which are the criteria for any moral evaluation or choice.

Clearly, all four agree that to be moral is to be rational. But it is noteworthy that they do not hold that immorality is irrational. For Hare the only thing which qualifies as immorality is inconsistency—between what I judge and what I do, between what I prescribe for you and what I prescribe for myself, between what I prescribe now and what I prescribe later. Apparent inconsistency, however, may in reality signify merely that one has changed one's mind or arrived at new fundamental decisions of value. Nothing makes it impossible or illegitimate to alter basic moral convictions from moment to moment. If this is true, it would seem difficult on Hare's theory to be immoral at all.

Again, Foot writes: "The fact is that the man who rejects morality because he sees no reason to obey its rules can be convicted of villainy but not of inconsistency. Nor will his action necessarily be irrational. Irrational actions are those in which a man in some way defeats his own purposes, doing what is calculated to be disadvantageous or to frustrate his ends. Immorality does not *necessarily* involve any such thing."[7] According to her view, all men do not have the same purposes or ends; nor do we all "care" about the same things. Morality may or may not fit in with our own most fundamental projects. This being the case, it is no more irrational for a man to discard moral considerations than to ignore the rules of etiquette.

Warnock's position is very similar to Foot's. He too holds that it would not be irrational to disregard the moral point of view, sometimes or even all the time, in favor of some other set of considerations or principles. He allows us this option. But we would be wrong were we to decide that moral reasons are no reasons at all. We must acknowledge that morality constitutes at least one set of reasons for decision and action, that it is one way of being rational.

Beardsmore comes closest to holding that to be immoral, as he would understand the term, would be irrational. It would be irrational, presumably, for a man who has learned within a moral community to value or to condemn certain sorts of things not to judge and act accordingly. But just as morality is essentially something contextual, so too is rationality. What makes sense, what counts as reasons, how one views human identity and destiny, even systems of logic—all depend on the form of life in which one participates.

(*c*) *The Importance of Morality.* It would be astounding, indeed, if moral theorists did not regard their subject as an important human concern. Clearly, the four philosophers see morality as a good and advantageous thing and want us to be moral. And, from what they reveal of their own positions on concrete ethical issues, they tend to be conservative and orthodox. Yet all back off when it is a question of assigning priority to moral considerations in life's affairs. We see this already in their common refusal to condemn immorality as irrational. What lies behind their hesitation seems to be a reluctance to consider the requirements of morality as absolute obligations or categorical imperatives. One wonders what accounts for this. Perhaps they feel that such a view would detract from man's autonomy and decision-making powers. Possibly they are worried that such a "stringent" conception of morality results in intolerance or even psychological illness. Or perhaps they simply share the philosopher's skepticism about absolutes. And, of course, they may be preoccupied and puzzled by the pluralism of modern society. One can only speculate.

Hare argues that morality should be classified with other sorts of evaluative language. Consequently, he is not particularly concerned to attribute to it any special distinctiveness or importance. (It must be acknowledged, however, that according to Hare morality supplies us with the principles by which we guide our lives. If questioned, he would doubtless agree that nothing could be more important.) Foot proposes that we should view morality as a system of "hypothetical imperatives," worthy of our allegiance if they happen to fit in with our own cares and concerns. Warnock looks on morality as one point of view, one set of principles or reasons, alongside other equally valid points of view or kinds of considerations; one makes a decision from among the alternative criteria according to what one "wants." Once again, Beardsmore comes closest to affirming the primacy of morality for human judgments and decisions. Yet even he seems to allow the possibility that a way of life may not include any recognizable morality at all. In any case, as soon as one emphasizes diverse "ways of life" and different, but legitimate, moralities, it would seem difficult to use the language of moral obligation or categorical imperative.

We can only conclude that a considerable distance separates the understanding of the words "moral" and "immoral" in ordinary language from the interpretations offered by these philosophers. This is not to say that their theories are therefore wrong. One of philosophy's tasks is to clear up conceptual confusions, and it may be that ordinary language has a distorted picture of morality from the start. This would doubtless be the contention of these philosophers. But we go on using "moral" and "immoral" with the assumptions described above and, as philosophers, we look with interest on theories which dare to attempt their justification. Let us now consider how one such theory might be justified.

ETHICS AND ANTHROPOLOGY

I shall begin with some general remarks which will be developed and defended in the remainder of this essay. As the preceding analysis indicates, I am in agreement with G. E. M. Anscombe when she writes: "it can be seen that philosophically there is a huge gap, at present unfillable as far as we are concerned, which needs to be filled by an account of human nature, human action, the type of characteristic a virtue is, and above all of human 'flourishing.' "[8] Anscombe made this comment a decade ago, but it could just as well be made today since the gap remains unfilled. Moreover, Anscombe suggests what seems to me the only possible way of closing the gap between moral theory and our ordinary understanding of moral discourse and the moral life: it needs to be shown that our ethical beliefs flow from a conception of man, of human nature, and of human flourishing. Or, to put this thought in the context already established: treating morality as nonarbitrary, rational, and of overriding importance is intelligible only if we can uncover and accept the view of man on which such assumptions are based.

I am assuming, then, that it is legitimate to ask the old Socratic question "How should life be lived?" and answer it by determining what it is to be human and how human beings flourish. Most of contemporary moral philosophy (including the philosophers discussed above) is in disagreement with this position, and so I have set a bold task for myself in defending it. As a first step in exploring the connection between morality and human flourishing, I wish to argue, against D. Z. Phillips and H. O. Mounce (who, incidentally, are Beardsmore's mentors), that we need not be put off by the notion "it pays to be (morally) good."

The central notion in the moral theory of Phillips and Mounce is that of "moral practices."[9] Moral practices are something one finds oneself "within," "of which one is a part," to which one "belongs." Moral practices are composed of a particular set of concepts (it is this point which Beardsmore develops)—"such concepts as honesty, truth-telling, generosity, etc." But moral practices are more than a certain range of concepts. They are also the varying "moral opinions people hold" and even "arguments . . . rooted in different moral traditions." Moral practices are readinesses to interpret, evaluate, and justify concrete choices in definite ways. Moral practices, as criteria for choices, are not themselves objects of choice or decision (*contra* Hare); they are something one learns, absorbs, assimilates by growing up and participating in a moral community. Moral practices, then, are the "moral viewpoints [which] determine what is and what is not to count as a relevant fact in reaching a moral decision."

Considerations such as these lead Phillips and Mounce to advance the following thesis: "particular judgments and conclusions arrived at within a moral practice, could only be justified or rendered intelligible if certain things are considered right or wrong without standing in need of further justification. It is these things which are our criteria for right and wrong in certain contexts, that go to make up our moral practices." [10] Now, I have no argument with Phillips and Mounce if the point of the above is that we explain and defend our moral judgments by appealing to certain concepts—"moral practices," if one prefers—the usage of which we have learned within a social context.

I disagree with Phillips and Mounce, however, when they refuse categorically to bring "moral practices" into question in any sense at all. They contend that "in order for a man to hold a moral position at all, there must be certain things it does not make sense for him to question." [11] This may be true, as long as we choose "to hold a moral position." But it often makes sense to re-evaluate "moral practices" when we have grounds for questioning the wisdom of morality itself. Consider the following examples.

(a) A merchant finds himself in competition with other merchants whose business practices he regards as immoral or amoral. Watching his own profits dwindle while his competitors thrive unimpeded, he might well begin to question his own (moral) practices; he might well ask himself: "Why be virtuous?" "Why be moral at all?"

(b) A pre-medical student is tempted to cheat on an important chemistry examination. Something inside him says "Why not?" Something else says, "No, be honest." He begins to wonder "Why should moral considerations be overriding?" "Why decide from the moral point of view?"

(c) Roman Catholic parents judge that they should not have any more children if they are to be responsible parents of the children they already have. Faced with a potential or actual unwanted pregnancy, they begin to question their church's proscriptions against birth control and/or abortion. They seek out and examine reasons for and against these moral practices in which they have been trained. They ask, "What is it that makes a practice moral or immoral?"

What all three of the above cases illustrate is that at times we do, and quite understandably, call into question our "moral practices"—for example, when morality appears to put one at a disadvantage in life's affairs (a), when conscience clashes with expediency (b), when so-called *prima facie* duties conflict (c). We find ourselves wondering: Just what is morality? What is the moral point of view? What is morality's focus? How to decide whether a particular practice is moral or immoral? Why be moral all the time? Furthermore, it seems evident that when we raise this sort of question we are really asking: What is the moral interest? What is it about man which makes him want and/or need to be moral? Why is it most truly human to be moral? Our answers to these questions must clearly be based on factual beliefs about man and about what it is to flourish as a human being.

My position is that ethics and anthropology are interdependent, that there must be congruity between moral beliefs and beliefs about the identity and destiny of human beings, about their authentic wants and/or needs. Interestingly, Phillips and Mounce are in explicit agreement on this point. But they take the position that the reason why there must be this compatibility between human wants and/or needs and moral judgments is precisely that anthropological beliefs are grounded in ethical beliefs. As illustration, they analyze a dispute between a Roman Catholic housewife and a "so-called scientific rationalist" on the morality of contraception.[12] The latter, to support his case in favor of contraception, points to the physical and economic harm which might result from too many births. But the housewife stresses the honor of motherhood and the importance of doing God's will. Phillips and Mounce contend that the root cause of the deadlock is that each party in the dispute belongs to a different moral community, to different moral practices. It is evident, they claim, that the rationalist and the housewife have the moral beliefs which they do, not because of their beliefs about human existence, about human wants and needs; instead, their differing views on man's identity and destiny are due to their differing moral beliefs, the moral practices and traditions to which each subscribes.

With W. D. Hudson,[13] I find Phillips' and Mounce's analysis of this typical case of moral disagreement, as well as the conclusion which they draw from it, unconvincing. As Hudson observes, surely "it would be putting the cart before the horse to say, for instance, that religious moralists believe man ought to obey God's will, and, since man could not do that unless he were a being who lived under God's governance, the religious moralist *therefore* believes that is what man is" (p. 322). In this light, it appears to make no sense to say that anthropological beliefs are grounded logically in moral beliefs. On the contrary, as Hudson points out, it is usual and unobjectionable procedure for one under attack for his moral beliefs to invoke his anthropological view to make his ethic intelligible and/or to justify it. Ultimately, the disagreement of the housewife and the rationalist regarding contraception is rooted in a disagreement concerning the facts of human existence. The housewife believes that she (and her children) has an immortal soul and that happiness, peace, and perfection are to be sought and found in obedience to God's will. The rationalist knows nothing either of an immortal soul or of God's will; he believes that his career as a man is limited to this life and that his survival and prosperity depend on his own intelligence and skills. In other words, both the housewife and the rationalist think that factual beliefs about human existence establish boundaries for what can properly be considered human flourishing—

indeed, as I am arguing, for what can intelligibly be said to be moral or immoral action.

Hudson explores these connections between anthropological and moral beliefs by inviting us to examine imaginary conversations similar to the following.

A_1: Jones believes that it is better to suffer injustice than to do injustice.
B_1: Really? That is not very realistic.
A_2: For him it is. He believes that to do injustice introduces disorder and unrest into the spiritual part of his being. He believes that spirit is more important than body, and in fact he looks forward to its continued existence after the body dies.
B_2: Oh, I see.

How is it, asks Hudson, that A's mention of Jones' beliefs about man's identity and destiny is enough to make it understandable to B why Jones has the moral beliefs he does? Hudson suggests that factual beliefs (e.g., A_2) function as the minor premiss in a practical syllogism of which the conclusion is the particular moral position (e.g., A_1) taken. The problem, of course, is to identify the understood, but unstated, major premiss. Hudson's "tentative" proposal is, "Whatever will give rise to the flourishing of man, as what he is taken to be, ought to be done" (p. 324). Thus, Jones's full explanation of his position in the example above would run something like this:

(a) Whatever will give rise to the flourishing of man, as what he is taken to be, ought to be done.
(b) Man is taken to be a being of spiritual and bodily dimensions, the spiritual dimension of which makes him unique among other bodily beings and is likely to survive the passing of the body.
(c) Therefore whatever will give rise to the flourishing of man as a being uniquely spiritual, with the prospect of an afterlife, ought to be done.
(d) Not to do injustice, which causes spiritual disorder and unrest—even if this involves suffering injustice, which merely affects the body—assures the flourishing of man as a being uniquely spiritual, with the prospect of an afterlife.
(e) Therefore, it is better to suffer injustice than to do injustice.

Hudson does not deny that "flourishing" is an evaluative word. Still, he insists, and quite correctly it seems to me, that "this major premise recognizes a limit on what, for any given moralist, may count as 'flourishing' " (p. 324). It just would not make sense for someone such as Jones above to make the claim that men flourish by doing injustice, even when threatened with suffering injustice themselves. And this is true not simply because Jones accepts the moral principle "it is better to suffer injustice than to do injustice" but also because Jones has beliefs about who man is both actually and potentially—in this case, that man is a spiritual being whose flourishing does not depend essentially on fulfilling his bodily needs. As Hudson puts it, "given that you say . . . that this is what man *is*, you cannot (logically) go on to say that he flourishes by not being this" (p. 325).

Hudson makes several additional points which are worth summarizing. First, he calls subscription to his major premiss ("Whatever will give rise to the flourishing of man, as what he is taken to be, ought to be done") a "test of rationality" (p. 326). He argues that this moral principle must be fundamental to any ethical system if it is to be intelligible. For surely it would be a sign of madness or confusion to use moral terms to commend what does not contribute to human flourishing. Hudson states his conclusion in this way: "Using *moral* terms like 'good' and 'ought' in order to commend the flourishing of man *as what he is taken to be*, is 'the thing to do' with such language. If anyone is not doing this, then what he is doing does not make sense to us" (p. 328). Secondly, Hudson points out that these considerations open up a path for discussion in a moral dispute. We can always ask an opponent to show that his moral beliefs are consistent with his anthropological beliefs (a strategy, incidentally, of which even Phillips and Mounce would not disapprove). As Hudson writes: "Whatever a man says in terms of 'is' may not be formally contradicted by whatever he says in terms of 'ought' " (p. 328). Finally, Hudson suggests that all the preceding "makes some foundation in fact for moral judgment at least conceivable" (p. 328). This much is surely correct. Insofar as there is consensus on the questions of the identity and destiny of man, to that extent there are limits to what can be called human flourishing, and, hence, to what can be commended by means of moral terms. Hudson concludes by proposing that we seek this consensus on the facts of human existence through the physical sciences, the social sciences, and even religion (p. 328).

My attempt, with the help of Hudson, to show the inadequacy of some of the positions taken by Phillips and Mounce has required a discussion of the connection between ethics and anthropology. But what of our original question whether a theory of morality may properly make the claim that "it pays to be good"? I think enough has been said to justify the claim that, to be adequate, it must. After all, if the "thing to do" with moral terms is to commend human flourishing, it would seem permissible to use the slogan "it pays to be good" as a valid, if somewhat inelegant and possibly misleading, way of expressing the connection, described above, between flourishing and morality. To be moral is to choose to act in a manner most conducive to the realization of man's authentic destiny as a human being. Morality, insofar as it is a rational enterprise, is simply unintelligible as anything else than this.

THE MORAL PARADOX

The principal objection, of course, to the position that "it pays to be good" is that morality, understood in this way, might seem reduced to a kind of enlightened selfishness. But this would indeed be a distortion, for it goes without saying that it simply would not make sense in terms of ordinary moral discourse to describe the moral attitude as anything else than unselfish and disinterested. Thus, a paradox begins to emerge. On the one hand, the authentically moral agent is concerned with human flourishing; on the other, his orientation is essentially non-egotistical. To put it more provocatively: morality presumes that it is in man's interest to be disinterested. Let us examine this curiosity more closely.

I assume that if some choice or action (or what is related to choice or action) is called "moral" or "immoral" then it is always legitimate to ask "What makes you say that?" and that it is always reasonable to expect a response which will point to certain features of the matter in question. But which features? As I have already argued, it is surely acceptable to explain moral judgments by appealing to the action's capacity for advancing or impeding, in some serious way, human well-being. In other words, our beliefs about what is humanly good function as criteria, generate reasons, for our moral evaluations.

But the issue is more complicated. Our language also supplies us with a special set of terms for rendering intelligible and justifying our moral judgments. I am referring to what Beardsmore calls the "range of concepts . . . which are in some sense constitutive of a morality." Thus, if asked what makes us say that some instance or kind of human action is the "moral" thing to do, we typically respond that the action in question is the honest (or just, chaste, respectful, loyal, courageous, kind, generous, humble, or temperate) way to act. Similarly, we say that some action is "immoral" because it is dishonest (or unjust, unchaste, disrespectful, disloyal, cowardly, unkind, selfish, vain, or intemperate). Such explanations make sense. There is, moreover, a kind of finality about them—at least as long as we assume a moral point of view. Ordinary moral discourse does not question the relevance of these concepts or characteristics for supporting assertions that something is or is not morally commendable.

An inspection of these specifically moral concepts (really a listing, in adjectival form, of what are commonly regarded to be virtues and vices) reveals another important distinction. Though it does ring true to say that something is moral or immoral because it displays courage, loyalty, temperance, etc., nevertheless these modes of behavior, these character traits, may serve immoral ends. Moral action will usually require such qualities; but, strictly speaking, their possession does not guarantee morality. With justice, respect, kindness, etc., it is another matter. The just, respectful, kind action *is* the moral action. The just, respectful, kind man *is* the moral man. Concepts such as these exercise a primacy when it comes to making moral judgments and offering reasons for those judgments.

Is it possible to say what is distinctive about these primary moral concepts? I suggest that they all are used to characterize dispositions toward, relations and dealings with, other people. In fact, when we say that someone in his character, choices, and actions is honest, just, kind, respectful, etc., we mean that he takes into consideration and views positively the wants, needs, interests, concerns of others. When we say that someone is dishonest, unjust, unkind, disrespectful, etc., we mean that he ignores the wants, needs, interests, concerns of others or subordinates them to his own. In a word, what I call the primary moral concepts have the function of designating those actions or character traits which are oriented to the protection and strengthening, or weakening and destruction, of human relationships—of, I would add, friendship among men.

What the preceding analysis indicates, I hope, is that in the moral evaluation of possible choices and actions one brings to bear as final criterion the conception of a human ideal. The moral interest is to realize this ideal in the world, to make it happen. But, on examination, such a conclusion appears infected by a kind of antinomy—the same antinomy which is reflected in the perennial debates of teleologists and deontologists regarding the norm of morality. For my argument is twofold. (*a*) Authentic moral evaluation is made with a view to human flourishing; those choices and actions are (morally) "good," "right," and "ought to be done" which contribute to the enhancement of human life and to the realization of what are "taken to be" the genuine needs and wants of human beings. (*b*) Morality, with its emphasis on justice, honesty, generosity, etc., proposes as normative for judgment and decision a particular conception of the virtuous man. A choice or action is "moral" to the extent that it displays the qualities and orientations of this ideal moral agent. How to reconcile these two conclusions? Or more to the point, how is it that, with Hudson, I can still offer, as a formulation of the fundamental moral principle, "whatever gives rise to the flourishing of man, as what he is taken to be, ought to be done"?

It seems to me that the moral point of view, when correctly understood, already carries with it a particular notion of "human flourishing." In general, a human being flourishes inasmuch as, in the quality of his life and in his commitments, choices, and actions, he approximates what are considered to be the dispositions and characteristics of the ideal human being. Human flourishing takes place in the measure to which the human ideal is realized in our lives. The moral point of view, however, assigns primacy to qualities like justice, honesty, and generosity. Courage, self-discipline, loyalty; health, education, the development of talents, etc.—such features also characterize and concern the ideal human agent, but only secondarily. Morality presupposes that human flourishing is to be understood chiefly as the possession and expression of justice, honesty, generosity, and the strictly moral virtues. In sum, the moral interest, understood as the readiness to take positive account of other people's interests, assumes that virtue is its own reward, that virtue, if not identical with human flourishing, is its heart and center.

Perhaps by a brief discussion of the moral *ideal* and the moral *purpose* I can express in slightly different fashion how this reconciliation of the teleological emphasis on the good and the deontological emphasis on virtue are provided for in my account. Let us inspect again what might be called the dynamic of moral evaluation, particularly the role of the criteria which govern decisions on moral issues. On the one hand, according to my interpretation, the agent evaluates various options with a particular *purpose* in view. In most general terms, he inquires as to their capacity for giving rise to the flourishing of man. Thus, I include and stress the central tenet of teleological ethics: that the moral is intimately connected with the realization of the humanly good. On the other hand, in my theory, the agent also evaluates the various possible options against the requirements of an identifiable *ideal*. He wants to know the extent to which the available choices in themselves are consistent with the motivations and dispositions of the virtuous man. In this way, I avoid the pitfalls signaled by the deontologist—for example, to reduce choices and actions to mere neutral means or to overlook the character and commitments of the agent himself. In other words, the criteria for moral evaluation are a distinctive moral ideal and a distinctive moral purpose. But, and this is the key point, what prevents my account from presenting itself as a kind of two-headed oddity is the claim that the moral ideal and the moral purpose are actually one and the same. The ideal, in the light of which moral evaluation of human choices and actions is made, turns out to be, essentially, the evaluator's conception of what human beings should become. It is the agent's purpose in choosing and acting morally to achieve, in his being and activity, the ideal of the morally good man. The ideal which is normative for moral evaluations of human conduct is also the goal or objective which the moral interest aims to realize.

If the foregoing is correct, it allows me, I believe, to say quite a bit more than Hudson does regarding the required compatibility between ethical and anthropological beliefs. Since the very adoption of the moral point of view commits one to view positively the interests of others, even when those interests conflict with one's own, it is obvious that only certain types of beliefs will qualify as authentic moral beliefs. Similarly, it is equally obvious that there will be restrictions on the range of anthropological beliefs which can be compatible with authentic moral beliefs. Specifically, by making qualities such as justice, honesty, kindness, etc., the most important and indispensable concerns of man, morality already embodies a general understanding of the human identity and destiny, of the fundamental and authentic wants and needs of human beings.[14] Morality assumes that the singleminded pursuit of one's own selfish interests is a serious mistake concerning the way in which human beings can improve their situation in the world. Morality already "takes" man "to be" a being with certain characteristics and potentialities which are only, or at least best, realized as he turns from narrow self-interest to a wider interest in others. The corresponding conception of human flourishing will have to include a community dimension; according to the moral point of view, man flourishes only when he lives in cooperative interaction with his fellows.

I shall conclude this section by returning explicitly to the two points with which it began. First, the "pay-off" in human flourishing, which the moral interest has in view, is not selfish or egocentric. I have tried to show how it would be legitimate to say "it pays to be good" without distorting the real nature of morality. Secondly, with its simultaneous emphases on achieving good and being virtuous, there is surely something paradoxical about the moral point of view. Here, too, I have tried to show that this paradox makes sense only if it is true to say that man is such that he flourishes by being just, that individual and community flourishing somehow are always compatible and interdependent.

THE "WHY BE MORAL?" QUESTION

It may be well to summarize the lines of argument in each of the preceding sections with reference to the familiar "Why be moral?" question. My objection to contemporary theories of the moral life, such as those proposed by Hare, Foot, Warnock, and Beardsmore, amounts to this: by treating the "Why be moral?" question as futile, senseless, and unanswerable, they are unable to give a satisfactory account of what I have termed the common assumptions of ordinary moral discourse. My argument that ethical beliefs are grounded in anthropological beliefs suggests that the only way to respond to the "Why be moral?" question is this: moral behavior and moral choices are demanded by what man is; they are the essential ingredients for authentic human flourishing. Finally, since concern for others is central to the moral attitude, an answer to the "Why be moral?" question explains paradoxes such as these: self-fulfillment lies in virtue, public and private interest coincide.

By way of conclusion, I wish to address explicitly the "Why be moral?" question. First, I shall attempt to make clear what I take the question to mean. Then, lest it seem merely a philosopher's puzzle, I shall urge its contemporary relevance. Finally, I shall make some suggestions as to how the question might be dealt with in the future by philosophers.

It has been pointed out that this question is really two questions.[15] One might be asking why *people* should be moral, why morality should exist at all. There is no great problem here. Hobbes's prediction that life without morality would be "solitary, poor, nasty, brutish, and short" is at least plausible. But instead one might be asking why *I* should be moral—especially when no one else seems to be consistently just or honest or concerned about others, when, it seems, being just or honest or concerned about others is often to one's disadvantage. The question becomes more difficult where it is clear that injustice, dishonesty, and selfishness will go undetected or unpunished, or might even be praised and rewarded.

There is, of course, nothing new about all of this. Socrates and Plato distinguished the second meaning of the "Why be moral?" question centuries ago. They put it more dramatically: "Both are dreadful, but which is worse—to suffer injustice or to do injustice?" Their intuition was that to do injustice is always the greatest of evils—for the individual as well as for the state—even when remaining just hurts, even when others act unjustly and their injustice touches the just man. For Socrates and Plato, the Just and the Good are intimately related. Their dedication to philosophy was motivated largely by the need to discover what it is about reality, human identity, and destiny which makes intelligible and justifies such moral beliefs.

We can appreciate the practical importance of Socrates' and Plato's questions by means of a general observation. People talk a great deal these days about a decline in morals. On the surface, they mean such things as changing sexual mores and the rampant injustice and materialism in our society. But on a deeper level this talk expresses the intuition that there has been widespread loss of understanding and appreciation of the moral point of view, the moral interest. Indeed, there are signs that a society-wide weakening of commitment to a moral way of living and of looking at things has taken place. It is as if we have grown rusty in our knowledge of some foreign tongue in which we were once fluent or have become weary with a style of life which once had meaning. Men still speak the language of justice, honesty, fidelity, and generosity, but we often sense something hypocritical or hollow about it. In a word, we seem to have lost our "feel" for the language of morals and, as a consequence, it threatens to become a dead language.

If we are troubled by this state of affairs, what would have to be done to strengthen commitment to the moral point of view, to revive the language of morals? Among other things, we need to articulate the view of man and the world which underlies the moral attitude.[16] Why should I be moral and just unless it makes sense in terms of the way I understand myself and my world? To show that it makes sense is no easy task, of course, for morality already embodies an extraordinary and paradoxical view of man: that it is in the interest of human beings to be disinterested. Yet if we are to awaken our sense of justice, it is important that we recognize, examine, and seek to verify the beliefs about man which justice already assumes. We need to understand and appreciate this peculiar vision of the human identity and destiny if we are to rediscover the moral point of view and the language of morals. In a word, with Socrates and Plato, we need to see why it is that the egoism of Callicles and Thrasymachus is wrong—that is, inhuman.

Philosophers should concern themselves with the "Why be moral?" question—in the second sense as well as the first. More precisely, philosophers should investigate the connections between ethics and anthropology; they should probe the moral paradox. As a small contribution to this inquiry, I wish to make some recommendations and suggest some possibilities for the direction and methodology of this inquiry.

1. It is possible to argue that the question "Why be moral?" is the same as the question "Why be just?" I have already indicated my agreement with Beardsmore's notion that a particular range of concepts is "constitutive" of morality. I went from there to point out that certain of these concepts exercise a primacy within the moral point of view: justice, honesty, and respect are more central to morality than courage, temperance, or patience. Might not further analysis make it reasonable to subsume honesty, respect, and the other primary virtues under justice? After all, it would seem to make sense to appeal to considerations of justice in response to the (not altogether unintelligible) questions "Why be honest, or respectful, etc." If this is so, then justice would seem to be the fundamental moral concept or virtue. To ask "Why be moral?" would then be to ask "Why be just?"—and vice versa.

There is more to say in this context. Earlier I claimed that what distinguishes justice (and other primary virtues) is its positive view of the interests of others, the protection and strengthening of human relationships. This suggests at least some overlapping of justice with love, a concept which is, as Iris Murdoch has said, "so rarely mentioned now by philosophers."[17] And mention of love immediately brings to mind the idea of good. My discussion about the connections between human flourishing and the primary moral virtues has already pointed to some coincidence between the notions of good and justice. In any case, it seems to me that adequate treatment of the "Why be moral?" question will require an exploration of the relationships between and the unity of the concepts of justice, love, and good. This is, of course, to call for a return to the philosophical tradition of Socrates and Plato.

2. I take it as unobjectionable that morality's function is not only to define and regulate men's dealings with one another, but also to improve these relationships. At the same time, I say, with Hudson, that the "thing to do" with moral terms is to commend the flourishing of man as what he is "taken to be." To answer the "Why be moral?" question involves putting these two statements together. It is to attempt to justify morality's conviction that human flourishing—for the individual as well as for society—depends necessarily on mutual cooperation and companionship. It is to attempt to justify the anthropological beliefs, underlying the moral point of view, that the individual's being and flourishing are inextricably and intimately linked to the being and flourishing of others.

It strikes me that the starting point and categories of personalist philosophy may prove most suitable for this project. In most general terms, personalism "takes" man "to be" one who is conscious, self-conscious, intelligent, rational, free, intentional, responsive and responsible, creative, capable of love—in short, a self, a person. But he grasps his selfhood and becomes a person only in relation to other persons, only in community. Since man is and flourishes as "person-in-community," then whatever promotes community also promotes personal life; and whatever promotes personal life promotes community. I believe such an approach would help to illumine the moral paradox.

It is not my purpose here to examine and evaluate the personalist philosophy of man. But I would like to return briefly to the issues discussed in the first part of this essay. Recall the three questions, the response to which, according to my analysis, separates the theories of Hare, Foot, Warnock, and Beardsmore from the assumptions of ordinary moral discourse: (a) whether moral disputes are always, in principle, open to right solution; (b) whether it is irrational to be immoral; (c) whether moral considerations have overriding importance for affairs of practical judgment. Notice what happens if we accept an anthropology in which community and personalness identify the "interest-structure"[18] fundamental to human existence. Certainly we would then be in possession of an independent criterion, however general and distant from concrete issues, for deciding the rightness and wrongness of moral judgments and decisions. We would have a standard for determining the content of morality as well as for judging between conflicting values. Furthermore, it would be irrational to choose to act in ways which are not consistent with our own most fundamental interest. And, finally, what could be more important than that point of view and range of considerations which have to do with our basic identity and destiny as human beings?

3. Here I wish simply to stress a recommendation which Hudson has already made. Whatever the advantages of a particular philosophical system, such as personalism, it is probably true that, in an age of positivism such as our own, philosophers will not be heard unless they consult and make use of the findings of the empirical sciences. It seems obvious to me, in any case, that philosophers should regard the various techniques and methods of modern science as an indispensable aid in determining how man is "taken to be" and, thus, how man flourishes. To this call for an interdisciplinary approach to the "Why be moral?" question, I would add two points. First, with L. C. Becker,[19] I expect that psychology and cultural anthropology, among all the disciplines, would have the most potential for contributing to a suitable philosophy of man. Second, I mention again my position that morality already presumes a general (if unspecified) and paradoxical conception of man. In using the empirical sciences, the moral philosopher should try to test the validity of this conception and, with the help of the evidence of these sciences, begin to unfold this conception in more detail.

4. My criticism of Hare, Foot, Warnock, and Beardsmore is that, in spite of their interest in good moral reasoning, they, nevertheless, are intuitionists; they stop too soon in the process of reason-giving for the justification of moral judgments. When, in moral reasoning, one reaches Hare's "decisions of principle" or Foot's "hypothetical imperatives" or Warnock's "four fundamental principles" or Beardsmore's "concepts constitutive of a morality," one presumptively reaches rock-bottom. There is nothing further to investigate. In the light of their criteria, one simply sees whether a choice is moral or immoral. (For Foot and Warnock, of course, there is the further question whether one "cares" or "wants" to be moral.) I would label this kind of conclusion intuitionism—an unjustifiable intuitionism in that it fails to recognize that morality has logical connections with how man is "taken to be" and how man "flourishes."

But my suspicion is that even if moral philosophy acknowledges its dependence on anthropology, it will never fully escape the charge of being intuitionist. In their account of the reason-giving process for the justification of moral judgments, moral philosophers will still have to offer as final criteria what might accurately be called "intuitions." I have suggested as the fundamental moral principle Hudson's formula: "Whatever will give rise to the flourishing of man, as what he is taken to be, ought to be done." But I quickly add that the moral way of life already assumes and includes definite beliefs about what man is "taken to be," his interests, and the nature of human flourishing. I emphasize the paradoxical nature of those beliefs—once again, that it is in man's interest to be disinterested, that individual and communal flourishing are interdependent. We need to explicate and explain the congruence of these personal and community dimensions of human life, to unfold this way of "seeing" human existence which is the moral point of view.

But is this vision of things true? How do we justify this way of "seeing" human life? Certainly the cooperation and fellowship envisioned as man's common destiny are so far distant as to seem practically impossible to attain. Certainly there are numberless counterexamples, real and imagined, which could be offered to challenge the belief that it is in one's interest to be disinterested or that personal and community flourishing coincide. It seems to me that faced with these difficulties all one can do in defense of this view of life is to reveal it in all its dimensions, demonstrate its inner coherence, and show its foundations in the facts of human life as they are disclosed through common sense and the more sophisticated investigations of science. Finally, however, all this is really an invitation for one to ask and to decide for oneself: Does this account of man and morality match one's own experience? Do similar intuitions emerge when one reflects on the whole of life?

NOTES

1. See his *The Language of Morals* (New York: Oxford University Press, 1964) and *Freedom and Reason* (New York: Oxford University Press, 1965).

2. See especially "When Is a Principle a Moral Principle?" *Proceedings of the Aristotelian Society*, Supp., 28 (1954), 95–110; "Moral Arguments," *Mind*, 67 (1958), 502–13; "Moral Beliefs," *Proceedings of the Aristotelian Society*, 59 (1958–1959), 83–104; "Goodness and Choice," *Proceedings of the Aristotelian Society*, Supp., 35 (1961), 44–60.

3. See *Contemporary Moral Philosophy* (New York: St. Martin's, 1967) and *The Object of Morality* (London: Methuen, 1971).

4. See *Moral Reasoning* (New York: Schocken, 1969).

5. Here I am thinking also of general terms such as "good," "right," "ought," and their contraries when the words "moral" and "immoral" can be substituted for them without substantially changing the meaning.

6. See "Morality as a System of Hypothetical Imperatives," *Philosophical Review*, 81 (1972), 305–16.

7. Ibid., 310.

8. "Modern Moral Philosophy," in *The Is–Ought Question: A Collection of Papers on the Central Problem in Moral Philosophy*, ed. W. D. Hudson (New York: St. Martin's, 1969), p. 194.

9. *Moral Practices* (New York: Schocken, 1970), pp. 7, 60, 59, 54.

10. Ibid., p. 19.

11. Ibid., p. 17.

12. Ibid., pp. 58–59.

13. *Modern Moral Philosophy* (Garden City, N.Y.: Doubleday, 1970), pp. 320–29. Subsequent references to this work will be given in parentheses in the text.

14. It may seem that in saying this I have returned, covertly, to the position of Phillips and Mounce: namely, that anthropological beliefs are grounded in ethical beliefs. But this is not the case. I am insisting merely that if a man espouses morality, in a recognizable sense of this term, it is because he already views human existence in a certain way.

15. Kai Nielsen, "Why Should I Be Moral?" in *Moral Philosophy*, ed. Jack Glickman (New York: St. Martin's, 1976), pp. 191–204.

16. I do not wish to imply that philosophers should become propagandists for the moral point of view. Philosophy remains a science with its own (oftentimes fuzzy and/or disputed) rules for what constitutes good evidence, good method, good argument. At the same time, no one, I think, would deny that philosophy can and does have significant overflow influence in altering, reordering, or reinforcing people's beliefs about morals and other issues of practical import. Philosophy at its best forces us to look at the world and human existence in new ways.

17. *The Sovereignty of Good* (New York: Schocken, 1971), p. 46.

18. I am borrowing this term from my colleague Robert O. Johann. See his "Person, Community, and Moral Commitment," in *Person and Community*, ed. Robert J. Roth, S.J. (New York: Fordham University Press, 1975), pp. 155–75.

19. *On Justifying Moral Judgments* (London: Routledge & Kegan Paul, 1973). Becker is one contemporary moral philosopher who has made some beginnings on the project under discussion here.

4

Toward Integrity and Wisdom:
Justice as Grounding Personal Harmony

LEONARD C. FELDSTEIN

Fordham University

THE HISTORY OF PHILOSOPHY has been pervaded not only, in the Greek tradition, by the quest to understand the true, the good, and the beautiful, and, in the scriptural tradition, their affective correlates of trust, hope, and love, but, more fundamentally, in the Greek perspective, by a seeking after the *good life*, and, under the scriptural perspective, after *its* correlative, the *pious life*—in both instances, man quests after justice, integrity, and wisdom.[1] Despite the designations "good" and "pious," this inclusive quest transcends the sphere of morality as such, and I designate it the *spiritual life*. In the argument to be presented, I exhibit this consummation of human existence as stressing varying modes of balance between diverse human virtues; and virtue, in the generic sense of power, is surely not restricted to the moral domain. Further, each constituent of this fruition of life—namely, justice, integrity, and wisdom—expresses an aspect of that life; each aspect subsumes both traditions, the Greek and the scriptural. In the context of a life which is both good and pious—hence, in the larger sense, spiritual—every factor in the complexes which these traditions propose acquires a distinctive import. Yet justice, integrity, and wisdom are closely related notions. For its explicit and most complete formulation, each presupposes and requires the others. Nevertheless, my concern in this essay is essentially with the first member of the triad—namely, *justice*—though to characterize this notion, I must indicate its connections with the remaining notions.

I

From the point of view which I develop, justice pertains to a quality of the person, and, hence, of interpersonal relations; and, ultimately, of the community itself. Since its primary role is to specify the conditions under which personal harmony may be attained, it is, above all, a cognitive category. For it seeks to disclose the factual circumstances which ground personal harmony; in this capacity, it aims at the widest possible understanding of human being, both in its frailty and in its strength. Yet justice is a quite special kind of cognitive category. Its concern is also with that rectification of wrong which alone will allow for such harmony to be attained; and it aims at restoring a kind of balance or equity within the person, between persons, and for the community as a whole. Hence, a judgmental component involving morality is necessarily interwoven with the cognitive component. Finally, since no means may, in the largest sense, effectively flow toward an end—in this case, *harmony*—unless it partake of the quality of that end, justice also involves an aesthetic component. In short, justice requires that the truth of the other be grasped as a representation of the interplay of the powers of both, a representation which is self-emending.[2] In consequence, justice presupposes the idea of *participatory* truth: namely, that kind of mutual entrusting which is suffused by hope and, in the last analysis, identical with love, though love in a narrower sense than that kind of love which qualifies integrity, and, in its supreme form, pervades wisdom. It is under this perspective that I examine justice and explore its relationship to both integrity and wisdom.

Against customary accounts of justice, I am claiming that justice hardly stands in opposition to love; nor must it be conceived as merely tempered by or attuned to love. And only in a restricted sense is it bound to hope (or, often, to hopelessness). Quite the contrary. For justice is intimately interwoven with both love and hope. Correlatively, although, *qua* cognitive, it concerns truth, and hence always presupposes an attitude of trust with respect to truth's gathering, reception, and impact, justice is surely as intimately as, though more restrictedly than, integrity and wisdom interwoven with both beauty and morality. In this essay, it is my task to exhibit these peculiar concordances, the special ways in which justice is indeed a cognitive category interfused with the moral and the aesthetic, and the kinds of relationships which it bears to integrity and wisdom. Throughout, the theme of the person as seeker will be the dominant motif linking justice, integrity, and wisdom.

Some preliminary comments on my use of the terms "integrity" and "wisdom" are in order. In a large sense, integrity treats morality, but that generalized type of morality which incorporates truth and beauty; in addition, it stresses hope, hope woven of trust and love. In this respect, integrity comprises all members of the Greek and the scriptural triads, though always under the perspective of both goodness and hope. For integrity is concerned with that orientation toward objects which apprehends their mutability with respect to one's own best interests—i.e., one's interests conceived in the light of an ideal, an ideal "within" which all members of the community, in principle, participate, and which affords one authentic personal equanimity. Accordingly, hope always dominates the attitude of integrity—hope pervaded by trust and love. For, in the stance of integrity, the participants shape an ideal of peership in which this principle is affirmed: mutual loyalty will provide the conditions under which both parties may flourish with their fullest potentialities[3]—i.e., as whole and, therefore, *wholesome* human beings. In sum, integrity expresses the mutuality of participatory goodness.

Analogously, and as the culminating member of the triad which characterizes the spiritual (or essentially Christian) life, wisdom, in a large sense, deals with beauty and its correlate, love. Beyond that, it is interwoven with trust and hope, orientations toward the person which ground the possibility for the attainment of both truth and goodness. In wisdom, a person ceases to fragment experience; he enjoys its wholeness, its aliveness, and its unconditioned worth.[4] One becomes human freedom incarnate. For in wisdom the *fullness* of participation is achieved; in rhythmic alternation between inwardness and outwardness, a reverent bond to the other is established.[5] In effect, "One surrenders oneself to existence, to Rilke's 'imperishable invisibility' into which one has transfigured the visible and in which one always participates."[6] Implicating the aesthetic, in its most inclusive sense, wisdom nonetheless subsumes, without negating, the cognitive and the moral. Transcending both, it interrelates these enterprises, while denying the essential autonomy of neither. Indeed, by no arbitrary choice does Kant make his *Third Critique* the crown and glory, the very keystone for the understanding, of his entire work, the fullest and most satisfying presentation of the noumenon. Nor is Hegel succumbing to an inflexible dialectic when, of the moments of consciousness which unfold as his *Phenomenology*, the earliest pertain to sense, perception, and understanding, the intermediate to custom, morality, and statesmanship, and the culminating to art, religion, and philosophy. The last, for Hegel, constitute spheres of existence in which, by stages, the dialectic replicates itself, on successively higher levels, as wisdom itself unfolds toward its own consummation in the *Absolute*: the great cosmic ferment of participation *par excellence*, participation of creatures interfusing as they themselves are benignly suffused by the Creator.

In brief, justice is that preliminary search of human being, the latter's initiating phase, which, in its own unfolding moments, points toward and prefigures the stages which will succeed it—namely, integrity and wisdom—and grounds the very possibility for the realization of those stages. The *path* which one must traverse in order for the higher components of a life which is both good and pious—hence, spiritual—fully to be attained, justice, in *its* very essence, is nonetheless woven into that life's essence. Hence, justice is not so much a state, either of persons or of communities, as a process and a dynamism. It is the movement and the flow *toward* integrity and wisdom; yet it is always permeated *by* integrity and wisdom. Accordingly, the just person is one who so coordinates the life, on the one hand, of the true, the good, and the beautiful, and, on the other, of trust, hope, and love, that the quest toward the culmination of that life in wisdom is facilitated and, indeed, made possible.

In this sense, justice is a means to an end; it is an actual state of dynamic relatedness, within oneself to oneself, and within the community to another, a state which grounds the possibility for the attainment of an ideal. Still, as I have stated, no means can be employed toward any end unless it, in fact, partakes significantly of qualities belonging to that end. Hence, to be just, one must never desist from imbuing one's life with concrete anticipations of that of which both integrity and wisdom consist. For one thus imbued, justice, insofar as integrity and wisdom are ideals, is itself ideal. To that extent, its status is normative. In effect, it is an *ought*—indeed, by implication, the quintessential ought of human existence. Yet, as an end achieved, justice is an actuality. It is, I stress, the concrete condition whereby integrity and wisdom become possible. Moreover, even they, those moments in searching's process higher than justice, themselves partake of the character of both ends and means. For, once attained, integrity itself, now sublating justice as one of its essential constituents, serves as means whereby wisdom's end may be attained. Hence, integrity, too, exhibits a dialectical interplay between *is* and *ought, actual* and *ideal*, the *descriptive* and the *normative*. But even when wisdom is attained—this pinnacle of human existence with respect to which justice and integrity are but penultimate moments— a new unfolding occurs; and the dialectic of *is* and *ought* replicates itself anew.

Accordingly, in every instance, these phases, which are at the same time contemporaneous aspects of the life which is good and pious—hence, spiritual —bring about, by their inmost natures, the engaging of ideal and real. In each case, a transition is effected. At bottom, this transition is a mediation, involving the mediated passage from a state of disharmony, relatively speaking, to a state of harmony, relatively speaking. Once integrity has been attained, a new context is provided within which more inclusive modes of justice become possible; once wisdom has been attained, an analogous context is provided within which more inclusive modes of integrity and of justice become possible. Yet, throughout this process, all three ingredients of the spiritual life are present; and, as *com*present, they are dialectically interrelated. My aim is to explicate this dialectic from the point of view of but one member of the triad: namely, justice.

II

Reflection on the etymology of the term "justice" discloses an aspect of this preparatory stage of the journey through the realms of spirit—namely, those realms suggested by integrity and wisdom. Deriving from the Latin *ius*, meaning "right in the sense of joining" (or fitting), and, before that, from the Sanskrit, meaning "to join,"[7] *justice* may be regarded as *uniting* in several ways: *qua* solitary, a person reveals his diverse parts as coordinated to an integral and harmonious whole; *qua* interpersonal, he relates to another in ways which are woven to a unitary and cohesive fabric; *qua* social, a person dwells in a community which exhibits a scheme of equilibrium within which he may find a uniquely appropriate role and function; *qua* cosmic, a person is brought into relationship with the universe in a larger sense—for κόσμος, that attunement of seemingly disparate realms, shapes the ultimate ground whereby the less inclusive harmonies of community, interpersonal relation, and personal makeup may be achieved. In general, therefore, justice implies mutual affinity and participation. It is striking to note that, from an etymologic point of view, symbol, deriving from συμβάλλειν, also means a joining together. In consequence, in this essay I regard "justice" and "symbol" as though they were cognate terms; and I develop a context of thought in which I show that, correctly deciphered, the symbolisms of the presence and compresence of persons are, at one and the same time, marks of the justice of a person—his justice with respect to himself, to his fellows, to his community, to the world as a whole.

Adverting to the common etymologic ingredient in "justice" and in "symbol"—namely, *joining*—I may affirm: various ways of joining characterize human being. In effect, they are patterns of balance and imbalance, and they express modes of coherence with respect to the arrangement of his functions, his parts, his aspects. It is as though a scarce commodity, namely, *anima*—that which animates and ensouls the person as person—is distributed to these factors in accordance with a principle of equity. The analogue of a corresponding principle for securing justice for society, this principle likewise has its correlate in a principle governing the interwovenness, order, and mutual affinities prevailing throughout the cosmos. Indeed, personal harmony, interpersonal attunement, social equity, and cosmic order are coordinate and mutually presupposing notions. Each mode of "joining" represents a dynamic state of some class of entities. And not only do these states mirror one another, they interweave and interpenetrate. In this essay, I am concerned (primarily) with how equity, expressing a *preliminary joining of issues*—a co-adaptation of responsibilities and an attunement of diverse conflicting interests, activities, and dynamisms—grounds integrity; and (secondarily) with how, as a result, integrity, expressing the transmutation of conflict to contrast, shapes that unique and individual cohesiveness which itself grounds the flowing forth of wisdom.

Since justice is but the first phase of a process, it is impossible fully to characterize this phase without predelineating certain qualities of the succeeding phases. For justice is but the initial stage setting in motion an experiential journey into the self and the unfolding of the moments of this journey toward integrity and, ultimately, wisdom. To take Dante's *Commedia* as concrete exemplar of such journeys: the *Paradiso* expresses man's strivings toward final wisdom; the *Purgatorio*, his strivings toward mediating integrity; and the *Inferno*, his strivings toward the acceptance of the justice meted to him consequent upon his recognition of the truth of his actions. Now, I outline, as it were *in abstracto*, the main problems associated with the initiation of this quest.

In my account, justice pertains to man's whole being: not merely to his body as such, in its soul-informed πρᾶξις—his physical and practical actions—or to his soul as such, in its body-informed θεωρία—his spiritual and intellectual actions. Hence, justice concerns *anima*, the spirit which animates body and soul; and it treats the way in which, by a principle of equity, *anima* distributes, as it were, in appropriate (i.e., fitting or just) proportions, symmetries, harmonies, and (in a word) balances to a person's integral being. Ever torn among conflicting options, each person is compelled to choose. His tendency to be torn asunder pertains quite as much to his body as to his soul. Many forces play upon him. Depending upon the resilience and sturdiness of his body and his soul, his actions exhibit different grades of congruity among themselves. Diverse tendencies, compulsions, and powers are at work within him. Indeed, so strong is a person's need to conform to the demands of his environment, giving himself up to whatever he perceives to be its factuality, and hence genuinely persuaded of his attitude of truthfulness, that he becomes too easily *deformed* in his inmost being. For reality's distorted sectors work so massively upon the person that he readily declines to a "scotosis of truth,"[8] eclipsing, by the imagery of deformation, existence's significant regions. Hence, justice pertains to a person's opening himself up, by an act of free will, to his being informed of reality's ever wider aspects and humankind's ever broader concerns. It thereby enables him to rectify deformation and to bring into more synchronous relationship hitherto incongruous regions of his being. In this manner, justice prepares the way which must be traversed that, by the unitary impact of *responsibly* interwoven parts—i.e., parts authentically responsive to reality's deeper textures—he might, in integrity, achieve more potent, durable, and clarified commitments.

By integrity, I intend a double meaning: *integrality*, in the sense of one and indivisible; *integument*, in the sense of a covering sensitive to touch. Hence, the integrated person is one who, as a *totum* resonating to his world's textures, responds appropriately to their impact. The just man prefigures the man of integrity, as the latter prefigures the man of wisdom. He is a contemplative man: one who contemplates various possibilities of action, and interweaves as a coherent assemblage his specific choices for action. In addition, he is a practical man who perceives plausible courses of action: namely, those which conduce to more durable commitment. As contemplative, the just man envisages such factors of his existence as might be woven into his shaping acts; he surveys the facts and he selects what is appropriate and fitting—always guided both by those of his options which he adjudges will best adapt themselves to those facts, and by those schemes of co-adaptation which will allow for more inclusive harmonious arrangements. Led by the vision of ever larger schemes, i.e., the aesthetic, the just person will mediate his πρᾶξις through his anticipatory θεωρία, and he will mediate his θεωρία by the concrete appraisals of his πρᾶξις. In this sense, he achieves a kind of balance between πρᾶξις and θεωρία. But this balance is weighted on the side of θεωρία. For, first and foremost, justice requires acknowledgment of the facts: his own existence, with its possibilities and its constrictions. Accordingly, since these facts must be known as grounding all action, though ultimately they can be *fully* known only in the context of prior action, justice is primarily the quest for truth: that, in hope, the good will flow from that truth; that perspectives of love and beauty will envelop it.

In justice, the person attains first a balance, fragile and precarious but true and valid, between πρᾶξις and θεωρία, the dialectically interwoven "divisions" of his being. Like a pendulum, the swing tends first toward θεωρία —a rendering of a judgment, a discernment, an acceptance of the facts; then, by way of compensation, toward πρᾶξις. Now, in accordance with the ideal of harmony, the world is reshaped. Yet this activity is already prefigured in the state of justice by the *idea*. For no *is* may long be kept apart from the *ought* toward which it flows, and into which it blends. Hence, coherence, attunement, and balancing of the facts precede the reconstituting of facts. A perceived inner congruity between the physiognomic symbols of every person reveals the interwoven patterns of rhythmic balance: body patterns as physique; soul patterns as psyche; numberless intermediate patterns partaking of the nature, on varying levels of corporeality or spirituality, of body and soul. When facts apprehended as coherent are transformed into facts shaped as coherent, the stage of integrity is attained. Often, the ideal itself falls into discord with the facts. To achieve a more satisfying concordance, a new balance between *is* and *ought*—idea and ideal—must be effected. Subsuming the true, hence trusting, person, conveyed by justice's orientation, and the good and hopeful person, enhanced by integrity's orientation—each orientation itself woven of its own truth, goodness, and beauty, and, correlatively, its own trust, hope, and love—and sublating all moments and stages, the integral person becomes luminous with wisdom's rhythms. Now, man, community, and universe harmonize. Pervading successively more advanced levels of equilibration, each firmer and more subtle than its predecessor, the three themes—justice, integrity, and wisdom—in succession dominate. Each a relative invariant, all comprise a common thread which passes through, and binds to unity, the correlated triads, Greek and scriptural.

III

Referred to the person, justice, I repeat, pertains to modes of distributing to his diverse parts a scarce commodity—namely, *anima*—in accordance with a principle of equity. In what sense may "commodity," "equity," and "part" be applied to the person? Certainly for communities those social arrangements are deemed just in which social equity prevails. By this I mean: a community's every member is accorded his due, for something is owed him by society; in the measure to which he has received, each person accordingly becomes indebted to society; as he, in turn, gives *to* society, society once again incurs a debt to him; hence, reciprocity prevails between community and person, a symmetry of obligation. Justice ascertains (and enforces by communally sanctioned means) the factual basis upon which this symmetry rests—though its modes of enforcement must, to be themselves just, be compatible with the kinds and qualities of obligation which it endeavors to sustain. Analogously, each "member" of a society, itself a kind of person (for it is composed of both psychic and physical parts—parts which are but loci on a continuum of personal "resonances"[9]) is under existential obligation (or even compulsion) to sacrifice a measure of *its* autonomy that the continued welfare of the whole, construed as person, be assured. Conversely, the person himself *qua* person is under personal obligation so to orient himself toward his every part that each part receives, by virtue of such orientation, *its* due within that whole. For, as with community and person, whole and part are in reciprocal and dynamic relatedness; neither ought, according to the principles of equity, to function in any way which will violate the integrity of the other. Moreover, the different parts of a person exhibit varying degrees of independence. Hence, in proportion to their intrinsic autonomy, these parts are in varying conditions of bondage: i.e., bonded, or "joined," in the etymologic sense of justice, to the whole.

With respect to a person's physical aspect: if, for example, certain anatomical structures were to be amputated, regeneration would occur. For the organism is empowered to produce virtual duplicates of such of its structures as possess relative autonomy, hence independence of the context provided by that organism. It is as though they are enabled vicariously to survive even their own destruction, to survive in the literal sense of *super-vivere*: a (substitutive) living beyond the most severe of crises of their own natural history; *a fortiori*, persons themselves survive such partial dissolution. Likewise, persons replicate themselves; despite the perishing of their individual members, communities survive with essentially stable institutions. On the other hand, persons survive symbolically (and in a deeply poetic sense) in their progeny; indeed, even a kind of biologic—or genetic—survival supervenes. But these analogies may not be pressed too far. For persons exhibit identities in a sense transcending the sense in which parts of persons exhibit identities. Yet a lesson is to be learned from these analogies, however limited their scope. Too, were they to be disrupted, certain biologic functions may readily be compensated for by other functions. On the other hand, some structures and functions, like those of the central nervous system, are radically dependent upon a person's total configuration; they are intrinsically incapable of regeneration. Hence, in the measure of their intrinsic degree or mode of autonomy, each structure and each function "owe" their own integrity to the totality of which they are constituents. Likewise, the totality reciprocally "owes" the appropriate "quantity" of *anima* to its every part. For, to be responsible for their well-being—since each part is, after all, in some measure intrinsically weak or un–self-sufficient—the requisite biochemical energies must be "fairly" (i.e., with equity) distributed to all parts.

Accordingly, the person owes hierarchically ordered obligations to his diverse physical parts. When, with respect to persons, I speak of independence and dependence, and the corresponding "obligations" of parts to whole, the analogy to the community of persons again breaks down. Only to a minimal extent does each part manifest anything resembling "free will." Accordingly, the whole person works in and through his every part, conferring upon it an essential context for its appropriate activity, the conditions under which, by its genetically determined composition, that part may indeed "act" autonomously. In other words, in the realm of personal being, parts provide their own contexts of activity to an incomparably less extent than do their analogues, persons, in the realm of community being. Still, up to a point, this analogy does hold. For a society imposes upon its members at least some significant patterns of determined behavior. Surely, it may modify their power for free will by, in part, depotentiating that power, and thereby lessening the scope of their options. Hence, societies as well as persons provide contexts for the activities of their relevant constituencies. Nevertheless, in general, far more than societies, the person as a whole energizes his every part. Displacing energy from one part to another, he effects all manner of energy transfer—always, of course, within the limits imposed by both the physico-chemical and the biological makeup of each part. Moreover, a part which has succumbed to pathologic processes resists every effort of the person to invigorate it and to restore it to its "natural" mode of functioning. Alternatively, were the person afflicted by psychic pathology, he himself might resist his inclinations to activate a part which would, under conditions of psychic health, overcome its *own* pathology.

Clearly a person's psychic "parts" are interwoven with his physical parts. Just as he can orient himself toward this or that bodily structure, and energize or de-energize it, as the case may be, so a person may assume similar attitudes toward his psychic parts. Thus, he can allow himself to be enveloped by an idea, consumed by it, or he can dwell upon it in such fashion as to bring to fruition its germinal content. In short, a person may permit that mental element to make *its* distinctive contribution to his overall being. Alternatively, as with physical parts, ideas may be deformed in varying degrees and ways, and brought into different kinds of conformation with the totality. Should a person dwell excessively with his own ideation, he may even deflect his attending to or from some relevant physical factor—in effect, remove the requisite *anima* or animating energy. For example, in the phenomenon of the phantom limb, a person may perpetuate beyond what makes ecologic sense for him (i.e., to the point of disrupting a prevailingly wholesome ecology of his parts) the illusion of a limb which, having been amputated, is *de facto* non-existent. He may waste his ideas on thought perseveration with respect to this preoccupation, allowing for an irrelevant and unwholesome efflorescence: a bizarre fungosity, so to speak, like a cancerous growth in a body. Always, the issue is one of balance, attunement, rhythm. Beyond that, it is a matter of the way in which a person conserves *anima*. True, his energetic power to animate is limited and, in the final analysis, distributes a scarce commodity. For life is short; all manner of affliction may impinge upon one. Dramatically or insidiously, these afflictions take their toll. Yet, as overall energy diminishes, novel schemes may be devised to conserve what energy remains. More important, subtle nuances of increasingly imaginative creative expression may be discovered. In this sense, the possibilities for such expression are numberless; the mysterious reserves of imaginational, and valid, cosmic representations are fathomless.

In general, justice orients itself toward conserving energy, securing itself on already established bases and perpetually appealing to tradition. In its subsequent evolution, different schemes of integrity, each grounded in and arising from foundations which it has secured, will point the way toward that liberalizing of justice which alone may reveal its concrete new forms. But, at this point, wisdom will already have been attained, with all *its* unfolding moments.

Through his energy conservation, a person builds up a reservoir from which he may deflect, in appropriate increments, such "energies" as are required for his new needs, bodily and psychic—needs which reveal themselves through tension within the already established scheme of equilibrium. Always, his problem is to achieve equity—the equity which lies at justice's very core. By equity, I mean this triphasic process: (*a*) anticipating possible new needs, estimating the likelihood with which these needs arise and deciding the way in which they are to be ranked with respect to their importance for a person's integrity; (*b*) conserving sufficient stores of energy, by such techniques as meditation or *t'ai chi*, so that, in quiet relatedness to the cosmos, energies are not actually bound, but held in abeyance; and (*c*) distributing the relevant energies, each weighted in accordance with a plan which requires continual modification as it is put into practice, as actual need arises, by a person's deliberately placing himself now in this part of his being, now in that. In principle, equity synchronizes the workings of these diverse parts, and thus harmoniously orders and coordinates his body activity and his soul activity.

IV

Earlier, I wrote of justice as concerned with facts; it treats the linking or cohering of facts. Always conditioned by hope and goodness (i.e., concern), and, more inclusively, by an overarching vision of beauty woven with love, justice seeks truth: the factual ground for human equilibrium and disequilibrium. Too, I referred to the interpenetrating themes of transcendence (or, in effect, fructification) and conservation. Though the latter theme dominates the explicit quest for justice, the former works immanently and pervasively to guarantee justice's dynamism. For all parts of the person strain, as it were, toward their mutual integration, that full integral personhood be achieved. Pathology alone, that of the person as a whole or that of any particular sector of the person, diminishes that straining's efficacy. By *straining*, I imply that an implicit intentionality is at work within a person's part: as long as that part is not disconnected from him—as long, that is, as it is functioning within a context provided by the person's living presence. Thus, a dead and amputated limb bears only the appearance, never the substance, of the limb as it actually functions. In general, no part of the person is a part save insofar as it is a part *of* the person: that is, operative as continually affected by that person—in other words, *in situ* or *in vivo*, rather than in isolation and *in vitro*. Accordingly, *fructification* expresses the principle by which, to achieve equity, no part of the person may be conceived as *merely* functioning. Like surviving, straining implies a going beyond any particular state of activity already achieved by any particular part. In brief, it is as though every part, insofar as it is an element within a pattern governed by equity, strives toward transcendence—i.e., toward its own ever more potent energy state.

Just as I have spoken of a principle which is the analogue of the law of energy conservation, so I now invoke a principle analogous to the law of inexorably increasing entropy; in particular, I treat the meaning for living, especially human, processes of the connection between these principles. Granted, the province of justice is fact, and its end is to adjudicate between conflicting construals or interrelations of fact. Nonetheless, its mode of governance cannot be wholly determined by a criterion which refers to stability of a past ecologic arrangement of the parts of either person or community. For, by the second law of thermodynamics, in its most general form, the overall quantity of energy available for use diminishes in time—granted, in isolated systems. On the supposition that person and community are partly isolated systems, *utilizable* energy for distribution among their respective parts cannot be presumed as a constant. For justice to prevail, and for equity to reign, different modes of apportioning energy over time must, in consequence, be adopted. Under the assumption of a quasi-entropic personal system, no static equilibrium suffices; passage must always be toward such conditions of equilibrium as will tend either to "coarsen" the parts, lessening subtle differentiations and finer nuance, or, alternatively, to "etherealize" the parts—so to heighten differentiation that ever more delicate nuance is achieved.[10]

In consequence, in its actual governance, justice always confronts a fundamental choice. On the one hand, it may opt for conserving a given equilibrium. In this case, the subtler distinctions among a person's parts (or, for that matter, a community's parts) will inexorably diminish. Alternatively, it may opt for fructification. In the latter instance, justice fully acknowledges that, though governed by sheer factuality, it is, nonetheless, haunted by hope and by love: that integrity might prevail, a *better* arrangement of the relevant factors is sought; that wisdom might prevail, the *best* arrangement which a refined vision can afford for ordering those factors is sought. With respect to the concept of justice as grounding personal harmony: though justice must attend the limiting circumstances of conservation, and, hence, is obligated to economize equity, it must also be inspired by the potentialities for fructification. Hence, justice must temper its tough-minded obeisance to fact, thus *idea*, and ought never to desist from a tenderhearted cognizance of the *ideal*. To know the latter, it must seek instruction from the ideal's exemplar, wisdom.

Concerned as they are with a species of justice in the sense of harmony, the complementary roles of physician and philosopher both illustrate and amplify my argument. Whether one consider the healers of antiquity, their herbs and their incantations, or the first great physician, who was also among the first great philosophers—namely, Hippocrates—medicine originally aimed at restoring equilibrium, at providing the person with a suitable ground for continued efficacy of action. It rectified pathology; it restored health. But not only were the great Asclepieia of ancient Greece sanctuaries of healing herbs and mineral waters, they were repositories of temples and statuary. Located to afford inspiring vistas of mountain, land, and sea, they were eminently conducive to states of psychic harmony—as in the mother Asclepieion at Kos, its great landscapes stretching toward Halicarnassus where Herodotus dwelt, his fantasies first dawning of distant lands and fructifying new modes of civilization and civility; as in a daughter Asclepieion adjacent to the Greek theater at Epidaurus, where justice—itself given by the gods out of their wisdom's fullness—was, embodied in the drama, often enacted as the dominant theme of an Aeschylus or a Sophocles. Surely, the philosopher instructs the physician concerning experience's finer nuances—given the rectification of their frailities, physical or mental. Analogously, the just man, who perforce is both the man of primordial integrity and the visionary who perceives ever more inclusive modes of integrity, must also be affected by a touch of wisdom. So judges must be instructed by poets; so every judge must himself be poetic; so, beginning his career as a competent judge, one who correctly and fairly—i.e., in the light of equity—appraises a situation must culminate his career in the deeper perceptions of mystic and poet.

Dwelling in *Inferno*, man acquires a sense of justice. Perceiving his flaws, he tries ways of rectifying them. Freed from their encumbrance, and accompanied by Virgil—Reason's poet—he journeys to *Purgatorio*'s threshold. There, he prepares to purify himself; he allows flaws to perish. Now forgetting his affliction by pathology, he is led (and he who is led, we must recall, is Dante the poet!) to Beatrice. It is she who is the multiple incarnation, at first, of schemes of integrity, and then, as *Paradiso* is entered, of successive levels of poetic purity, philosophic comprehension, religious piety, and, at the end of the way, mystical compassion. In the last analysis, the very watchword is compassion, compassion in the light of reverence: reverence for man; reverence for his family; reverence for his friends; reverence for his personal community; reverence for the larger human community; reverence for all that lives and breathes and for all that is animate as well and, in its own manner, all that merits our respect and our affection; reverence for the Creator—fount of love and beauty synthesized, without sacrificing justice or integrity, to wisdom. Dante's vision is of justice brought to fruition, of justice's endlessly novel efflorescences. Dante's journey is a growth through justice, in all its variegated forms, so that, at the end, he is *beyond* justice.

V

Previously, I referred to a person's ecology. By this I meant the unfolding balances of his structures, his processes, his rhythms, his functions. These balances ceaselessly shift; they transform themselves in response to a continually altering environment which imposes ever new demands upon him. Because of the displacements of the schemes of co-adaptation which result from these changes, every part of his body and his soul undergoes its own re-adaptations, both among themselves and with respect to the milieu relevant to the proper functioning of each. In consequence, the person is always poised to effect some new ecologic arrangement. His evolving life processes are composed of continual sequences of such arrangements, each required by environmental contingencies. By analogy, the community, whose parts are persons, must, by submission or by combat, come to terms with dangerous external forces, uncontrollable alien influences which threaten to disrupt it. Such factors may so impinge upon the community as to cause it, that it may protect itself, to mobilize countervailing forces. That a new and more realistic mode of equity may prevail, the community might even be compelled to shape new institutions for guaranteeing its internal security. Likewise, persons are communities of parts, parts which are so mutually implicated in relationships of reciprocal participation and interdependence—though always with a certain hierarchical ordering—that they may be regarded as virtually "communing" with one another. When a particular part is threatened, as the physique by antigen invasion, the reticulo-endothelial system, ever attuned to the dangers of the destructive forces, sets in motion, to avert catastrophe, such *intra*personal organismic activities as will effectively ward off danger; or when an emotional trauma strikes the psyche, repressive dynamisms are set up, lest the person succumb to a too fragile re-equilibration. Specific traumata are dissociated from awareness. Relegated to an innocuous region of the psyche, they activate a defensive reaction by which the threat, symbolized as psychic defenses, is reduced without at the same time failing to register, by psychic representation, its continued presence within the person. Yet that very defense incorporates his strivings to overcome the threat.

Accordingly, every person builds layers of symbols. By his essence, he *is* an activity of continual symbol creation. And, by these symbols, he expresses, however circuitously, the entire factual state of his being, physical and psychic. By the ways in which his symbols are layered, one upon another, to form an intricately laminated fabric, the justice of the person *qua* person is revealed. For this fabric discloses his characteristic mode of coordination, his style of balance. His diverse parts are more or less congruous; the kind of congruity which they display exhibits schemes of interwovenness which reveal his most fundamental rhythms. A person's psychic aspects and his physical aspects are themselves but functions, more or less complicated, of those rhythms. I cannot sufficiently stress their primordial character. By an argument which I developed elsewhere, the person, in his inmost core, *is* rhythmicality; his very substance is constituted by rhythmic cyclicities, rhythmic spirallings, rhythmic orchestrations, rhythmic synchronicities.[11]

Of these configurations, the "coarser," so to speak, are the physical; the more "ethereal" and the more evanescent are the psychic; those which mediate the physical and the psychic are, in effect, his unconscious activities. For, I am assuming, by a position elsewhere stated,[12] that mind *is* body etherealized and that body *is* mind in its weightiness. I use the metaphors of gravity and levitation to suggest, first, that a continuum prevails between mental acts and physical acts, and, secondly, that both the mental and the physical are attributes, in a Spinozist sense. They are but aspects of one substance, a substance which transcends each realm while containing, as immanent within it, both realms; yet, in this very immanence and in this very transcendence, substance, as it were—though its *emanata* are physically modal or psychically modal—encloses endless mysteries, mysteries *transcendental* with respect to either realm: mysteries, indeed, enclosed within mysteries. At the same time, sufficiently penetrated, both realms, mind and body, lead to the very heart of substance. Fully explored in its consummate form, each realm reveals substance in its entirety; each flows into, becomes interwoven with, and blends with substance; each manifests the full character of substance: a character which is dynamic, organic, dialectical, processive. Under the perspective of the modal intertwinings of substance, its vicissitudes and its depths, its possibilities and its powers, the modal character of mind and body, understood in their variegated schemes of balance and imbalance, expresses the nature of *justice as grounding personal harmony*.

Hence, the just person is the one who represents himself, to himself and to others, authentically and without deceit. He expresses himself in ways which accurately correspond to the facts of the case; he unreservedly manifests his rhythmic nature's true cast. Neither does he willfully dupe nor does he use contrivances for concealing his actual state. On the contrary, he endeavors to present his substance, which is his distinctive rhythmicality, in its flaws as well as in its perfections: truly and without reservation. When Thrasymachus argues that the happiest man is the one who gives the appearance of being just, and thereby gains the advantages which would accrue to such a *persona*, yet, in actuality, possesses the powers, hence the advantages, of the unjust man, he postulates a person so split asunder within his substance that the dynamism by which the succeeding stage of integrity would otherwise unfold is impeded or, indeed, negated. Such a person would ineluctably be arrested in his growth toward wisdom. For, in this contradiction within him, the person so divides himself from himself that by thus seeming to acquire *two* sets of advantages, each by a means opposed to the other, he immobilizes himself; he becomes frankly impotent. He loses the capacity for potentiating those distinctively human powers which will allow him to bring to fruition his uniquely human destiny.

Basically, it is a matter of means and ends. For a means to conduce to a given end, I repeat, it must be qualified by qualities which resemble, and do not too greatly deviate from, the qualities imparted to that end. Otherwise, that means would conduce to an end opposite to the end presumably intended. On the other hand, were the means not, by a small increment, slightly less perfect than the intended end, it would lack the motive force, the dynamism, to attain that end. Finally, if the qualities of means and end were identical, the former would, in effect, collapse into the latter; no distinction would obtain between means and ends. Indeed, in the final analysis, no end can remain as such. Through subtle disequilibration, it has, once achieved, already become a new means directed toward a new end. For means and ends shape a continuum; they are organically and dynamically interwoven. Thus split asunder, the Thrasymachian man splits asunder this continuum of his own actions.

What is the connection between these brief reflections on means and ends and the theme of justice, especially of justice as the way toward integrity and wisdom? Focally concerned with truth, under the perspective of goodness and beauty—i.e., a trusting, pervaded by hope and by love, that all relevant facts will be disclosed—justice employs *par excellence* the method of ratiocination. For the end of justice is so to order facts that the configurings of ideas which represent those facts will ground the values implicit therein; it is accordingly oriented toward the drawing forth of ideals profoundly interfused with facts, and never radically severed from them. By dispassionate reason, appraisals are made. Yet the rational means employed by justice's attitude must be qualified by a double orientation: hope that knowledge of the facts will transform the knower to a better, hence more integral, person—i.e., a person of greater integrity; and love for that person in his human essence, that the beauty of that essence might flow into novel and ever more inclusive schemes of wisdom: that, in effect, the factual status of man will be reconciled to his ideal status.

Accordingly, the means used to lead the person from his merely factual status toward an ideal immanent within and germinating through that status, namely, *reason*, is converted, once the end of integrity is attained, to a new means, namely, *intuition*: that means which incorporates ever larger visions of what man is capable of attaining in his growth toward wisdom. Hence, reason directed by trust in the healing force of truth so conduces to the end of integrity, the healed condition, that the latter, once attained, itself becomes a new means, namely, intuition, which, directed by hope and a perception of the possibility of love, points toward the most generalized perceptions of all—those inherent in wisdom's beauty. Therefore, the journey which Dante undertakes is a preparation for his own final encounter with all aspects of his being. According to his vision, bound together by love, the numberless layers of man's symbolisms will cohere as a single, indivisible unity, but without sacrifice of the numberless nuances which these symbolisms never cease to exhibit. All this, a fusion of unity and plurality, is orchestrated to organically interwoven strands of means and ends, and a continual growth of the former to the latter and of the latter to the former: growth initiated in justice, growth brought to its first consummation as integrity, growth culminating in wisdom's dynamics. Thereby, human being is irradiated with the fire of the universe's divine center.

In sum, I have spoken of justice, and the immanence within justice of integrity and wisdom, in a merely abstract way. For my account to be more compelling, it must be supplemented by an experiential depiction of the actual journey from justice, through integrity, to wisdom; it must enumerate and specify the phases and moments of this quest. But, for the quest to begin, justice must prevail as primordially grounding personal harmony. For justice is the quest's very catalyst; and the quest itself must be portrayed. In it, man undertakes an arduous journey. Indeed, he proceeds upon a double journey. On the one hand, he explores the facts, the intentions, the yearnings, of his own interiority; on the other, he searches into those external circumstances which allow his potentialities to effloresce. Thereby, he depicts the multiple layerings of the world within him and the world without. He reveals each route of this twofold journey as veridical complement to the other. In the last analysis, he aims his ultimate end at self-disclosure *in concreto*: his most inclusive harmonies, his symmetries and his attunements.

In this process, a life is achieved which surpasses the spiritual life in the same measure as *that* life surpasses both the good life and the pious life. For wisdom itself unfolds in unpredictable ways, ways which lead it to modes of existence which cannot yet be foreseen. Perhaps, ultimately, a synthesis of those approaches to life, and perceptions of reality, which incorporate Eastern as well as Western modes of philosophy must be concretely envisaged—that the horizons of what constitutes justice and integrity as well as wisdom be extended to what, under present perspectives, seem limitless, and even awesome.

"When a man grows old his joy," declared Yeats:

> Grows more deep day after day
> His empty heart is full at length
> But he has need of all that strength
> Because of the increasing Night
> That opens her mystery and Fright . . .[13]

Yet, when his life is just and illumined by integrity, he may, with "grace abounding,"[14] presume, with Dante, "to fix his look on the eternal light,"[15] and "within its depths,"[16] see "ingathered, bound by love in one volume, the scattered leaves of all the universe."[17] And now, at last, he may affirm:

> Omai sarà più corta mia favella
> pure a quel ch'io ricordo, che di un fante
> che bagni ancor la lingua alla mammella.[18]

And, in the fullness of his being, he can at last utter:

> O luce eterna, che sola in te sidi,
> sola t'intendi, e da te intelletta
> ed intendente te, ami ed arridi![19]

Truly, justice as grounding personal harmony is a stage along life's way toward integrity and, in the end, toward that wisdom with which Dante concludes his surpassing journey:

> All' alta fantasia qui mancò possa;
> ma gia volgeva il mio disiro e il velle,
> si come rota ch' egualmente è mossa,
> l'amor che move il sole e l'altre stelle.[20]

NOTES

1. See my "Personal Freedom: The Dialectics of Self-Possession," in *Freedom and Value*, ed. Robert O. Johann (New York: Fordham University Press, 1976), pp. 61–85.
2. See ibid., p. 81.
3. See ibid., p. 82.
4. See ibid., p. 83.
5. See ibid.
6. Ibid.
7. Eric Partridge, *Origins* (London: Routledge & Kegan Paul, 1958), p. 325.
8. See the discussion in Bernard J. F. Lonergan, s.j., *Insight* (New York: Philosophical Library), pp. 191–203.
9. See my "Luminosity: The Unconscious in the Integrated Person," in *Mental Health: Philosophical Perspectives*, edd. H. Tristram Engelhardt, Jr., and Stuart F. Spicker (Dordrecht: Reidel, 1976), pp. 177–88.
10. Ibid.

11. In my *Homo Quaerens: The Seeker and the Sought; Method Become Ontology* (New York: Fordham University Press, 1978), human rhythm is treated from a methodological point of view; in *The Dance of Being: Man's Labyrinthine Rhythms; The Natural Ground of the Human* (New York: Fordham University Press, 1979), from an ontological point of view.

12. See my "Luminosity," pp. 177–88.

13. "The Apparitions," *The Collected Poems of W. B. Yeats* (New York: Macmillan, 1940), p. 332.

14. *Paradiso*, 38.82.

15. Ibid., 38.82–83.

16. Ibid., 38.85.

17. Ibid., 38.86–87.

18. Ibid., 38.106–108.

19. Ibid., 38.124–26.

20. Ibid., 38.142–45.

II
LEGAL, CONSTITUTIONAL, AND MORAL THEORY ON JUSTICE

5

Relocating Justice

JOSEPH V. DOLAN, S.J.

Fordham University

FOR BOTH ARISTOTLE, who judged it an institution of nature, and Hobbes, who traced its origin to a social contract, civil society was a critical factor in the maintenance of justice. But for different, indeed opposed, reasons. For Aristotle man was by nature social, a ζῷον πολιτικόν; apart from society, he was outside his natural element "like an isolated piece at draughts." Separated from law and justice, he disintegrated to become "a lover of war," transformed from the best to the worst of animals. For the Englishman, on the contrary, man was the natural enemy of his kind. The original condition of nature was a war of all against all. Only with the pact to surrender the "natural right" of each individual to wage this war was the way paved for the emergence of the state as a purely legal entity and for a human existence no longer "solitary, poor, nasty, brutish and short." For the *Politics* the state[1] merely actuated the latent tendency of man to justice:

> It is characteristic of man that he alone has any sense of good and evil; of just and unjust, and the like, and the association of living things who have this sense makes a family and a state [Book I, chap. 2].

But for the *Leviathan* a justice prior to covenant would be unintelligible; it would have no conceivable object:

> To this war of every man against every man this also is consequent: that nothing can be unjust. The notions of right and wrong, justice and injustice, have there no place. Where there is no common power, there is no law: where no law, no injustice. . . . It is consequent also to the same condition, that there can be no propriety, no dominion, no *mine* and *thine* distinct; but only that to be every man's, that he can get; and for so long as he can keep it [Part I, chap. 13].

It is therefore of great, if currently neglected, significance that Western political thought—from Plato, Aristotle, Cicero, and Aquinas up to the authors of the classical treatises *de jure et justitia*—had always approached the treatment of justice by first establishing its character as a moral virtue and in accord with a definite conception of man. Before attacking the political and legal problems proper—a complicated business as the treatises themselves witness —it was necessary to understand justice as a disposition of the soul. It is Plato's preoccupation with justice "writ small," as a state of the soul, which prompts the search for its counterpart in the polis where it is found writ large (and there, too, as a moral condition). Despite its name, the *Republic* is primarily a treatise on moral education and for that reason a treatise on politics. Again, it is justice as ἕξις or moral habit which Aristotle, after treating fortitude and temperance, first examines in Book V of the *Ethics* before exploring the different forms of "objective" justice. Like Plato's, his political philosophy was a function of his philosophy of man and was developed in the context of his moral doctrine. The same is true of Cicero's *De legibus*: "We are born for justice, and right is based not on opinion but on nature," as evidenced by human fellowship founded on a common human nature.[2] The *Digest* defines jurisprudence as *ars boni et aequi*. And the *Institutes of Roman Law*, the textbook which shaped the legal thought of the West, opens with the famous definition of justice: *constans et perpetua voluntas ius suum cuique tribuens* ("the constant and permanent *will* to give each his due").

It was because justice was viewed in the first place as a quality perfective of man as a naturally political animal, related to his fellows on a societal as well as on an individual, one-to-one basis, that the tradition recognized the necessity and importance of a distinction between legal (or general) and particular justice and the division of the latter into distributive and commutative.[3] These terms, representing long and careful reflection, have about disappeared from political vocabulary. When they do appear they are either perfunctorily defined and dismissed or substantially (and unwittingly) altered—as is only to be expected when the principles and perspectives which gave rise to them have themselves been supplanted.

A problem arises as soon as we begin to probe, and attempt to ground, the classic definition already cited: justice is to give each his own, his due or right (*ius suum*). At first sight, the definition appears circular—"the emptiest of tautologies" (Kelsen)—in equivalently saying that justice consists in being just. For what else is "one's own" but what belongs to him in justice? It requires no long scrutiny to realize that with these notions—right, due, one's own—we are dealing no longer with merely factual, descriptive, and empirically observable data but with the category of relations. In other words, a man is not said to *have* or to *own* a house in the same way as a cat is said to have a tail or *its own* eyes. To *belong* in the juridical as distinct from the grammatical sense, and not as a mere physical property, means that even if they are permanently stolen a man's purse and good name are still *his*. *Res clamat domino*. But where are we to find the root of this persistent relation?

If we are to say with the legal positivist that the right which is the object of justice originates in human law itself (by supposition the only law there can be) or—what amounts to the same thing—in an enabling constitution or Bill of Rights, then rights derive in the final analysis from will; which means that law itself is lawless will (*stat pro ratione voluntas*). For right, then, to be objective—that is to say, not dependent on human will as something to be enjoyed at the state's or society's discretion—there must be a *ius* or right antecedent to, and itself normative for, the constitution and laws which ramify therefrom.[4] Otherwise, to say that justice is binding on the state or society and that there are objectively unjust political regimes (e.g., ones which sanction genocide) would amount to saying that the state can obligate or bind itself since it would be the ultimate source and foundation of authority and right. Justice Holmes was thoroughly consequent with his positivism when he drew the lesson for jurist and court:

What I can't understand is the suggestion that the United States is bound by law even though it does not assent. What I mean by law in this connection is that which is or should be enforced by the courts and I can't understand how anyone should think that an instrument established by the United States to carry out its will and that it can dispose upon failure to do so, should undertake to enforce something that is *ex hypothesi* against its will. It seems to me like shaking one's fist at the sky when the sky furnishes the energy that enables one to shake the fist. There is a tendency to think of judges as if they were the independent mouthpieces of the infinite, and not simply directors of the force that comes from the source that gives them authority. I think our Court has fallen into the error at times and it is this that I have aimed at when I said that the common law is not a brooding omnipresence in the sky and that the United States is not subject to some mystic overlaw that it is bound to obey.[5]

This is the flaw in any theory of justice grounded on contract, whether this be conceived as real event or simply as logical postulate. We may contract to acknowledge rights, and some rights can flow mediately from contract but not as from their originating principle. How would the contract itself be binding on the parties? By another implicit contract to abide by contracts *et sic ad infinitum*? And what could we make of the notion of *unjust* contract? The inference is inescapable that if justice is not finally a mere fiction of law, having its sole "authority" from man's will and thus man-disposable, then the human person must have a natural *suum*—something inviolably his own, in the juridical sense of *his*—which the first act of justice on the part of either individual or community with respect to him must suppose as already founding a claim. As Thomas Aquinas argues in showing that creation had to be a free act of God in no way owed in justice to the creature:

Since an act of justice "renders to each his own," it is preceded by an action through which something is made one's own, as is clear in human affairs. By

laboring, one deserves to have as his own that which the act of justice gives
him in recompense. Thus the act whereby something becomes one's own in
the first place could not be an act of justice.[6]

We must ask: What is this prelegal title or transcendent basis for one's right
to just treatment? The urgency of this question is by no means universally
appreciated, and some react to it with annoyance. Several reasons account for
this. Justice is an elementary notion which, like all "self-evident" and universally experienced realities, is difficult to analyze. Furthermore, it is a *value* and
a primary datum of moral consciousness. And since it is an irreducible first
principle of practical reason, connaturally grasped by a kind of attunement to
reality or *per inclinationem*, people tend to think that they also *see* its necessity
with their speculative intellect and that they have a reflex understanding of
its essence (which may explain a curious kind of schizophrenia which makes it
possible for people of just and even gentle disposition to adjust mentally to
theories of man and society which are of direst logical consequence).

The principal obstacle to dialogue, however, is the prevailing legal philosophy, which is resolutely positivist and which rejects our question out of hand
as metaphysical and therefore meaningless—one betraying a superstitious men-
tality associated with long discredited natural law jurisprudence. Thus Karl
Olivecrona, the Scandinavian realist, in his *Law as Fact* dismisses as "pure
superstition" the notion of a normative law "endowed with supernatural
power":

> If we discard the superstitious idea that the law emanates from a god, it is
> obvious that every rule of law is a creation of men. . . . Every attempt to
> maintain scientifically that law is binding in another sense than that of ac-
> tually exerting a pressure on the population, necessarily leads to absurdities
> and contradictions. Here, therefore, is the dividing-line between realism and
> metaphysics, between scientific method and mysticism in the explanation of
> the law. The "binding force" of the law is a reality merely as an idea in hu-
> man minds. There is nothing in the outside world which corresponds to this
> idea.[7]

Not only is it false to say that law is founded on an abstract norm of justice
"existing by itself *in nubibus*"; our moral ideas and feelings are themselves to
a large extent "a consequence of the 'administration of justice' through regular
infliction of punishment and extraction of damages."[8]

Before venturing our own exposition, we might briefly note some abortive
efforts to give the idea of justice an objective standing and therefore to make
it normative for the legal order. First, it is of no help for exposing the root of
justice to explain it simply as being fair. Whether we take it as referring to the
agent's own disposition or to something objective (as in "a fair wage"), as
soon as we look to the meaning of "fair," we see that things are the other way
around. Instead of explaining justice as being fair, we should say an action is

fair when it is just and renders what is due. We cannot, for example, be fair or unfair to animals since we cannot be just to them or unjust (although there are moral norms for our treatment of them). As we shall explain later, animals lack the basis for a claim to a having of something as *their own*.

Nor, despite an early established and significant connection between just and equitable (*justum et aequum*), can we say simply that to be just is to treat equals equally. Not until we have identified a special feature of this equality and understand the expression to mean treating equal *men* equally. There is, again, no obligation to treat plants and animals of the same species or the same ontological status equally.

Where, then, are we to locate our ultimate *titulus juris*, the radical capacity or formal *ratio* for a "having as one's own" and thus for claiming that an object, action, or abstention is owed one on the part of another? Our thesis is that it is to be found in the simple being of the human person as such. To be a person is by that very fact to have a *suum* and to be absolutely and immediately—i.e., without any further mediating condition—the subject of rights. This is what the Declaration of Independence equivalently affirms in stating that *all* men are endowed *by their Creator*[9] with certain inalienable rights. And although the metaphysics, theology, and anthropology which originally shaped —and which alone can sustain—this position are no longer the object of a consensus, legal terminology itself continues to associate the notions of person and *sui juris* (as in designating corporations as "artificial persons"). It is this same conception which formed the original content of the expression "human dignity"—another term of ancient coinage now debased.

The word "dignity," from the Latin *dignitas*, translates the Greek ἀξίωμα and means inherent worth or excellence to which recognition and honor were due. In the ancient Christian liturgies God Himself was pre-eminently ὁ Ἄξιος (a sense carried over in our "dignitary"). The axioms (ἀξιώματα) of geometry—their Latin counterparts were the *dignitates*—were by metaphor so called because, being first principles, they were *self*-evident truths standing on their own, independent, and in no need of support by argument through the mediation of others;[10] on the contrary, other truths resolved in them as in their foundation. They were by analogy *sui juris* and not subject to challenge.

To claim a dignity for the human person is, then, to assert its intrinsic worth in this absolute sense and prior to any human conferral or further acquired "accidental" dignity of office, accomplishment, or graceful bearing. To press the term: the person is self-justified; he shares in a "realm of ends" and is not ordered as a means to the advantage of others. He may be legitimately subordinated—as a child to parent, subject to superior, citizen to the common good—but even this ordering must be finally justified as furthering the good of the person himself.

So much for the idea of dignity. But is human dignity real or merely postulated, in the manner of Plato's noble and necessary lie, as a supportive political myth "by which we might tell one genuine lie worthy of the name and persuade the rulers themselves that it is true, or at least persuade the rest of the city" (*Republic*, 414B)? May not the perception of dignity be a mere projection, and the instinct for justice a species-specific imprinting through which nature preserves *Homo sapiens* ("apart from law and justice the worst of animals") from self-destruction? Or are there cogent grounds for affirming that the person is uniquely worthy? We shall propose two characteristic and correlative features of human personality which indicate its dignity and inherent inviolability: (*a*) its power of self-determination or freedom of will; and (*b*) the existence of moral obligation as regulative of this freedom.

(*a*) The significance of man's freedom in this regard is most readily appreciated by contrast with the animal's. The animal is without any such power of decision. Its activity is completely determined by the environment, its future programed by its biology. Lacking a true self or ego, it is unable to "reflect"; nor can it perceive the good as such (*bonum in communi*) in terms of which it could judge objectively, i.e., in abstraction from an immediate particular and sensibly attractive good (*bonum delectabile*). That is why the animal can neither make progress nor develop a culture. Without "reason and hands," it can develop no art, not even a servile art to emancipate it from the determinations of the material environment, remaining totally passive before it even in what appear superficially to be active responses.

To be free, on the other hand, is to be left in the hands of one's own counsel, to be able to deliberate and weigh alternate courses of action in the forum of one's own interior tribunal, to refer them to one's own personally sanctioned standard of goodness and then commit oneself by acceptance or rejection. Instinct, appetite, and the will's own inclination await this final decision. In a more profound sense than the state of nature understanding of it, man's natural state is to be free. For Hobbes, this freedom consists in the mere absence of external constraint; its only guarantee is in the same physical might with which one individual can invade the freedom of another and in the resultant standoff of antagonistic mights. Here, however, we are speaking of an essential interior freedom "to make up one's mind" which is constitutive of human action and a requisite for human growth. This freedom is nature's witness to man's status as *sui juris* and to the corollary fact that he is meant to be least left alone when he implements that freedom in external action (without prejudice, that is, to the like freedom of others). All this is but another way of saying that man has rights.

(*b*) A moral obligation to make the right use of one's power of choice evidently implies a correlative obligation on the part of others to respect it and to place no obstacle in the path of the person's fulfilling it. (Indeed, the ultimate basis of natural rights is this basic natural duty of the human agent, and a strictly inalienable right is such because we cannot alienate the duty from which it originates.) Moral obligation thus implies that inviolability of the person which is but another term for subjective (i.e., personal) right: the moral power to do, possess, or exact something as one's own. (It is called moral power because, in contrast to physical might *in corpus*, it falls upon another's will.)

But we are now concerned with a deeper significance of moral obligation as being *simply and in itself*, despite the immediate connotation of subjection, the witness to human dignity. Man is under obligation because a rational nature (or person) is meant to possess moral values as its own immanent good and as disposing for a final possession of a Supreme Good. Man's specific perfection, in other words, is in the moral sphere, in the acquisition not of external or morally neutral goods but of *bona honesta*. The possession and, importantly, the privation of these affect him in a more essential way than does either the presence or absence of health, charm, or intellectual or artistic talents. They affect him at the core of his being, in a "personal center," and make the whole difference between a good and a flawed *man*. Though the good of another is the object and norm of justice, obligating because the other is a person to whom it is due, the virtue or *habitus* of justice is the subject's own good, for the same reason that injustice, while *injuring* another, is an even greater evil for the unjust agent himself. For the injustice leaves him, unlike his injured victim, an evil man.

It was this historic thesis—that it is a worse evil for a man to commit than to suffer injury—which so amazed and angered Callicles, the resourceful apologist for "the natural right of the stronger," and which Socrates relentlessly pressed "with arguments of steel and adamant" (*Gorgias* 509A). And the down-to-earth Aristotle makes the equivalent point. Without arguing the position or taking the trouble to compose it with his eudaimonist conception of ethics, he insists that certain actions (theft, murder, adultery) are never justified and that some ought not to be performed even to avoid "the most terrible sufferings and death" (*Ethics* 1110A26). Neither Plato nor Aristotle, it should be noted, is thinking here in utilitarian terms. The consequences of evil action which concern them are not the social ones but the ravages which it effects in the agent himself (simply because it is evil, whether or not the damage is observable or experienced).[11]

Agere sequitur esse. This fact which is uniquely true of man—that the law of his activity is a moral one not, as with the animal, aimed at biological survival but obligating him to forgo all other advantage to "save his own self" (and not, as utilitarian ethics would have it, to avoid external evil effects)— evidences his unique constitution as body–spirit. There is in him an element which transcends time, space, and matter, and which therefore is imperishable. Were this not the case, it would make no final difference whether a man turned out good or evil, and he would be of no intrinsic worth or dignity but at best a disposable instrument of some further cosmic purpose indifferent to him. A scrapheap is not a proper repository for beings endowed with dignity. Subsistence (or immortality) and dignity imply each other; one is the obverse of the other.

This resolution of the notions of justice and right in a dignity which is prior to, and normative for, all political arrangements and which is real, not just postulated as logical support for an established legal order, clearly entails a realist metaphysics.[12] It means that there is such an extramental reality as "human nature" with an intelligible structure and finality and with a real relation to an intelligibly structured universe or cosmos (both terms imply a principle of order). To put this another way: both state of nature (or contract) theories, which know only isolated and essentially unrelated individuals, and legal positivism, for which right and justice are legal fictions, are the logical and historical issue of nominalism.[13] Nominalism holds that only individual material substances are real, that there are no true universals and hence no *humana natura absoluta*. Consequently, there can be no real moral order since there is no objective good bearing a real relation to a real human essence. Given this ontology, right—the cardinal notion of jurisprudence—necessarily turns out to be a mere logical category or function of a state of affairs to which there corresponds no independent "abstract" value or moral exigency. Jurisprudence is no longer defined, as in the *Digest*, as *ars boni et aequi*.

> The object of our study [jurisprudence] is prediction, the prediction of the incidence of the public force through the instrumentality of the courts. . . . The primary rights and duties with which jurisprudence busies itself . . . are nothing but prophecies. One of the many evil effects of the confusion between legal and moral ideas . . . is that theory is apt to get the cart before the horse, and to consider the right or the duty as something existing apart from and independent of the consequences of its breach, to which certain sanctions are added afterward. But, as I shall try to show, a legal duty so called is nothing but a prediction that if a man does or omits certain things he will be made to suffer in this or that way by judgment of the court; and so of a legal right. . . . The prophecies of what the court will do in fact, and nothing more pretentious, are what I mean by the law.[14]

It may require some reflection to appreciate the full import of what is being argued here: namely, the separation of the juridical from the moral order and their mutual independence. This, of course, was already accomplished with Kant. But, while contemporary legal positivism has thick roots in the soil of Kantian criticism and moral theory, we are concerned here with some more particular reasons why the separation of law and morals may appear reasonable and innocent and why it is welcomed in many quarters as a healthful development bringing legal thought to maturity and guaranteeing the integrity of the judicial and legislative processes in thus isolating them from contamination by ideological interests and atavist extralegal influences.[15]

A first reason for plausibility is the fact that the moral and juridical orders are not coextensive. The first extends to the whole of human activity. Its sphere is the interior human act of the will in its relation to the dictate of right reason; an action can be formally just or unjust in the properly moral sense (or cowardly or brave) only insofar as it flows from a just or unjust (or cowardly or brave) disposition of the will.[16] But justice—which is the laws' whole concern—has a narrower sphere. Since it regulates action with reference to another, it has as its object only external activity which alone can benefit or injure another and which alone the laws can control.[17] Laws must therefore follow an observable external standard with an eye not to the individual's good or bad intentions—except as inferrable from external acts—but to the common good as affected by outward behavior. However, this is a limitation imposed by the nature of justice itself and in no way implies the laws' indifference to, much less independence of, the moral order. It means only that the moral and juridical orders are not simply identical but related as whole to part. One set of moral imperatives orders a man immediately with respect to himself; another orders him with respect to his fellow-man (and consequently, of course, to himself as well).

A second, related characteristic of justice provides perhaps the most occasion for the unwitting judgment that the considerations of jurisprudence are essentially amoral. In contrast with other virtues such as temperance and fortitude which establish a right order within the agent himself, justice—as far as its object, the *debitum*, is concerned—looks to the good of another and is satisfied with the appropriate external action regardless of the agent's good or bad will in placing it.[18] Actions are temperate through their accordance with the promptings of the well-ordered appetite of the temperate man himself. And since this order is determined and imposed by reason, the mean of this virtue is said to be a *medium rationis* which is relative and subjective inasmuch as it will vary from man to man.[19] An amount of wine suitable for inducing reasonable euphoria in one may prove too little or too much for another. It is impossible for an act to be temperate where the appetite defining it is itself disordered. Refraining from adultery is not an act of temperance when owing to thwarted plans to accomplish it. Similarly, it is not an act of courage to remain at one's dangerous post out of fear of court-martial; one cannot place a truly brave act without being bravely disposed. But justice follows a different norm. Here the mean is an objective *medium rei* determined without reference to appetite or moral disposition (although these will evidently affect one's perception of the mean). The amount owed a man for his labor is determined not by my generosity or selfishness but by the value of the labor itself. Even if I have the continuing will to withhold it and to pay him only under duress, once I have done so, he no longer has a claim; he has his own and I no longer owe. Although I remain unjust, justice itself is satisfied and so is the law.

This feature of justice, its embodiment in an external "impersonal" reality, is of no trivial consequence for the philosophy of law. It has everything to do with determining whether or not justice is real (in the sense which we have

been claiming for it). Because he missed the implication—although it was remarked by Aristotle and explored by St. Thomas—Justice Holmes was led to
conclude from it that law was reckless of moral considerations or purposes.
This is the burden of the doctrine of "the external standard" elaborated in his
much-admired classic *The Common Law* and proposed as offering the only
sound interpretation of legal history. The argument is that because "a man may
have as bad a heart as he chooses if his conduct is within the rules," and because he is allowed to inflict some harms even wickedly[20] but, whatever his
moral handicaps, must at his peril conform to a minimal standard of conduct
and be liable for lapses from it even "without moral stain," the law is shown
to have a purely external pragmatic purpose; there is no "mystic bond between
wrong and punishment." Harms to persons, reputation, or estate are indemni-
fied "not because they are wrongs but because they are harms."[21] All forms of
liability, in fact, have a common ground in the primitive appetite for revenge
which they seek to accommodate in socially acceptable ways.

This conclusion would in any case be imposed by Holmes's Darwinist anthropology. Here it is achieved through gross inflation of its premises (which
themselves require important qualification). There is, in the first place, a failure
to notice that the actions commanded by law constitute just conduct—our
medium rei—or something *owed*. A law's purpose is no less moral for being
realized in external performance. Secondly, the "harms" which the law pun-
ishes with such seeming indifference ("robbery or murder . . . taking and keeping other men's goods, or the actual poisoning, shooting, stabbing, and otherwise putting to death of other men") are not just unwelcome morally neutral
evils but injuries, i.e., injustices and violations of individual or public rights.
An external standard of liability is perfectly consistent with such an understanding and, indeed, demanded by it. Its application supposes that human
agents are normally responsible for their acts and that these correspond to intention. In both civil and criminal law the standards for liability reflect the
attempt to find reasonable norms for estimating responsibility. In those instances, of growing frequency in a complex industrial society, in which liability
is assigned without imputation of fault and even in clear absence of it, the law
is not reckless of moral considerations but seeks to distribute burdens equitably
on the basis of distributive justice. The criminal process in particular is characterized by its effort to establish on the basis of general experience a link between external deed and malice in one or another degree. And penalties here
are not mere fines but formal punishments.

There is still a third argument advanced for regarding justice as an amoral
empirically grounded reality pragmatically fashioned by law as its own creation
without reference to any presumed supralegal moral standards.[22] These, whatever their value for individual personal development, are held to be of no
relevance for the real world with which legislation and adjudication must deal
in balancing competing interests. Of what use is an ideal transcendent justice

or abstract moral principle for designing anti-trust laws or for deciding a complicated case of civil liability?[23]

This protest is really aimed at eighteenth-century rationalist types of natural law theory and the associated abuses of mechanical and conceptual jurisprudence. Here the general principles of "natural law"—in fact, they were only those of the state of nature school and of laissez-faire capitalism—were viewed as containing virtually within themselves the solution to particular legal problems and as governing concrete arrangements with the same rigid necessity, sureness, and uniformity as that with which axioms determined the conclusions of geometry. The judicial function in particular was viewed as simply declaratory—to "ascertain" the law, as if in a general statute the right particular disposition of a case were already contained and simply waiting for the court to discover it. It was this style of juristic thinking which prevailed in American courts during the heyday of economic liberalism and well into the present century. The efforts of state legislatures to meet the urgent needs of a new industrial era were repeatedly thwarted as the Supreme Court, in a string of notorious "Fourteenth Amendment cases," consistently struck down minimum wage laws and statutes regulating working conditions for women and children as violations of due process and of the right to property and to freedom of contract.[24] In applying these spacious "natural law concepts" no account was taken of the uneven conditions under which a powerful management and an individual prospective employee conducted their bargaining. As Justice Stone acidly observed in his dissent in *Morehead* v. *Tipaldo*: "There is a grim irony in speaking of the freedom of contract of those who, because of their economic necessities, give their services for less than is needful to keep body and soul together."[25]

Although many are now aware of the vast difference between them, this repudiated rationalism is still widely taken as the very model of natural law jurisprudence—"the natural error of the schools."[26] And the stigma attaching to it is still a large factor in the uneasiness caused by occasional recurrent signs of a revival of "natural law thinking." It is regarded as just another oppressive ideology—a "tyranny of concepts" hampering social progress by the "imposition of moral patterns on the flux of law." Its advocates are "the *a priori* men."[27]

"The life of the law has not been logic: it has been experience." This thematic sentence in the opening passage of *The Common Law*—it has since acquired the status of an apothegm—is frequently cited by legal realists to point out the futility of attempts to make sense of the legal order or to provide for its healthy development through any reference of it to a supposed natural law as its source.

> The felt necessities of the time, the prevalent moral and political theories, intuitions of public policy, avowed or unconscious, even the prejudices which judges share with their fellow-men, have had a good deal more to do than the

syllogism in determining the rules by which men should be governed. The law embodies the story of a nation's development through many centuries, and it cannot be dealt with as if it contained only the axioms and corollaries of a book of mathematics.[28]

This was considered a remarkable insight in 1881 and a thesis to be developed. But it would have come as no news to the scholastic expositors of natural law. Certainly after St. Thomas it was commonplace to point out the critical differences in the methods of speculative and practical science in their movement from principles to conclusions, or from the general to the particular. (In this they were developing an important methodological point which Aristotle made at the outset of the *Ethics* [see 1094B19ff.].) Natural law precepts, i.e., those grasped naturally (*per inclinationem*) without need of scientific reasoning (*sine omni deliberatione aut sine magna*), were of very general character (*communia*): to be just and polite; to care for one's children (*ST* I–II 94, 2, c). And even of these, some—the so-called "secondary" ones (e.g., to return borrowed goods)—held true only "for the most part" (*ut in pluribus* —Aristotle's ὡς ἐπὶ τὸ πολύ).[29] Since, being general, they did not reach to particular actions in all their variable particularity, they required adjustment to circumstances of time and place, factors which are not involved in geometry. Moral precepts had to be given a definite shape and be spelled out or "determined" as far as practicable in well-framed laws. The term "jurisprudence" itself indicated that these were not deduced *more geometrico* as logical conclusions from general premises but crafted on the basis of experience and by application of the legislator's *prudentia regnativa*. Justice in itself, or in idea, is invariable and ever exigent inasmuch as, by definition, it always "renders what is due." But it must locate this *debitum* amidst a welter of shifting relationships and impose it as a measure for actions which themselves have to do with variables. It will therefore be concreted in a wide variety of *just* but varying legal arrangements. And these uneven and often necessarily imperfect incarnations encourage the notion, especially among the empirically minded, that justice in itself is at best an abstraction—that real justice is wholly relative and not only settled or "determined" by law but indeed created by it.[30]

This line of thought is not altogether new. When Thomas argues for the position that all human law derives from natural law and depends on conformity with it for its own validity as law—otherwise it would be a *legis corruptio* (*ST* I–II 95, 2, c)—he has to meet two objections which proceed from a confusion of speculative and practical reason. The first argues that positive and natural law are disparate because the former is variable, the latter is the same everywhere (*eadem apud omnes*). Thomas answers simply that general principles of natural law cannot be uniformly applied because the concrete conditions of application differ so widely (*ST* I–II 95, 2, c., ad 3um). And in reply to a further "rationalist" objection based on the seemingly arbitrary character of human laws—the venerated *Digest* itself recognizes that for some statutes no reason (*ratio*) can be given—he grants that this is true, in a sense, of "particular determinations of natural law." Reason does not arrive at them by a deductive process since the principles of practical reason (or of natural law) do not contain conclusions in the same determined way as the axioms of geometry involve the conclusion that $a^2 + b^2 = c^2$, no more, no less. Thomas then goes on to add that these positive laws do, however, have their own "principle" in practical reason, i.e., the informed judgment of the legislators whose experience and prudence enable them to perceive immediately what sort of disposition a situation demands (*ST* I–II 95, 2, c., ad 4um).

This observation is still appropriate. General practical principles are relatively empty of specific content (*minus utiles* Thomas calls them);[31] they cannot substitute for empirical knowledge and good judgment (σύνεσις). And this unreadiness to yield specific directives in the form of apt laws—contrasted with the ability of experienced lawmakers and judges to shape suitable legislation and wise decisions without consulting "some mystic overlaw"—is taken as proof of the irrelevance of a natural law jurisprudence to the actual concerns of politics. This evaluation overlooks the basic difference in the roles of speculative and practical principles in the discourse of reason.[32] And this in turn occasions disregard of an important aspect of what, for want of a better term, we may call the metaphysics of action.

The trouble seems to be with the overtones of our English term "principle," which has lost much of its original sense of ἀρχή—of ontological source or causal beginning—and now rather suggests the notion of static formula or proposition, e.g., the "principle" of the excluded middle. This is a *logical* principle or external guide for reason proceeding *speculativo modo* from one truth to the discovery of another. But practical principles are real principles. They can be *expressed* verbally in propositional form, e.g., stealing is wrong; and, thus formulated as "truths," they can serve as guiding "premises" for a "conclusion"[33] in the form of another speculative–practical proposition declaring that a particular act of theft is wrong. But when we cast a real practical principle into language we are dealing with it then as information or as a *principium speculativo-practicum* and, so to speak, a step removed from its reality. However, when talking of laws, whether natural or positive, as practical principles in the proper sense of *practical*, we are no longer considering propositions but active ordinations or directives of practical reason. Intellect here is no longer merely reporting but effecting. It is a genuine ἀρχή μεταβολῆς functioning as formal cause in charge of the will (man's specifically rational appetite) in its movement toward the good—a movement generated by the good itself as final cause and real principle of will's desire. "The good has thus been aptly defined as that at which all things aim." So when we say that "Good is to be done and evil avoided" is a first principle of practical reason (or—what amounts to the same thing—of natural law), we are not talking of an apparently tautologous proposition (what else can "evil" mean but "what ought to be avoided"?) or of a logical principle containing other deducible ones virtually within it. We are rather referring in language, in order to talk about it, to what is in reality an immanent activity.[34] It is a composite but unified action to which will and practical intellect simultaneously make their distinctive contributions,[35] with will, as efficient cause, providing the motor power and intellect, as formal cause, directing or "commanding."[36]

This active direction is our real *principium*. Its momentum powers and pervades all specific directives for situations in which concrete good and evil are encountered and recognized, just as the power of a distant generator is mediated through step-down transformers to activate an individual toaster or vacuum cleaner. Positive laws are among such directives. They are *ordinations* emanating from the legislator's practical reason aiming at the common good as immediately attracting final cause and ultimately (and so first of all) at a *summum bonum* which alone is capable of originating the will's movement.[37] These ordinations of legislative reason must, of course, be promulgated by means of language in order to be transmitted as effective directives obligating the wills of individual human agents.[38] And this freezing of a vital activity through translation into written statutes generally framed and addressed to a whole multitude may account for the impression that these represent a kind of impersonal force. But law in reality is the order itself (*lex active sumpta*), not the law clothed in language.[39] The latter stands in somewhat the same relation to the real ordinance as a printed text of the *Republic* to Plato's real ideas; in each case we are dealing with signs, not the original law or idea.[40]

We are calling attention here to the fact that legislation is a human action or form of πρᾶξις; it is a choice of alternative means to an end and thus a value judgment. True, when legislators enact laws, they are in a sense *making* (especially if we think of law primarily as written statute). But as human agents they are first of all *doing* and doing in a different sense from one *doing* geometry. They are in pursuit of a good—which means that the will is being drawn by it[41]—and under its real influence the entire legislative process (counsel, deliberation, and final prescription) is initiated and prolonged. The first principle —the good—continues to energize the process (as final cause) just as, in the parallel case of a speculative science, the axioms control the prolonged reasonings of the geometer. Speculative and practical principles are alike in that they are general in scope and known *per se*. And because we come by them naturally and unreflectively, we are not directly aware of their input and their influence on the discourse of reason. The geometer need not formally advert to his axioms. But just as in geometry we begin with what is immediately and *per se* evident and work downward through middle terms to conclusions which participate in the light of our principle and are thus secured only by resolution in it, so practical reason in its practical moment is operating under the influence of its principle (the good) in order to reach proper "conclusions."[42] Only, now, the conclusions are not affirmations but actions,[43] i.e., choices of concrete goods which attract in virtue of their participation in and linkage to the universal good (*bonum in universali*).

However, the parallel character of the two processes should not obscure an important difference. For since practical reason is involved with action and in the order of final causality ("the good is that at which all things aim"), we are no longer working down from but up to the principle. As in the discourse of speculative reason, e.g., mathematics, there must be a starting point in a *primum intelligibile*—a truth first and immediately known—so in the discourse of practical reasoning, i.e., of things to be done (and this includes legislation and the judicial process), there must be a *primum amabile*, a good (end) which is first, immediately, and absolutely *desired*. As not all knowledge depends on a previously known (whereas all instruction and argument does)—this is the point made at the outset of Aristotle's *Posterior Analytics*—so not all that we desire is desired as a means to some other desirable. 'Ανάγκη εἶναι; there must be something first loved and for its own sake. Otherwise desire would go to infinity, and we would never reach a point where the order of intention could be converted to the order of execution. Since desire would be in endless pursuit of an indefinitely receding object, we would never begin to deliberate about means to achieve it and so could never choose. Subtract the first of a series of dependent causes such as we have here, and effects are likewise canceled. These are the simple psychological and metaphysical necessities of human action from which neither legislators nor judges are exempt. Whether aware of it or not, in each particular choice they are in pursuit of an ultimate good—our principle—to which they are directed not by election but by a natural dictate of reason.[44] Laws and decisions are thus implementations of a natural ordinance to pursue (or do) good and to avoid evil. Which is but another way of saying that positive laws derive from the natural.

All this may be of small immediate consequence for the practitioner involved in workaday transactions which call only for expertise in mastering complex particulars according to the norms of an established legal system. The same may be true even for the more creative function of legislator and judge where connatural perceptions and good instincts combined with intelligence and experience can suffice for their roles in preserving and promoting justice and the common good. But they are of immense consequence for the philosophy of law and for the closely involved "public philosophy" as well. The history of political thought should prove instructive. One may note in particular, for what concerns us here, the impact of individualist state of nature doctrines on the structure of Western institutions and on the shaping of social patterns.[45] Prominent among the agents of these transformations have been the decisions of higher courts revising customs and precedents, and prescribing new norms in the spirit of these theories. Ideas have their consequences even if, by the time they are realized, collective amnesia has already set in and sight has been lost of their watershed.

Implicit in every decision where the question is, so to speak, at large, is a philosophy of the origin and aim of law, a philosophy which, however veiled, is in truth the final arbiter. It accepts one set of arguments, modifies another, rejects a third, standing ever in reserve as a court of ultimate appeal. Often the philosophy is ill–co-ordinated and fragmentary. Its empire is not always suspected even by its subjects. Neither lawyer nor judge, pressing forward along one line or retreating along another, is conscious at all times that it is philosophy which is impelling him to the front or driving him to the rear. None the less the goad is there. If we cannot escape the Furies, we shall do well to understand them.[46]

It will make a crucial difference for a finished, integrated, and self-consistent jurisprudence whether the juridical order is regarded as being at its immediate source a product of human will and contrivance or whether, at the point of human initiative and creativity, art is seen as being in continuity with nature—nature as normative—and as doing "what nature would if it could." Only on the latter supposition are the state, its institutions, and its laws anchored in an objective order of justice prescribing the ends and limits of a political order.[47] For only then are the *prima directio* of practical intellect, which is the source of regnative prudence in the statesman and of political prudence in the citizens, identified as obligating norm, and the basis established for genuine moral authority binding on state and citizens alike. Otherwise the most fundamental standards of individual and public right stand revealed as mere *de facto* mores subject now *de jure* (as they will always be *de facto*) to revision at the will of the *de facto* power in the community, be this monarch, dictator, tyrant, army, or "we, the people." "Force, mitigated so far as may be by good manners, is the *ultima ratio*,"[48] and efficacy the ultimate validation of law.

What is here chiefly important is to liberate law from that association which has traditionally been made for it—its association with morals. . . . In its proper meaning, as distinct from that which it has in law, 'justice' connotes an absolute value. Its content cannot be ascertained by the Pure Theory of Law. Indeed it is not ascertainable by rational knowledge at all. The history of human speculation for centuries has been the history of a vain striving after a solution of the problem. That striving has hitherto led only to the emptiest of tautologies, such as the formula *suum cuique* of the categoric imperative. From the standpoint of rational knowledge there are only interests and conflicts of interest, the solution of which is arrived at by an arrangement which may either satisfy the one interest at the expense of the other, or institute an equivalence or compromise between them. To determine, however, whether this or that order has an absolute value, that is, is "just," is not possible by the methods of rational knowledge. Justice is an irrational ideal. However indispensable it may be for the willing and acting of human beings it is not viable to reason. Only positive law is known, or more correctly is revealed, to reason.[49]

Here we are at the dead end of a "pure theory of law"—the most erudite and sophisticated attempt to date to make intelligible and tolerable a juridical positivism with its idea of a wholly self-contained legal order. It is committed to this mission, of course, by its *a priori* rejection of a realist metaphysics and its exclusion of any non-material element in man or any transcendent point of reference for our concepts of law, justice, and right.

Early in his work *De legibus*, Cicero perceptively observes that questions about the nature of justice are finally questions about the nature of man (*natura iuris explicanda nobis est eaque ab hominis repetenda natura*—1.4.17) and about ultimate realities. Where is the fountain of law and justice to be found? Laws, of necessity, reflect a vision of human purpose. If man turns out in last analysis to be just one nature among others, one more empirical *fact* in a radically meaningless, and therefore valueless, "universe," and with no transcendent element in his composition to found a non-empirical value, then he must expect to be handled as such—and all the while with impeccable due process (as human fetuses are being handled now). Man is fair game for man since nature can be legitimately extended to include man himself where men— natures without obligations—manipulate other men—natures without rights.[50] The Pure Theory of Law admits no ground for protest. Where there is no natural *suum* there is no natural right. Where no right, no justice. No injustice either.

NOTES

1. Following common usage, we employ the term *state*, by metonymy, as a shorthand, non-technical, equivalent for *civil society* (or *community*) or *body politic*. Yet there are important differences between the state and society, and social contract theories have prospered through the confusion. The state is the body politic's organ of administration and is contained within it as a part within the whole. As such, it is a legal entity, a creation of man's, and a product not of nature but of art. See Jacques Maritain, *Man and the State* (Chicago: The University of Chicago Press, 1951), pp. 9–19.
2. See *De legibus* 1.7, 10, and esp. 12, where community of nature means community in reason and, therefore, in a natural law which founds a natural justice.
3. See Jeremiah Newman, *Foundations of Justice* (Dublin: Cork University Press, 1954).
4. For a development of this point, see Edward Corwin, *The "Higher Law" Background of American Constitutional Law* (Ithaca: Cornell University Press, 1967).
5. *Holmes-Laski Letters: The Correspondence of Mr. Justice Holmes and Harold J. Laski, 1916–1935*, ed. Mark DeWolfe Howe, 2 vols. (Cambridge: Harvard University Press, 1953), II 822.
6. *Summa contra gentes* II, 28. See also *Summa theologiae* I, 21, 4 (hereafter cited as *ST*).
7. (London: Oxford University Press, 1962), pp. 16–17. See also Dennis Lloyd, *Introduction to Jurisprudence* (New York: Praeger, 1959), which contains extensive extracts from past and contemporary writings in legal philosophy.
8. Olivecrona, *Law as Fact*, p. 151.
9. The endowment is not to be understood as a further act consequent upon

creation. However, since a contingently existing human nature cannot be founded upon itself, it cannot supply the *ultimate* basis of rights either. In other words, the dignity of the human person (the basis of rights, as we are about to explain) is founded upon the essential relationship of the rational creature to Creator. The nature of this relation is also the reason for the *inalienability* of certain natural rights; dissolution of these would imply dissolution of the relationship. For all this, see Josef Pieper's brief but excellent *Justice*, trans. Lawrence Lynch (New York: Pantheon, 1955), esp. chap. 1, "On Rights."

10. Thus Aristotle uses the term ἀξίωμα for *self*-confidence (*Ethics* 1117A24); his ordinary word for confidence in general is θάρρος.

11. See J. A. Stewart, *Notes on the Nicomachean Ethics*, 2 vols. (Oxford: Clarendon, 1892), I 301–302, at 1117A35, for the analysis of courage as at once pleasant and painful.

12. For positivism the person as ὑπόστασις (or *naturae rationabilis individua substantia*, Boethius' classic definition) is inevitably dissolved and pronounced a legal fiction. "The person as a holder of obligations and rights is not something that is different from the obligations and rights, as whose holder the person is presented—just as a tree which is said to have a trunk, branches, and blossoms, is not a substance different from trunk, branches and blossoms, but merely the totality of these elements. The physical or juristic person who 'has' obligations and rights as their holder, *is* these obligations and rights—a complex of legal obligations and rights whose totality is expressed figuratively in the concept of 'person.' 'Person' is merely the personification of this totality" (Hans Kelsen, *Pure Theory of Law*, trans. Max Knight [Berkeley & Los Angeles: The University of California Press, 1967], pp. 172–73). See also the extract from the same author in Lloyd, *Introduction to Jurisprudence*, p. 317: "The freedom or autonomy of the physical person, which is the juristic parallel of the ethical dogma of freedom of the will, is rejected as an illusion from the domain of legal theory."

13. See John Wild, *Plato's Modern Enemies and the Theory of Natural Law* (Chicago: The University of Chicago Press, 1953); and A. P. D'Entrèves, *Natural Law* (London: Hutchinson University Press, 1970), pp. 69–72. See also Plato's *Laws* (889B–890A) where the point is made that if reality is at its root irrational —if, that is, chaos and not design is the "first principle" and mind an accidental product of blind evolution—then "there is absolutely no such thing as a real and natural right." The "really and naturally right" is the life of domination over others.

14. Oliver Wendell Holmes, "The Path of the Law," *Collected Legal Papers* (New York: Harcourt, Brace, 1921), pp. 167, 168–69, 173. This essay is reprinted in Max Lerner, *The Mind and Faith of Justice Holmes* (New York: Modern Library, 1954).

15. See, for example, William Ebenstein, "Hans Kelsen," in *International Encyclopedia of the Social Sciences*, ed. David L. Sills, 17 vols. (New York: Macmillan, 1968), VIII 360–65 at 365. For Kelsen's statement on this point, see Lloyd, *Introduction to Jurisprudence*, pp. 310–11. In his *What is Justice?* (Berkeley & Los Angeles: The University of California Press, 1957), p. 22, Kelsen defends his "relativist philosophy of justice" against the charge of amoralism: "On the contrary! The view that moral principles constitute only relative values does not mean they constitute no value at all; it means that there is not one moral system but that there are several different ones, and that consequently, a choice must be made among them." On what basis? As A. P. D'Entrèves notes (*Natural Law*, pp. 104–105), the failure to face this issue exposes the Achilles heel of modern legal positivism "for the recognition that the ultimate test of the validity of law lies *beyond*

law itself is nothing but a natural law proposition." Continuing the analysis, he remarks: "It is tragically significant that the country where formal jurisprudence was developed to its utmost perfection was also the country where legality offered least resistance to the challenge of new and disruptive forces. Events seem to have brought us back once again to long-forgotten responsibilities."

16. Moral acts are those which make a person good or bad as man, i.e., rightly or wrongly ordered with respect to the true human good or final end. Morality is therefore *per prius* a quality of the will-act establishing the right or wrong relation. However, from this interior act of the will a moral quality derives *per posterius* to the external act which it effects as well, e.g., the actual inordinate consumption of alcohol. Moreover—an important point neglected by "the morality of intention" and the type of legal theory which we are considering—the external act, independently of its relation to the will or to "good intention," is itself objectively good or bad depending on its conformity or difformity with an objective order of relations or, in scholastic language, with the "order of right reason." "Bonitas autem vel malitia quam habet actus exterior secundum se, propter debitam materiam et debitas circumstantias, non derivatur a voluntate, sed magis a ratione" (*ST* I–II 20, 1, c). This latter order is normative for the will's own goodness in the first place: "Illa autem [bonitas] quae est ex debita materia vel circumstantiis dependet ex ratione: et ex hac dependet bonitas voluntatis, secundum quod in ipsam fertur." A human act cannot be morally good without good intention, yet it can be morally bad even with it; to be simply good, it must be wholly good. "Ad hoc quod aliquid sit malum sufficit unus singularis defectus; ad hoc autem quod sit simpliciter bonum, non sufficit unum singulare bonum, sed requiritur integritas bonitatis" (*ST* I–II 20, 2, c).

17. The relationship of justice to the other virtues is nicely expressed in *ST* II–II 58, 8, c. For the limitation which this relationship imposes on law, see *ST* I–II 91, 4, c (*tertio*).

18. This point is made in the initial article of the treatise on justice in the *Summa* (II–II 57, 1, c) where Thomas is determining the specific object of justice.

19. See *ST* I–II 60, 2, c; 64, 2, c; and esp. II–II 58, 10, c.

20. (Boston: Little, 1881), pp. 38–50, 144–49, 161. The pertinent passages are also found in Lerner, *Mind and Faith of Justice Holmes*, pp. 51–70.

21. *Common Law*, p. 49.

22. See Roscoe Pound, *Justice According to Law* (New Haven: Yale University Press, 1951) pp. 9–14.

23. "Each side of many a bitter controversy argues with assurance that its case rests upon eternal principles of right and justice. Each identifies its claims with unchallengeable dictates of morals. If nothing else the everyday discussions between employers and employees would convince us that this sort of natural law can do very little for the lawyer. It is because there is no 'natural' guide to solution of so many of these conflicts and overlappings of competing claims and expectations that we must have positive law or go back to private war" (ibid., p. 15).

24. For a detailed examination of this abuse, see Arthur North, s.j., *The Supreme Court: Judicial Process and Judicial Politics* (New York: Appleton-Century-Crofts, 1966); and Roscoe Pound, *Interpretations of Legal History* (Cambridge: Harvard University Press, 1946). Lerner, *Mind and Faith of Justice Holmes*, pp. 127–288, contains abundant illustrations from the Supreme Court record during the period of Holmes's incumbency, mostly in the form of his dissenting opinions. There is also substantial commentary.

25. 298 U. S. 587 (1936), as cited by Lerner, *Mind and Faith of Justice Holmes*, p. 75n.

26. "Path of the Law," p. 180.

27. "Natural Law," *Collected Legal Papers*, p. 314. The essay, which originally appeared in the *Harvard Law Review* (1918), is reprinted in Lerner, *Mind and Faith of Justice Holmes*.

28. *Common Law*, pp. 1–2.

29. *ST* I–II 94, 4, c: "Apud omnes enim hoc rectum est et verum, ut secundum rationem agatur. Ex hoc autem principio sequitur quasi conclusio propria, quod deposita sint reddenda. Et hoc quidem ut in pluribus verum est; sed potest in aliquo casu contingere quod sit damnosum, et per consequens, irrationabile, si deposita reddantur, puta si aliquis petat ad impugnandam patriam." For Aristotle, see *Ethics* 1094B21.

30. "If we may learn anything from the intellectual experiences of the past, it is the fact that only relative values are accessible to human reason; and that means that the judgment to the effect something is just cannot be made with the claim of excluding the possibility of a contrary judgment of value. Absolute justice is an irrational ideal or, what amounts to the same, an illusion—one of the eternal illusions of mankind. From the point of view of rational cognition, there are only interests of human beings and hence conflicts of interests" (Kelsen, *What Is Justice?*, p. 21).

31. "Sermones enim morales universales minus sunt utiles, eo quod actiones in particularibus sunt." *ST* II–II, prologue.

32. See *ST* I–II 94, 4. This article—an acknowledged *locus classicus*—was one of those which stirred the astonished admiration of the Kantian jurist Rudolf von Jhering, when they were called to his attention in a review of his famous *Der Zweck im Recht*. This was the work which asserted the claims of realism against the notion of an "immutable" natural law and the jurisprudence of conceptions (*Begriffsjurisprudenz*). In a lengthy appreciative footnote to a second edition (2 vols. [Leipzig: Breitkopf & Härtel, 1886], II 161n) Jhering paid generous tribute to Thomas and went on to state that had he been acquainted earlier with these texts, he might not have written his own book "for the basic ideas which I was treating are found there already expressed with perfect clarity and in the most pregnant style by this powerful thinker" ("denn die Grundgedanken, um die es mir zu thun war, finden sich schon bei jenem gewaltigen Denker in vollender Klarheit und prägnantester Fassung ausgesprochen"). "In astonishment I ask myself how was it possible for such truths, once they had been uttered, to have been so completely forgotten by our Protestant scholarship? What mistakes it could have been spared had they been taken to heart!" ("Staunend frage ich mich, wie war es möglich, dass solche Wahrheiten, nachdem sie einmal ausgesprochen waren, bei unserer protestantischen Wissenschaft so gänzlich in Vergessenheit geraten könnten? Welche Irrwege hätte sie sich ersparen können, wenn sie dieselben beherzigt hätte!").

33. The analogical character of these terms is noted in *ST* I–II 90, 1, ad 2um.

34. I find some approach to this sense of the word "principle" in an expression of Locke's: "to principle and guide" (*Essay Concerning Human Understanding*, 1.3.25).

35. Aristotle analyzes nicely this relationship of practical reason and appetite as mutually related co-causes of action in *De anima* 433A8–25.

36. Much confusion surrounds this notion of command. "Command theories" of law, for example, are generally voluntarist or "will theories" holding that law

is an act of will rather than of reason. However, the command (*imperium*) is the function of practical intellect; it is the intellect's direction or "ordering" of the will's activity. See *ST* I–II, 17, 1 and 90, 1.

37. Since the will is the appetite corresponding to intellect, its object is the universal good, *universale bonum*, corresponding to the object of intellect, *universale verum*. Since we are dealing with real causes of real movement, such a universal good must be concretized in a real *summum bonum*. See *ST* I–II, 2, 8.

38. It should be noted that since the promulgation of the legislator's original order (*lex ut in regulante*) is to *rational* individuals, it continues to exist there also (*lex ut in regulato*) as a principle of reason and therefore formally as law (not just by analogy) itself actively ordering the subject's own activity. That is why man is at once subject to natural law—it is "impressed" on intellect and he is not its author—and also a law to himself (*sibi ipsi lex*). In heeding it, he is following "his own direction" and in violating it, he is, as Cicero put it, fleeing his own self (*ipse se fugiet*). This is the point missed in systems of "independent morality" and complaints about the "heteronomy" of natural law ethics. See *ST* I–II 91, 2, c, and ad 3um.

39. Cicero points out the difference in *De legibus* 1.6.19. After stating that law is mind and reason (*mens ratioque prudentis*), itself measuring right and wrong (*ea iuris atque iniuriae regula*), he excuses himself for having to follow popular usage (*populariter loqui*) and to "give the name of law to that which in written form decrees what it wishes either by command or prohibition; for such is the crowd's understanding" ("appellare eam legem, quae scripta sancit, quod vult, aut iubendo aut prohibendo, ut vulgus appellat").

40. Failure to attend to this relationship of the statute, impersonalized and fixed *per firmitatem scripturae* (I–II 90, 4, ad 3um), to the original imperium accounts in great part for the excesses of analytical and mechanical jurisprudence as theories of interpretation of law. It also explains Olivecrona's facile designation of laws as "independent imperatives" i.e., not genuine commands but mere sentences in the imperative mood. As though the imperative mood of a sentence corresponded to no distinct mental act but was self-generating. Cf. his *Law as Fact*, pp. 35, 43: "A command presupposes one person who commands and another to whom the command is addressed. . . . A command in the proper sense implies a personal relationship. The command is given by one person to another by words or gestures meant to influence the will. Now the same kind of words is also used in many connexions where no personal relations whatever exist between the person who commands and the receiver of the command. The words can nevertheless have a similar, if not identical, effect. They function independently of any person who commands. We may in this case speak of 'independent imperatives' in order to get a convenient term. As an example of independent imperatives may be cited the Decalogue. It cannot be said that Moses is commanding us to do this or that. . . . In reality the Decalogue is a bundle of imperative sentences, formulated several thousand years ago and carried through the centuries by oral tradition and in writing. They are nobody's commands, though they have the form of language that is characteristic of a command. The rules of law are of a similar character."

41. The proper causality of the final cause is its *ipsum appeti*—the attraction undergone by the efficient cause (which is why the final cause is prior in nature or *causa causarum*). The will is not free to seek or not seek its natural object.

42. See *ST* I–II 90, 2, ad 3um (a text admired by Jhering; cf. note 32).

43. See *De anima* 433ʌ16: "The last point in the process of practical thinking is the starting point of action."

44. See *ST* I–II 91, 2, ad 2um. See also 95, 2, c (on the derivation of positive from natural law).

45. For a development of this point as it bears on the American "consensus," see Walter Lippmann's *The Public Philosophy* (New York: New American Library, 1962), esp. chaps. 8–11, and John Courtney Murray, S.J., *We Hold These Truths* (Garden City, N.Y.: Doubleday Image, 1964).

46. Benjamin Cardozo, *The Growth of the Law* (New Haven: Yale University Press, 1963), pp. 25–26.

47. Kelsen himself has made the point: "The ideological function of this whole contradictory conception of subjective right is clear enough. It is intended to uphold the idea that subjective right, that is, private property, is, in respect to objective law, a transcendent, *a priori* category—an impassable obstacle to the construction of the content of the legal order. This conception of a subjective right different from and independent of the objective law becomes the more important when the latter is recognized to be a constantly changing order, created by men and founded neither on nature nor upon the eternal and divine will, particularly when the construction of the objective law proceeds in a democratic fashion. The conception of an independent subjective right, which is even more 'just' than the objective law, is a device to protect the institution of private property from damage at the hands of the legal order" (cited from *Pure Theory of Law* by Lloyd, *Introduction to Jurisprudence*, pp. 315–16).

48. *Holmes–Laski Letters*, II 36.

49. Cited from Kelsen, *Pure Theory of Law* by Lloyd, *Introduction to Jurisprudence*, p. 310.

50. On this point, see the final chapter of C. S. Lewis' *The Abolition of Man* (New York: Macmillan, 1970), esp. pp. 82–91.

6

Reverse Discrimination and Compensatory Justice:
Constitutional and Moral Theory

DAVID A. J. RICHARDS

New York University

THE RELATIONSHIP OF MORAL AND LEGAL IDEAS in constitutional law is currently undergoing a striking and suggestive theoretical re-examination. In contradistinction to Learned Hand's influential legal positivist indictment of all forms of "natural law" ideas in understanding constitutional law,[1] recent commentary urges "the strength of our natural law inheritance in constitutional adjudication," which it is "unwise as well as hopeless to resist."[2] The theoretical focus of this re-examination is a needed "fusion of constitutional and moral theory, a connection that, incredibly, has yet to take place," without which "[c]onstitutional law can make no genuine advance."[3] A natural form of this theoretical re-examination is the application of moral theory to the analysis of particular constitutional provisions. Obviously, the relationship between morality and constitutional law is not exact.[4] Nonetheless, a number of provisions of the Constitution presuppose strong substantive moral ideas and conceptions so that the analysis of underlying moral ideas fundamentally clarifies the interpretation of the constitutional provision.[5]

Morally informed constitutional provisions differ importantly in their historical relationships to substantive moral ideas. The First Amendment, for example, clearly rests on the substantive moral conception of basic human rights familiar to educated men of that time from the widely read relevant works of Milton[6] and Locke,[7] among others. But the original Constitution did not consistently extend these rights to all moral persons; the institution of slavery, for example, was nowhere condemned, but rather at several points impliedly endorsed.[8] This moral lacuna in the constitutional charter of basic moral rights was only resolved by the Civil War and the constitutional amendments which followed in its wake.[9] Of these amendments, the due process and equal protection clauses of the Fourteenth Amendment have been an especially fertile source of the enlargement of constitutional rights. The equal protection clause, for example, has been interpreted to require forms of equal treatment well beyond the original intent to abolish slavery and concomitant state practices.[10] Not only has the due process clause been interpreted to require the application of many of the original amendments comprising the Bill of Rights against the states, it has been viewed as a source of rights not expressly articulated in the Bill of Rights.[11]

This gradual evolution in the development of the constitutional conception of moral rights typically rests on constitutional provisions strikingly general in form ("freedom of speech or of the press"; "due process of law"; "equal protection of the law") and often lacking any convincing legal history regarding the intended specific application of the provision. A consensus, to the extent it existed, was on the generalities of a political compromise which concealed future divergences of interpretation.[12] Even when there is definitive legal history to the effect that a certain interpretation of a constitutional provision was not contemplated, such legal history is not decisive in the Supreme Court interpretation of those provisions.[13] The Supreme Court has the seminal role in the development of constitutional doctrine in the light of its independent competence and responsibility. Within the framework of such general constitutional provisions, typically ambiguous legal history, and ultimately independent Supreme Court decisional authority for the development of constitutional doctrine, the explanation of underlying moral ideas has a remarkable clarifying force both in the interpretation of general structural features of constitutional adjudication and in the progressive evolution of constitutional doctrine.

The purpose of this essay is to elaborate a variation on a theme defended elsewhere: namely, that contractarian moral theory has a peculiar explanatory force in understanding both the structure of constitutional law (as a limitation on majoritarian power) and specific problems in constitutional adjudication.[14] We focus here on the moral interpretation and analysis of the equal protection clause of the Fourteenth Amendment, clearly among the most morally informed provisions of the federal Constitution. As one seminal commentary notes:

> It [the equal protection clause] was placed in our Constitution as the culmination of the greatest humanitarian movement in our history. It is rooted deep in our religious and ethical traditions. Is any other clause in the Constitution so eminently suited to be the ultimate haven of human rights?[15]

In particular, we shall examine the vexing problem of the constitutionality under the equal protection clause of programs of reverse discrimination. This problem has elicited sharply conflicting viewpoints regarding the fundamental morality of such programs, which has received natural expression in legal disagreement over the constitutionality of such programs under the equal protection clause of the Fourteenth Amendment. On the one hand, commentators argue that programs of reverse discrimination represent constitutionally forbidden classification by race or ethnic group, abandoning the fundamental moral principle (embodied in the equal protection clause) that persons are to be treated as individuals on their own merits, not as members or representatives of groups.[16] On the other, such programs are defended on the ground that they represent a consistent working out of the moral principle underlying the equal protection clause: namely, that disadvantaged minorities should be accorded special protections against majoritarian oppression, or the vestiges thereof.[17]

This moral and constitutional controversy most recently was crystallized in litigation in *DeFunis v. Odegaard*,[18] in which DeFunis argued that the minority preferential program of the University of Washington Law School unconstitutionally deprived him of admission to that school. The *DeFunis* record revealed that in 1971 the law school had essentially two pools of applicants.[19] The Admissions Committee considered the applications of blacks, Chicanos, American Indians, and Philippine-Americans separately from other applications. Although no minimum quota had been set for applicants who were members of these minorities, thirty of the thirty-seven accepted would probably have been summarily rejected if their records had been treated like those of white applicants, since their "predicted first year grade averages," based on Law School Aptitude Test scores and college grades, fell below the effective cut-off point for virtually all white applicants.[20] Many white students with substantially higher predicted averages, including DeFunis,[21] were also denied admission. If the law school had treated minority group applications as it treated white applications, none of the eighteen minority students who actually enrolled would have been admitted.[22]

In a 5–4 decision, the Supreme Court refused to decide *DeFunis* on equal protection grounds, concluding in a *per curiam* opinion that since DeFunis clearly could complete his legal education, the case was moot.[23] Only Justice Douglas indicated his opinion on the substance of DeFunis' equal protection claim. In his view, the Constitution compels "the consideration of each application *in a racially neutral way*,"[24] which would require that each candidate be evaluated individually according to criteria applicable to all, and that race be eliminated as a factor—explicit or implicit—in admissions decisions.[25]

The Court in *DeFunis* clearly only postponed the disposition of the issue of that case: namely, the constitutional permissibility of voluntary preferential admissions programs to professional schools in the absence of evidence of racial discrimination in the past by the professional school. Yet, the general problem of the constitutionality of preferential programs has been a matter of recurrent judicial concern in related contexts. In the classic area of racial imbalance among public schools, the Supreme Court itself has squarely upheld the appropriateness of racial classifications to correct illegal *de jure* segregation among public schools[26] and has explicitly suggested that states may use racial

criteria to correct racial imbalance among such schools even when official
practices are not responsible for the original imbalance.[27] Similarly, lower
courts have approved racial quotas to correct employment discrimination under
Title VII of the Civil Rights Act of 1964,[28] even though some of the present
beneficiaries of preference are not the persons who suffered the original discrimination.[29] A similar approach has been adopted by courts concluding that
municipalities have engaged in unconstitutional employment policies.[30] Courts
sometimes find discrimination in the absence of any intentional disparity in
treatment, on the ground of state use of tests on which members of minority
groups fare badly or on the absence of positive efforts by the state to recruit
members of minority groups.[31] A similar way of thinking underlies the guidelines used by the Department of Health, Education, and Welfare for assuring
nondiscrimination in university faculty hiring. Goals are set for minority group
and female representation to test whether universities are hiring on a nondis-
criminatory basis;[32] in theory a university is required only to hire on an evenhanded basis, but if it falls below H.E.W. goals it may have a difficult time
proving non-discrimination.

In order to clarify the recurrent constitutional litigation over the permissibility of preferential programs, we must turn to the examination of the moral
debate underlying the constitutional disagreement. If this is in substance a
moral disagreement, as it clearly seems to be, moral theory may have cogent
force in bringing its insights to bear on this problem. We shall begin with a
general discussion of the special clarifying role of contractarian moral theory
in interpreting constitutional values. Then we shall discuss the general problem
of the interpretation of the equal protection clause and the continuing debates
among constitutional scholars regarding the proper interpretation of the equal
protection principles which outlaw forms of racial discrimination. Finally, we
shall discuss the role of contractarian principles in clarifying the constitutional
problem of reverse discrimination.

THE ROLE OF CONTRACTARIAN MORAL THEORY IN INTERPRETING
CONSTITUTIONAL VALUES

It may be clear, perhaps self-evident, that moral theory should significantly
clarify a disagreement which is in substance moral. But there are a number of
plausible normative moral theories—intuitionism, utilitarianism in one or another of its forms, and the like. How can one justify the choice of contractarian
moral theory in the analytic interpretation of constitutional values?

Whatever the adequacy of contractarian theory as a general moral theory,
it has an authoritative role in the interpretation of the constitutional order in
the United States. When the Founding Fathers adopted a Bill of Rights, intended to render certain rights immune from abridgment by legislative ma-

jorities, they echoed a contractarian line of thought familiar to them in the work of Locke[33] and developed as well by other philosophers.[34] Later amendments to the Constitution, notably the fourteenth, represent a natural extension of this general contractarian conception. Acknowledgment of the existence of contractarian moral ideas underlying constitutional guarantees is common in constitutional theory; but this acknowledgment is followed by either frank intellectual disavowal of them[35] or invocation of explanatory theories lacking the focal historic significance of contractarian theory.[36] The consequence not unnaturally has been constitutional theories which either sharply limit judicial review on constitutional grounds[37] or skeptically undermine in principle the very idea of judicial review of majoritarian laws or policies.[38] Having dissolved in cynical acid the moral ideas and conceptions intrinsic to the constitutional order,[39] they unsurprisingly find it difficult to justify or defend. Contractarian moral theory remedies these defects. Building on the moral conception historically underlying the constitutional order, this theory takes these moral ideas seriously in a way in which other constitutional theories do not. Perhaps contractarian theory is not the final word as a comprehensive moral theory.[40] Nonetheless, as a matter of constitutional theory, the choice of this moral theory is not an open question in the United States; more plausibly than any other moral theory, it is the theory of the Constitution and, as such, requires the most serious and sustained consideration.

Contractarian theory makes two kinds of major theoretical contributions to the analysis of constitutional law and values: (a) it explains certain structural features of constitutional adjudications which are otherwise inexplicable; and (b) it affords a method for clarifying the moral basis of particular constitutional values (e.g., the First Amendment free speech and press clause, Fourteenth Amendment due process and equal protection of law clause; and the like). Both aspects of the explicatory power of contractarian theory are relevant to the analysis of the problem at hand: the moral basis of equal protection of law as applied to programs of reverse discrimination. Particular constitutional values, like equal protection of law, exist within the framework of established constitutional traditions. A brief examination of the contribution of contractarian theory to the understanding of this larger framework will give structural background to the subsequent examination of a particular constitutional value (equal protection) constructed around this foundational framework.

In general, constitutional adjudication is characterized by two pervasive structural features. First, judicial review on constitutional grounds is fundamentally countermajoritarian. The idea of such review and invalidation of existing law rests on the Founding Fathers' deep distrust of absolute majority rule, and on their intention to afford institutional constraints on the capacity of majority will to trample on the rights of minorities.[41] Second, such judicial review is intended to protect certain kinds of moral rights. The Founding Fathers believed that the rights guaranteed, for example, in the Bill of Rights were natural moral rights which government had no right to transgress. Man, they supposed, is foremost a moral person, and secondarily a member of a political union; once having joined such a union, he retains his moral status as a person and his moral immunity from legal claims which violate his moral status. This is one of the basic ideas of the social contract theory of natural rights, familiar to the founders in the work of John Locke.[42] This moral perception underlies the idea of judicial review and invalidation on constitutional grounds. Literally, laws which violate certain kinds of moral rights are invalid.

Much currently available constitutional theory flatly fails to account for these general structural features of constitutional adjudication.[43] Such theory also fails to take seriously the countermajoritarian cast of the constitutional design, instead limiting or criticizing judicial review on the ground that it violates the majoritarian will of the people, which is the alleged fundamental premiss of the democratic order.[44] Correlatively, these theorists either admit the existence of moral rights in the contemplated constitutional design of the Bill of Rights but then evince utter skepticism about them,[45] or fail to give any weight at all to the existence of such moral rights,[46] sometimes substituting either purely procedural concepts of treating like cases alike or neutral principles.[47] Having thus denied or failed to take seriously fundamental structural features of the constitutional design, it is not accidental that these theories fail to do justice to the practice of constitutional law in the United States.[48]

Contractarian theory, in contrast, takes seriously the role of natural rights thinking in the history of the Constitution. Whatever the historical obscurities which surround the proposal and adoption of the Bill of Rights, there is little question that the Bill was part of and gives expression to a developing moral conception regarding the moral rights of men which had been elaborated by Milton[49] and Locke[50] and which was being given or was to be given expression by Rousseau[51] and Kant.[52] The Founding Fathers believed some such theory. It is not surprising, therefore, that contractarian theory naturally explains the general structural features of the constitutional order in a way in which other theories cannot.

Unlike other constitutional theories, contractarian theory does not start from the premises of the ultimate good of majority rule or of neutral principles; nor does the theory rest on skepticism about the possibility of giving reasonable expression to the moral notions implicit in the constitutional order. On the contrary, for contractarian theory, the foundations of constitutional democracy are the principles of justice, conceived as those ultimate standards of conduct which persons would agree to from a suitably defined original position, as the principles according to which, *inter alia*, the justice of institutional arrangements of mutual co-operation is to be assessed. Constitutional democracy is perceived, in the light of contractarian theory, as a reasonable attempt to realize the requirements of the principles of justice.

From the perspective of contractarian theory, it is unlikely that there is a unique solution to the problem of just constitutional design; rather, any one of a range of constitutions, involving different institutional frameworks, might be adopted compatibly with the principles of justice. But one form of constitution which is clearly justified by these principles would be one in which certain requirements of justice are embodied in the constitution itself as conditions of legal validity. As we shall see shortly, one central principle of justice, derivable from contractarian theory, is a principle of a greatest equal liberty and opportunity.[53] Constitutional delegates might justly and reasonably recognize the tendency of popular majorities to be short-sighted in not respecting the liberties defined by this principle. Accordingly, one just solution to the problem of constitutional design is a constitution like that of the United States in which the liberties regulated by this principle are themselves guaranteed in the Constitution, with a power of judicial review and invalidation on the ground of this principle of justice.

Using such ideas, contractarian theory accomplishes, in general, an account of the structural features of constitutional adjudication which other theories are unable to explain.

First, contractarian theory explains why judicial review is not suspect, being, as it is, countermajoritarian. Majority rule is not the basic moral principle of the constitutional order. The basic moral principle is the principle of greatest equal liberty. Majority rule is justified only to the extent that it is compatible with this deeper moral principle, which constitutes a standard of criticism for majority rule (for example, that the existent institution of majority rule violates underlying moral principles of weighing each person's vote equally).[54] To the extent that judicial review enforced the requirements of a greatest equal liberty in a way in which majority rule cannot (for example, remedying malapportionment in a way in which majoritarian political processes cannot),[55] judicial review is morally justified.

Second, contractarian theory explains in general the nature of the general moral rights which are implicit in the constitutional order. Moral rights, I take it, constitute moral reasons for action of a special weight and urgency: namely, moral claims to certain kinds of individual needs and concerns which must be satisfied prior to other kinds of moral claims and which justify the use of force, other things being equal, in support of the urgency which these moral claims involve.[56] The moral rights implicit in the constitutional order constitute a subclass of the larger class of moral rights: namely, those moral rights which are elevated into enforceable legal rights by constitutional principles. Contractarian theory explains how this is so.

The Constitution rests on the general contractarian idea that certain kinds of moral principles, derivable from some kind of social contract conception, should be recognized as the minimal benchmarks of decent cooperative life. One such principle is the principle of equal liberty, which is derivable from contractarian ideas because it gives expression to the intuitive moral ideas implicit in that conception. No other comparable principle coheres as well with the idea of the status of persons as being of equal moral worth. In particular, this moral principle expresses the idea that individuals, as such, have indefeasible, inalienable rights: utilitarian calculations of the greatest good of the greatest number as expressed in popular legislative or executive action notwithstanding, these rights are not to be transgressed. But this moral principle is a central constitutional principle underlying the constitutional order. As such, the principle of greatest equal liberty, which defines the moral rights to which individual persons are entitled prior to other kinds of claims, defines *pari passu* constitutional rights which ensure that certain kinds of individual concerns are not plowed under by majoritarian rule. The Constitution, being contractarian in principle, makes these moral rights into legal rights, whose urgency as rights appears in their enforcement by the judiciary against unjust majoritarian action.

If contractarian theory can thus clarify quite general structural features of constitutional adjudication, it may also cast light on the nature and scope of particular constitutional values. In the matter of equal protection of law under the Fourteenth Amendment, we focus this theory on a constitutional value not cited in the original Bill of Rights; indeed, as we have noted, the institution of slavery, against which the fourteenth and the associated Civil War amendments[57] are in large part directed, was impliedly endorsed by the original Constitution.[58] The Fourteenth Amendment represents an extension of the constitutional charter of basic moral rights, "as the culmination of the greatest humanitarian movement in our history."[59] In order to bring moral theory to bear on the interpretation of the new moral values introduced into constitutional law by this amendment, we must first turn to the exposition of constitutional law relating to the equal protection clause and to the problem arising from reverse discrimination therein.

THE CONSTITUTIONALITY OF FORMS OF RACIAL CLASSIFICATION UNDER EXISTING LAW

The equal protection clause of the Fourteenth Amendment provides that "[n]o State shall . . . deny to any person the equal protection of the laws." Being quite general, the language of this clause is susceptible to a number of disparate and divergent interpretations. Considered abstractly, "equal protection of the laws" might bear a plausible formal interpretation, requiring only that laws (whatever their substantive content) be impartially and dispassionately applied to all who come within their terms. On this interpretation, laws requiring racial segregation would satisfy "equal protection of the laws" as long as the substantive content of the law were impartially applied, segregating all persons of the relevant races as the law requires. On the other hand, another plausible interpretation of the language of this clause would put substantive constraints of some form on the admissible content of laws, forbidding those requiring racial segregation, whatever the impartiality of their enforcement applications.

Obviously, the rational application of such general language as "equal protection of the laws" calls for the development of more specific constitutional principles which courts may use in order to render such a generality into the determinate form required for enforcement by judges, legislators, executives, lawyers, and the citizenry in general. The history of a constitutional amendment is significant in evolving such determinate interpretive principles. The purpose of the Fourteenth Amendment was broadly humanitarian; its history evinces at least the post-Civil War desire to provide firm and undeniable constitutional guarantees for the congressional enactments effecting the abolition of slavery and concomitant state practices.[60] But the history of the passage of a constitutional amendment, though probative, is not decisive. The language of the Fourteenth Amendment, for example, is far broader than the original slavery concerns, and therefore principles of broader application must be developed. The ultimate decisional authority for the development of such interpretive constitutional principles is, of course, the Supreme Court. In order to understand the form of the development of these principles, we must turn to the decisions of the Supreme Court. Then we shall be able to consider the special constitutional problem raised by racial classifications.

A. *The Standards of Review.* Broadly speaking, the development of constitutional principles interpretive of "equal protection of the laws" has focused on the issue of legitimate and illegitimate forms of classification by the state. This development is usefully perceived in the light of Tussman and tenBroek's seminal distinctions.[61] Thus, laws typically use general language (e.g., "all vehicles using the street"), which identifies certain general classes of persons or things which fall within the law in virtue of their sharing some characteristic definitive of the general class (e.g., wheeled machines used to transport persons or things over streets). Let us call such a defining characteristic of a general class C. In addition, laws typically have certain purposes to achieve certain ends, which may be inferred from the law itself, the legislative history (if any), and/or the general operation of the law (e.g., the law "all vehicles using the street shall not exceed 30 m.p.h." has the purpose of minimizing traffic accidents). Let us call a purpose of this kind P.

Laws may be analyzed, for equal protection purposes, in terms of the relationships between the C's and P's underlying them: namely, whether or to what extent the general class identified by the C of a particular law achieves the purpose identified by the P of the law. Five possible relationships are identified by this analysis, namely:

(1) (CP)   : All C's are P's and all P's are C's;

(2) (C)(P) : No C's are P's;

(3) (P over C)   : All C's are P's but some P's are not C's;

(4) (C over P)   : All P's are C's but some C's are not P's;

(5) (P over C)   : Some C's are P's but not all C's are P's; and some P's are C's but not all P's are C's.

One of these relationships holds in the case of any legislative classification, which may be assessed in terms of varying degrees of reasonableness of fit between classification and purpose.

Situations (1) and (2) represent extremes of reasonableness and unreasonableness, respectively. In the first case, the classification of the law coincides perfectly with its purpose. No more can reasonably be asked. In the second, no member of the legislative classification is relevant to the legislative purpose. The classification is, therefore, perfectly unreasonable. Situation (3) represents the case of legislative underinclusiveness. Some of the persons or things identified by the legislative classification bear on the purpose of the law, but there are other persons or things, which equally relate to the purpose, which are not included in the classification.

Situation (4) is the case of legislative overinclusiveness. Some of the persons or things included in the legislative classification facilitate the legislative purpose; some do not.

Situation (5) is the mixed case of legislative over- and underinclusiveness. Some of the members of the legislative classification do not advance the law's purpose (overinclusiveness); and things or persons, as much facilitative of the law's purpose as the members of the legislative classification, are not members of the class (underinclusiveness).

All forms of under- and overinclusiveness violate the perfect equal treatment of like cases specified in situation (1). Underinclusive legislative classifications do not treat similar cases similarly: all persons or things, facilitative of the legislative purpose, are not identified by the legislative classification. Overinclusive legislative classifications similarly fail to treat like cases alike, including persons or things which do not relate to the legislative purpose. The Supreme Court's development of constitutional principles interpretive of "equal protection of the laws" takes the form of establishing principles of review which determine to what extent such *prima facie* violations of equal treatment are constitutionally permissible.

This development has taken the form of two different standards of equal protection review. The strict standard of review, or "strict scrutiny" test, is used whenever the Court finds that a legislative classification is "suspect" or involves certain "fundamental interests," such as voting rights,[62] access to the criminal process,[63] the right to travel,[64] and the right to procreate.[65] If this test is triggered either by a suspect classification or by a fundamental interest, the Court in general[66] requires that the law in question have as its purpose a valid state interest and that that purpose be pursued substantially without over- or underinclusiveness. For example, suppose there is a state law, intended to advance the compelling state interest of knowledgeability of local affairs, to the effect that voting rights may be exercised only by those who have lived in the state for more than one year. Since the exercise of voting rights is a "fundamental interest," the law in question is unconstitutional under the strict test, which is triggered by the presence of such a fundamental interest. The legislative classification (citizens of the state for less than one year) fails to include many citizens who are not knowledgeable (underinclusiveness) and includes many citizens who are knowledgeable (overinclusiveness).[67]

On the other hand, if a legislative classification is not "suspect" or does not trench upon "fundamental interests," the legislative classification is valid under the equal protection clause if and only if the classification has some rational basis. This is the rational basis or "weak" test. Effectively, if the rational basis test applies, a fair amount of under- and/or overinclusiveness is constitutionally acceptable. For example, on the assumption that traffic control is a legitimate state interest and that the right to advertise is not a "fundamental interest," a city regulation forbidding all vehicles in the city to display advertising on them, except self-advertising, is constitutional. The classification may be both underinclusive and overinclusive; forms of self-advertising may cause distracting traffic control problems, and forms of other advertising may not. Though the classification would be unconstitutional under the strict test, it is constitutional under the weak test; it is possible that the legislative body had some rational basis for supposing that self-advertising did not involve the magnitude of the problem posed by non–self-advertising.[68]

B. *The Constitutional Status of Racial Classifications: The Dilemma of Reverse Discrimination.* The constitutional status of racial classifications was classically raised by the school desegregation cases starting with *Brown v. Board of Education.*[69] At first, it seemed that the disposition of these cases might turn on some view of the status of education as a "fundamental interest," triggering the strict case. But subsequent cases extended the constitutional prohibition of state-required racial segregation well beyond the confines of education;[70] indeed, the Supreme Court eventually, for reasons of a perhaps dubious nature,[71] expressly refused to denominate education one of the "fundamental interests." Accordingly, the exacting constitutional scrutiny, to which official segregation was subjected, was interpreted as arising from the application of the "suspect classification" prong of the strict test, on which we shall focus here (putting aside the question of the application of the "fundamental interest" prong).

Herbert Wechsler, in an early critique of *Brown* and its progeny,[72] argued that *Brown* failed to rest on a neutral principle, of a kind which is required for the critical acceptability of a constitutional decision on the merits. Wechsler's conception of neutral principles arises from his attempt to defend the propriety of constitutional adjudication from the criticisms made by Learned Hand.[73] Hand argued that the exercise of judicial invalidation of laws on constitutional grounds was a judicial usurpation of a legislative chamber's essentially performing the legislative function of determining whether legislation is in the public interest—weighing the costs and benefits of legislation in their relation to goals of public policy. Wechsler argues that courts, in exercising their power of invalidation on constitutional grounds, do not decide cases on general grounds of public policy or legislative criteria of importance. Rather, courts are subject to a discipline of reasoning, to which legislators are not bound: namely, that the disposition of constitutional questions must be formulable in terms of some constitutional principle, which transcends the case at hand and is applicable to all comparable cases.

More generally, Wechsler's point may be characterized in terms of systematic institutional differences between legislative and judicial decisions at the stage of input to the decision, the process of decision, and the form of the decision itself. At the stage of input, for example, legislators, unlike judges, have broad fact-finding powers which enable them to sift complex situations of fact in an exploratory way; judges, in contrast, typically are limited to the disposition of a particular case before them as the facts of the case have been presented by the parties. In terms of the process of decision, legislators have a broad mandate to weigh considerations of the public interest and the claims of conflicting power and pressure groups; legislators are not required to reach their decision or to justify it in any way analogous to the intricate written opinions of judges, which endeavor to justify the conclusions of law, involved in the disposition of a particular case, as being compatible with established precedent in some rationally coherent way. Finally, the result of legislative decision is typically a quite complex and general statutory scheme with detailed rules and regulations and precise definitional schemes, involving elaborate coercive agencies and the spending of large sums of government monies; judicial decisions, in contrast, are typically of limited mandate (e.g., X must pay money to Y).

Wechsler's emphasis on the distinctive marks of proper judicial decision stresses the constraints and discipline which this process involves: the search for general principles, decisive of the case at hand but applicable to similar cases as well, and compatible with the body of existing principles embodied in past authoritative judicial decisions (precedent). In the area of constitutional adjudication, Wechsler conceives the search for neutral principles as an exigent requirement for proper constitutional decision, as a court must decide all cases properly before it in accord with applicable law, lacking any power to decline to decide cases on grounds of unprincipled expediency of a legislative kind.

Brown lacks such a neutral principle, Wechsler argues, because it is impossible to identify a defensible principle, supportive of the decision in that case, which the Supreme Court would extend to similar cases. Legislative motive, Wechsler suggests, cannot typically be taken into account; and he fails to see why the principle of separate-but-equal is a necessary denial of equality, supporting the point in *Plessy* (which established the propriety of the separate-but-equal principle, until reversed by *Brown*) that if "enforced separation stamps the colored race with a badge of inferiority" it is solely because its members choose "to put that construction upon it."[74] Would, Wechsler rhetorically asks, enforced segregation of the sexes be unconstitutional because females resent it?[75] Is a prohibition of miscegenation a discrimination against the black who would like to marry?[76] The only plausible neutral principle supportive of *Brown*, Wechsler argues, is the denial of the freedom of association (of blacks to associate, if they wish, with whites). But this principle is itself compromised by *Brown*, which respects the associational rights of blacks at the expense of the similar rights of whites. And how can this trade-off of rights be constitutionally defended? To justify this, for Wechsler, is the unmet "challenge of the school-segregation cases."[77]

Wechsler's challenge was met by two kinds of responses: first, attacks on the very idea of neutral principles,[78] and second, attempts to identify a neutral principle supportive of *Brown*.[79] One of the most notable of these later attempts was Alexander Bickel's suggestion that the neutral principle needed was a principle expressly outlawing all forms of racial classifications by the state.[80] The obvious counter-example to this neutral principle is, Bickel acknowledges, programs of racial preferences, designed to undo the effects of past unconstitutional segregation by race. Bickel acknowledges the force of this counter-example, but does not give weight to its force in modifying his formulation of the proper neutral principle for the desegregation cases. Bickel argues, rather, that the courts should exercise the "passive virtues" when such preferential programs are to be constitutionally scrutinized.[81] In effect, courts, at least for a reasonable time period until the beneficial effects of these programs are worked out, are not to decide cases involving preferential programs using racial classifications. The neutral principle (no racial classifications by the state are permissible), used to end segregation, remains uncompromised but inapplicable, at least until the effects of the unlawful segregation are ended.

Bickel's basic position regarding the neutral principle underlying *Brown* remained constant throughout his life, but his view of preferential programs changed during the 1970s. Thus, Bickel joined Philip Kurland to write the brief of B'nai B'rith, one of the amici curiae in *DeFunis* opposing discrimination against whites.[82] The day of proper exercise of the "passive virtues," vis-à-vis racial classifications, is over. Such classifications are to be constitutionally scrutinized on the merits, and found wanting.

The actual form of the argument, in the B'nai B'rith brief, is somewhat more complicated than Bickel's earlier position. The relevant neutral principle is not simply that no racial classifications by the state are permissible, but rather that racial classifications *per se* trigger the "suspect classification" prong of the strict test, and are unconstitutional under that test. This complication of the earlier proposed neutral principle was necessitated by the fact that earlier Supreme Court opinions expressly declined to espouse the position that racial classifications are *per se* unconstitutional. The most notable example thereof are the Japanese relocation cases, in which the Supreme Court permitted the use of a racial or national-origin classification (clearly "suspect") for determining who should be relocated and otherwise confined.[83] Other cases have permitted clearly underinclusive attempts to ameliorate burdens on the exercise of clearly established "fundamental interests," on the ground that the state may take one step at a time.[84]

Adopting this more complicated formulation of a neutral principle outlawing classifications by race, Bickel argues that preferential racial classifications, of the kind involved in *DeFunis*, fail to satisfy either of the aspects of the strict test: there is no compelling state interest which they pursue (analogous to that found in the Japanese relocation cases: namely, national security), and the interest which they do pursue is both overinclusive and underinclusive. The avowed purpose of the preferential scheme was to remedy the cultural disadvantage of certain groups. But, Bickel argues, the minority groups favored in the *DeFunis* preferential program do not include all persons who are culturally disadvantaged—for example, poor whites (underinclusiveness)—and may include minority group members who have not in fact been culturally disadvantaged (overinclusiveness).

The central gravamen of the Bickel argument is the appropriateness of the strict test. The main reason urged for the view that racial classifications *per se* trigger the strict test is stated as follows:

A racial quota creates a status on the basis of factors that have to be irrelevant to any objectives of a democratic society, the factors of skin color or parental origin. A racial quota derogates the human dignity and individuality of all to whom it is applied. A racial quota is invidious in principle as well as in practice. Though it may be thought here to help "minority" students, it can as easily be turned against the same or other minorities. The history of the racial quota is a history of subjugation not beneficence.

The evil of the racial quota lies not in its name but in its effect. A quota by any other name is still a divider of society, a creator of castes, and it is all the worse for its racial basis, especially in a society desperately striving for an equality that will make race irrelevant, politically, economically, and socially.[85]

It is important to see that not all forms of racial classification, even those used as part of preferential ameliorative programs, would be unconstitutional even under Bickel's conception. For example, in the case of classic *de jure* segregation by race, the use of racial classifications to remedy or end such illegal segregation would be constitutional under Bickel's formulation of the strict test. The purpose of such a remedial program (to correct the imbalance of all white and all black schools, which result from *de jure* segregation) would be precisely matched by the use of racial classifications allocating certain pupils to one school and others to another; the racial classification, being neither overinclusive nor underinclusive relative to a legitimate state interest, satisfies the strict test.[86] The problem for Bickel arises with preferential programs which have purposes which do not precisely match the racial classifications suggested.

The defense of preferential programs takes two forms: (*a*) the attempt to show that these programs satisfy the strict test; and (*b*) the argument that the weak rational basis test is the more proper standard of review for these preferential programs. The main thrust of the first group is that preferential racial classifications advance a compelling state interest, of a weight equivalent to that invoked in the Japanese relocation cases.[87] The usefulness of the analogy to these cases derives from the force which they gave to the presence of a compelling state interest: namely, that the racial classification is permissible even though it does not match the compelling state purpose pursued. For, in these cases, it is reasonably clear that the racial classification was overinclusive (including many quite loyal Japanese-Americans) and underinclusive (failing to include many Americans of an ethnic ancestry which might tend to make them less than enthusiastic in supporting a war against the country of their ancestral origin, for example, German- or Italian-Americans). If a compelling state interest could be sustained in the case of preferential racial classifications, then such programs would be sustained though they are over- and/or underinclusive.

Other supporters of preferential racial classifications argue that the strict test of equal protection review is not appropriate here, so that any over- or underinclusiveness of legislative classification should be assessed only for its rationality under the weak test. One striking form of this argument is that of John Hart Ely, who has argued that the "suspect classification" prong of the strict test turns on the presence of a strong we–they component in the legislative decision: namely, that those who made the decision to use a certain racial or other classification to disadvantage a certain group include no or few members of the group thus disadvantaged. Since this element is lacking in preferential racial classification (the we's are advantaging the they's, and disadvantaging themselves), there is no reason to apply strict scrutiny.[88] Another recent form of this argument is that of Owen Fiss, who suggests a radical reinterpretation of the traditional over- and underinclusiveness analysis of equal protection; instead of focusing on issues of fairness in and among legislative classifications, Fiss suggests that equal protection be construed as a principle ameliorating the position of worst-off groups. Since preferential racial programs do exactly this, they should satisfy equal protection under a rational basis analysis.[89]

An intermediate position between those who advocate the strict and those who defend the weak tests is the position that some form of intermediate test is required here, neither as exacting as the strict test nor as deferential as the weak. This position, recently suggested by Kent Greenawalt,[90] would uphold the principle of preferential racial classifications but closely scrutinize the particular form of the classification in question to see if its over- or underinclusiveness may be kept within reasonable limits. In general, however, the Supreme Court has not been receptive to the suggestion, first made by Gerald Gunther,[91] that intermediate levels of review be developed between the dichotomous strict and weak tests.[92]

The constitutionality of preferential programs obviously elicits divergent interpretations of applicable constitutional principles. Only remedial racial classification for *de jure* segregation seems acceptable on any theory of equal protection review.[93] The crux of the argument turns, I believe, on the application of the strict *vs.* the weak test. Proponents of preferential programs understandably try to render such programs compatible with the strict test;[94] but their arguments seem dubious. The analogy of the Japanese relocation cases seems forced. Those cases have been subjected to unremitting criticism since they were decided,[95] and, if of continuing validity, would probably be limited by the Supreme Court to their facts. This analogy aside, many preferential programs are clearly over- and underinclusive in the way the strict test forbids. Accordingly, the argument between proponents and opponents of these programs naturally turns on the issue of which standard of review, strict or weak, is appropriate in the case of racial classifications used in preferential programs.

Having thus set out the nature of the constitutional issue, we may turn to the exposition of moral theory and the light, if any, which it casts on this tangled dispute.

THE MORAL THEORY OF CONSTITUTIONAL EQUAL PROTECTION

We have argued in general that the moral theory of the constitutional order is premised on the contractarian idea that democratically elected legislatures and executives are limited by constitutionally imposed constraints which limit majoritarian political power, rendering fundamental civil and human rights legally immune from political bargaining. Majoritarian sentiments which would ignore and violate these rights notwithstanding, these rights are guaranteed, enforced by the legal power of a trained and politically independent judiciary to invalidate exercises of state power which violate them.

We turn now to the more concrete task of discussing how contractarian theory may clarify the interpretation of particular constitutional values, in particular, the equal protection clause of the Fourteenth Amendment and the problem of reverse discrimination thereunder. We begin with a general sketch of the principles of justice, and then turn to the moral theory of equal protection.

A. *The Principles of Justice.* This article employs a contractarian analysis, following the model of John Rawls,[96] which proposes the following approach: Moral principles are those which perfectly rational men, irrespective of historical or personal age, in a hypothetical position of equal liberty and having all knowledge and reasonable belief except that of their specific personal situation, would agree to as the ultimate standards of conduct applicable at large. Our concern is to apply this definition of moral principles to a theory of justice; we must therefore introduce into the original position the existence of conflicting claims over a limited supply of "general goods" and consider a specific set of principles to regulate claims on such goods. If there were general goods in abundant superfluity, or if people were more willing to sacrifice their interests for the good of others, the need for principles of justice might be nonexistent or significantly different.[97]

"General goods" are those things or conditions which are typically the objects of rational choices or desires or the generalized means to a variety of particular desires.[98] It is natural to classify liberty as one of these general goods. Liberty for A to do X implies the absence of constraint, either to do or not to do X; obviously, the existence of various rights and liberties is an important generalized means enabling each person to pursue his particular ends, whatever they are. The mature and reasonable man whose actions are specifically constrained by others in certain directions lacks an essential ingredient of deciding on and pursuing his individual happiness. Various liberties are, accordingly, indispensable to the formation of a self-respect based on full expression of the spirit (liberties of thought), self-direction (political liberties of voting and political participation), security of the person (civic liberties of impartial administration of laws protecting person and property), and the possibility of unhampered movement (freedom of physical, economic, and social movement).[99]

Similarly, it is natural to identify capacity, property, and wealth as basic distributive goods. Capacity, the physical, intellectual, and emotional competences necessary to rational action, is obviously a general means enabling people to pursue individual ends. Property, the possessions over which one has legally protected exclusive control and right of disposition, is in some form[100] a significant means enabling people to pursue their individual and disparate ends.[101] Wealth, including a medium of exchange, provides the wherewithal to pursue the ends which one desires.

In a discussion of such basic distributive goods, it is natural to regard a notion of basic opportunity as also of fundamental moral importance. An

examination of the ordinary language use of the word "opportunity" will clarify
the moral notion of opportunity which is central to this analysis. An opportunity, in the ordinary language sense, is a kind of good. An oncoming disaster
is generally not considered to be an opportunity, unless one regards it as af-
fording a spiritual exercise or a test of one's mettle. But an opportunity is a
special kind of good. In general, an opportunity for a person A to do X is said
or thought to exist only where some circumstance external to A exists, the
presence of which affords a chance of doing X. Thus, it is not normally proper
to speak of the internal capacities of A which enable him to do X as being
opportunities to do X.[102] Internal endowments—including attitudes, motivations, personality, and beliefs, as well as capacities—are at least as significant
as external circumstances in explaining why certain good-producing actions occur or are likely to occur, but these endowments are not identified by the normal concept of opportunity.

An opportunity for A to do X is thus an external circumstance which confers
a chance or an availability of doing X, which leads or is believed by the speaker-
thinker to lead to some good. A New Yorker, for example, may be described
as having a certain cultural opportunity, because New York City offers a
range of institutions which confer an availability for cultivating and pleasurably
exercising cultural sensibilities, the cultivation and exercise of which are, or at
least are believed to be, human goods.

The existence of an opportunity does not conclude the question of fair access
to that opportunity. A person in prison in New York has no access to that city's
cultural opportunities. Access would be similarly impaired by a lack of sensory
capacities. If a person were blind, he could hardly appreciate the formal beau-
ties of Balanchine's choreography at the New York City Ballet; if he were
deaf, the musical pleasures of hearing the New York Philharmonic would be
unavailable. Poverty might make access to the Metropolitan Opera, and even
to the New York City Opera, impossible. Further, if one were not in prison,
not sensorily defective, and not poor, a lack of experience and cultural training
might also limit access to New York's cultural opportunities.

The moral concept of opportunity is the type of external chance which is
naturally thought of in discussions of the general goods involved in fundamental
distributive questions.[103] Thus, one thinks of a broad class of external circumstances which facilitate full development and expression of the capacities involved in a rational life and afford unrestricted access to available goods. These
opportunities include the family opportunity which a child has for emotional
nurture, guidance, and training; the educational opportunity which a child has
for training in the basic skills; broad cultural opportunity; and the opportunity
to take fair advantage of the liberties formally available. The existence of these
opportunities, as in the New York example, obviously does not resolve the
question of fair access to the good life; opportunity is only one among the
general distributive goods. Opportunities of this basic nature are not only ends

in themselves (being ingredient to aspects of basic human fulfillment), but important instrumental preconditions to realization of the full value of available liberties. Voting rights are meaningless in a society whose population is illiterate. Freedom of thought is useless without the training which forms an independent intellectual conscience. Freedom of social and economic movement is of little value if institutions do not provide the training to make such movement more probable.

The original position presents a problem of rational choice under uncertainty: rational men in the original position have no way of predicting the probabilities which they may end up with in any given situation of life. If a person agrees to principles of justice which permit deprivations of liberty and property rights and later discovers that he occupies a disadvantaged position, he will have no just claim against deprivations which may render his entire life-prospects meager and bitterly servile. To forestall such consequences, the rational strategy in choosing the basic principles of justice would be the conservative "maximin" strategy:[104] make certain that the worst position in the system adopted is the best of all conceivable worst positions, that is, maximize the minimum condition. Thus, if a person is born into the worst possible situation of life allowed by the adopted moral principles, he or she will still be better off than in the worst situation allowed by other possible principles.

The application of the maximin strategy requires us to consider the interpretation and relative weight assigned the general goods by those in the original position. These dimensions will crucially determine the principles governing the distribution of general goods. In order thus to compare and weigh these general goods, we must consider the relevance of what I shall call primary human goods, understood as the fundamental (thus "primary") ingredients of mature fulfilled human personality. Self-respect is a primary good in this sense. For human persons, self-respect has its natural basis in our desire to exercise our capacities competently.[105] Human beings have complex capacities involving the capacity for thought and deliberation, the use of language, the creation of designed artifacts of a practical and aesthetic nature, the capacity to plan and shape life in terms of desires and aspirations over time,[106] and the like. A secure and confirmed confidence in our developed competence to exercise these capacities is the basis of self-respect and self-esteem, without which persons lack confidence in the basic competences in part constitutive of human personality. Deprived of the experience of personal competence and self-mastery, humans lack the experience of self-worth, the absence of which leads to the despairing inner death of apathy, cynical or stoical remoteness, the slavery of the soul.[107]

Self-respect, being a primary good, enters into the conception and weighing of the distribution of general goods by the principles of justice. In particular, consideration of this primary good enables one to determine which of the general goods are so fundamental that inequalities in their distribution are unlikely to secure the highest lowest: the person or class with lower amounts of them would be disadvantaged to a greater extent than by disparities in other goods. The notions of liberty and opportunity seem in this way more fundamental than other notions; the question of capacity is explicitly put aside.[108]

Self-respect, as a primary good, explains why liberty and opportunity justly have a strong grip on our moral imaginations. A society in which the liberties of thought are trammeled is one in which the basic need for expression of the spirit is frustrated, with the distorting rigidities of defined orthodoxies the result. A society without any voting rights is one in which a person's sense of autonomous self-direction shrivels into apathy.[109] A society which does not guarantee equal access to the criminal and civil law provides no security of the person. A nation which restricts the liberty of physical, social, and economic movement condemns each person to the fortuitous place, social class, and job of his birth, thus reducing horizons and prospects to a nullity and making effort and aspiration stupid because they are in vain. In short, all these liberties facilitate and nurture a basic sense of self-respect, a belief in the competence and integrity of one's person, without which satisfaction of needs is only an escapist refuge from an inner death.

Similarly, basic opportunities are at least as fundamental. They assure that persons, no matter what their natural endowments, are given a chance to develop a conception of their rational good and the capacity to bring it to realization. Without such oportunities, persons can develop no self-esteem in their competence as developed rational beings, including not only various occupational competences but those broader capacities which make possible a fully rational life (the use of language; the capacity to plan and adjust desires over time; the growth of special talents involving the pleasures of cultivating a craft, an art, an athletic prowess, and the like; and the development of emotional capacities of social feeling). In addition, such opportunities ensure that the underlying value of liberties is realized. Thus, it is no accident that voting rights do not exist as anything more than a plebiscitary sham, if at all, in a society whose population remains illiterate. In such circumstances voting rights may be a form of exploitation rather than a means of liberation. Freedom of thought has little value in the absence of a disciplined training which enables precise, intelligent, and plausible expression of an independent intellectual conscience. Freedom of social and economic movement has little value if institutions do not provide the training which makes such movement more probable. And civic liberty, like voting rights, lacks value where people do not have the fair opportunity to make use of it.

In matters involving the fundamental factors which shape a person's capacity to become a full rational being and to enjoy the life of such a being, the rational contractors of our model of political morality could not, consistently with maximining, agree to any principle except equality. Use of the maximin strategy in choosing principles relating to liberty and opportunity thus tends to eliminate the disadvantaged class; the highest lowest is equality for all persons.

By contrast, once a certain minimum level of property and income is guaranteed, the contractors of the original position would not find equality in income and property rational from the point of view of the original position. A relatively poor person, with full equal liberty and opportunity, may be better off in a system which allows inequalities in the distribution of wealth than in a system requiring equality; the effects of inequality may make him less poor over his life than if there were a mandated equality of wealth.[110]

The following principles of justice regulating the distributive shares of general goods would therefore be accepted in the original position:[111]

> *The principle of equal liberty and opportunity.* Basic institutions are to be arranged so that every person in the institution is guaranteed the greatest equal liberty and opportunity compatible with a like liberty and opportunity for all.

> *The principle of justified inequality.* Inequalities in the distribution by institutions of general goods such as money, property, and status are to be allowed only if those inequalities are a necessary incentive to elicit the exercise of superior capacities, and only if the exercise of those capacities advances the interests of typical people in all standard classes in the institution and makes the life expectation of desire satisfaction of the typical person in the least advantaged class as high as possible.

The principle of equal liberty and opportunity applies to three types of basic institutions: (*a*) the legal system, (*b*) the educational, cultural, and family system, and (*c*) the economic system of jobs. The legal system is required to guarantee by law the equal right of all persons to the liberties of thought and speech, civic liberties, political liberties, and freedom of political movement. In the second category, equal opportunity requires these institutions to allow children and young adults an equal opportunity to develop their sensitivities and capacities, particularly their rational concept of their welfare in terms of developing and realizing a coherent life plan. In the economic system of jobs, people are to have an equal opportunity to be selected for any job as long as their qualifications are equal. If the second principle applies, so that different social and economic classes justifiably exist, then every person is to have equal liberty and opportunity of movement within the class system consistent with his capacities.

This concept of opportunity must be distinguished from the notion of achievement, a related but not similarly morally fundamental notion. The moral concept of opportunity expresses the idea that people are entitled to whatever facilitates their development as rational persons. That a person may be more abundantly endowed with capacities, and thus have a higher potential achievement, is irrelevant to this notion; that one may in some sense achieve more with a certain basic opportunity than another person is similarly irrelevant. Unlike achievement, opportunity is governed by a principle of equality, not only because it makes liberties valuable, but also because it is a condition of a rational life in which a coherent development of desire and capacity is possible.

B. *The Moral Theory of the Standards of Equal Protection Review.* We have seen that the strict test of equal protection review, whether triggered by the "fundamental interest" or "suspect classification" prong of the strict test, requires a much more exacting standard of review for legislative classifications. A court, once it has decided that the strict test is applicable, carefully scrutinizes the classifications which a particular law employs—i.e., infers the policy which the statute pursues; if that policy is legitimate, assesses whether the legislative classification is overinclusive or underinclusive relative to the policy thereof; and if it is either or both, typically holds the law unconstitutional. On the other hand, if a legislative scheme neither trenches upon a "fundamental interest" nor employs a "suspect classification," the weak rational basis test is applied, under which broad constitutional tolerance is extended to "ill fit" between legislative classification and purpose.

In order to understand the moral basis for these different standards of review, we must focus on the question of why, morally, "ill fit" between legislative classification and purpose should be regarded as constitutionally dubious in the case of "fundamental interests" or "suspect classifications." In general, the constitutional concept of equal protection interprets the constitutional requirement of equality, mandated by the Fourteenth Amendment, in terms of the idea of treating all things or persons similarly relative to legislative purpose. Both underinclusive and overinclusive legislative classifications violate this idea in that, respectively, they group persons or things which omit items identified by the legislative purpose, or fail to omit items not so identified. But why should cases involving "fundamental interests" or "suspect classifications" be more exactingly held to this standard than other cases?

Understanding of this problem must begin with the contractarian conception underlying the constitutional order and the principles of justice, sketched above, which that conception places at the foundation of legitimate government. A contractarian conception of moral rights is, as a matter of historical and present fact, implicit in the constitutional order of the United States; accordingly, contractarian moral theory, built on the *same* historic conceptions as the constitutional order, naturally explains not only, as we have seen, various structural features of the constitutional order, but specific constitutional issues. In general, this historic conception rests on the idea that, majoritarian sentiments to the contrary notwithstanding, moral rights are guaranteed, enforced by a trained judiciary independent of the other branches and immunized from majoritarian political pressures. Thus, the notion of judicial supremacy has, from the first, been intended as a bulwark, as Alexander Hamilton put it, against "encroachments and oppressions of the representative body"[112] and "serious oppressions of the minor party in the community."[113] The judiciary, accordingly, is given the constitutional responsibility of determining, as a matter of progressively unfolding constitutional interpretation, the proper standards by which they are to determine such moral rights and defend them from state interference.

The equal protection clause of the Fourteenth Amendment represents an extension of the moral theory underlying the constitutional order. Moral rights, at best suggested in the initial Constitution and at worst impliedly denied,[114] are here expressly recognized and guaranteed. Thus, the equal protection provision was clearly intended to render illegal forms of state oppression of and discrimination against black persons, newly freed from slavery by the Thirteenth Amendment and guaranteed the right to vote by the Fifteenth. But, in form, the provision is quite general, speaking of "equal protection of the laws." Accordingly, the moral theory underlying this new constitutional provision has justly been taken by the Supreme Court to require articulation of a more general moral principle applicable at large to other situations and other persons. In articulating this principle, the Court, as already noted, evolved the strict and weak standard of equal protection review.

Initially, we must be clear that the principles of justice, derivable from the contractarian conception, apply not only to judges, but also to legislators, executives, and indeed the citizenry at large—all of whom are morally bound by their requirements. It follows that judges are not necessarily the only or the best enforcers of applicable principles of justice. The point may be put more strongly: the injustice of a law, determined on the ground of some violation of the principles of justice, should not be deemed sufficient for the state or federal courts to invalidate that law under the due process or equal protection clause of the Fourteenth Amendment or similar constitutional provisions. There are good reasons why this *should* not be so. If courts were used to attack all unjust laws, pressure on the courts for legislative change would become the rule rather than the exception, a mark of weakness in democratic institutions; judges would become the arbiters of complex social and economic issues which they are institutionally ill suited to decide;[115] and the power to govern would shift from elected representatives to an appointed judiciary. Despite these general considerations, there is no doubt that a strong and able judiciary can and should, on grounds of justice, perform a crucial constitutional function in remedying certain kinds of injustice which majoritarian rule is likely, unchecked, to work. The problem, analytically, is to articulate a defensible rule defining the circumstances in which judicial remedies should be available to override the injustices worked by majority rule; all such injustices cannot, compatibly with the considerations just adduced, be susceptible to judicial remedy.

Constitutional law well recognizes the distinction between constitutional principles which may and those which may not be enforced by courts. For example, the due process and equal protection clauses incorporate a state action requirement which renders certain injustices committed by the state, but not by private individuals, subject to constitutional attack[116] by courts; legislative power may reach farther.[117] In addition, before a case may be constitutionally scrutinized by courts, the case must be "justiciable"—a "case or controversy"[118] presented in a concrete dispute between adverse parties in a form susceptible to sound judicial examination; a plausible constitutional claim, no matter what its merits, may not be assessed by courts if it does not appear in proper "justiciable" form.[119] In some areas, notably "political questions," even where constitutional provisions clearly apply, the courts will abstain from judgment, because other governmental branches are putatively better final judges of the issues involved.[120]

Similar considerations regarding the proper role of courts in enforcing constitutional principles underlie the issue of the appropriate standard of review, the issue raised by the strict and weak tests of equal protection review. Certain kinds of cases, though involving plausibly construed violations of constitutional principles, elicit a deferentially weak standard of review under which they are upheld by courts; other cases are aggressively reviewed under stringent standards of review without the deference to legislative competence which the weak standard of review evidences.

Underinclusiveness of legislative classification relative to the law's purpose may occur for various reasons, some quite defensible, others less so. For example, the failure of the law to include all persons required by the legislative purpose may rest on grounds of administrative convenience; drawing a more precise classification would be too costly in terms of the needed administrative machinery relative to the gain thus secured. On the other hand, the underinclusiveness of a legislative classification may rest on less justifiable *political* grounds; for example, the limitation of a legislative classification to small businessmen as special treatment in order to guarantee re-election in an approaching election.[121] Such clearly political reasons for underinclusiveness seem to deny the kind of equal treatment which the equal protection clause *prima facie* requires: not treating all cases alike relative to legislative purpose. Close judicial scrutiny of such unfair classifications, insisting that legislatures treat like cases alike, might be a sound discipline; legislatures would be forced to decide whether the law's purpose was sufficiently weighty to be extended consistently, or whether, in fact, the law would not be maintained if the legislature were constitutionally compelled to extend the law to its fair extent. On the other hand, the free play and competition of supposedly equal economic and social forces in the democratic political process is an essential feature of sound and vigorous democratic processes; if one pressure group prevails over another in a fair competition for legislative influence, it may be unwise for a court to interfere. At bottom, "the pressure theory of legislation and the equal protection requirement are incompatible."[122] How they should be squared is a major problem of constitutional law and theory.

Overinclusiveness of legislative classification seems more clearly problematic: it burdens individuals with legislative penalties when they are not tainted by the evil which the law's purpose seeks to remedy, violating traditional ideas condemning guilt by group association.[123] Nonetheless, even such classification can within limits be justified on grounds of administrative convenience. The Supreme Court itself has allowed such classification even in quite questionable circumstances of supposed national emergency.[124]

The strict test of equal protection review, premissed on the violation of "fundamental rights" or use of a "suspect classification," is intended to identify those forms of under- or overinclusiveness which the Court, on the ground of the principles of justice following from contractarian ideas, is competent to assess and correct. The "fundamental interest" prong of the strict test, thus, rests on the special moral status and weight of the liberties and opportunities regulated by the first principle of justice—namely, that the distribution of those liberties and opportunities was to be in terms of a greatest equal liberty and opportunity for all. Inequalities in the distribution of these goods are presumptively unjust, so that the constitutional assessment of the distribution of these goods is judged under a very exacting standard of review, under which deviations from equality rarely pass muster.[125]

The "suspect classification" prong of the strict test, on which we focus here, may be similarly clarified by reference to the requirements of the principles of justice. But here the moral issue turns not on the nature of the liberty or opportunity unequally distributed (i.e., the "fundamental interest"), but on the morally irrelevant basis upon which people have been unequally distributed these and other goods of life.

Thus, the contractarian model of morality, from which the principles of justice are derived, importantly gives sense and specific content to the thought that morality involves viewing others as persons. The contractors of the original position, not knowing their specific identity, would not agree to ultimate principles of morality which differentiate among people on the basis of human characteristics which bear no relation to people's capacity to govern their conduct or to perceive others' interests and claims in terms of ultimate principles of conduct expressing a conception of fundamental human equality and liberty. On this view, the capacity to view others as persons turns on the capacity to see persons in terms of individual, possibly unique, characteristics of thought and action, which afford relevant considerations for moral discriminations (e.g., kindness, gentleness, generosity, fair-mindedness, industriousness, productivity, and the like). By contrast, viewing people in terms of morally irrelevant characteristics, which bear no connection to just moral discriminations among individuals, is to treat people in the way in which one treats things, as objects having generalized characteristics which one may manipulate to advance one's purposes or ends (e.g., tools, or tables and chairs, and the like).

From this perspective, the "suspect classifications" triggering the strict test identify the morally irrelevant characteristics in terms of which people's rights have as a matter of common fact been denied. Thus, the classic original "suspect classification," race, rests on a long history of racial prejudice against black persons rooted in institutions of slavery (abolished by the fourteenth and its companion amendments) and later institutions of economic and social segregation which have existed, in a *de jure* form, until relatively recently.[126] Persons, who happen to be of a certain race, are on that basis alone deprived of fair access to the goods of life. Similarly, prejudices against aliens or certain ethnic groups, on the basis of alienage or ethnicity alone, have deprived people of the moral consideration due them as persons. Accordingly, the "suspect classification" analysis has naturally been extended to alienage and ethnic origin.[127] Similar prejudices against people on the basis of sex alone are gradually leading the courts to apply a level of scrutiny to sex-based classifications which increasingly looks like strict scrutiny or some variant thereof;[128] commentators urge acceptance of other such suspect classifications on similar grounds, e.g., insanity,[129] poverty,[130] sexual preference,[131] and the like.

On this view, the strict test applied to "suspect classifications" rests on the existence, as a matter of historical and present fact, of widespread prejudices against certain groups of persons on the basis of morally irrelevant characteristics. Undoubtedly, there are some cases in which legislation clearly takes as its motive racial prejudice which cannot constitute a legitimate basis for state action under the Fourteenth Amendment, condemned, as it is, by the basic principles of justice embodied in this humanitarian amendment.[132] However, in many other cases, the attempt to prove such condemned legislative motives is difficult and sometimes insuperable. Accordingly, the "suspect classification" prong of the strict test was evolved in order to provide a judicially manageable standard of review in place of difficult attempts to infer legislative motive. Thus, given the realistic premiss that such racial prejudice exists and is powerfully operative in majoritarian politics (evidenced, for example, by the existence of slavery, subsequent *de jure* segregation abolished only relatively recently, etc.), legislative classifications, which themselves invoke the morally irrelevant characteristics associated with widespread prejudices, are viewed by the court with suspicion (thus, "suspect") when they are drawn unfavorably to the group in question.

The usual reasons which justify overinclusive or underinclusive legislative classifications do not obtain in the case of such "suspect classifications." If a statute, for example, places a certain burden on blacks alone (involving a "suspect classification") in the pursuit of a legitimate state interest which would reasonably include persons of other races as well, then reasons of administrative convenience seem, given the presence of familiar attitudes of racial hatred and opprobrium against blacks, hardly weighty. The usual argument, that the result of the putatively fair political competition for power among interest groups should be allowed to rest wherever it falls, is undercut here by the unfairness of the political competition which led to the use of such racial classifications; the groups in question are systematically denied the moral consideration due them and their claims as persons, often being isolated into a relatively powerless political group whose claims are not treated on a par with those of ordinary political bargaining. Such overinclusive classifications seem even more unfair: they do not just fail to treat the non-blacks on a par with blacks, relative to a legislative purpose which implicates both equally, but burden blacks with imputation of an evil of which they are wholly innocent.

On this view, the strict test applied to "suspect classifications" takes seriously social facts of forms of social prejudice and their unfair force in majoritarian politics in violation of fundamental contractarian principles. In contrast, Wechsler's criticism of the desegregation decisions, for lack of a neutral principle, fails to take seriously the Supreme Court's obligation to develop constitutional principles to deal with social facts. The "suspect classification" doctrine precisely allows the Court to give weight to a realistic assessment of legislative motive in the form of a quite neutral, judicially administrable principle: namely, the use of a classification, based on characteristics typically associated with familiar stereotyped social prejudices, to burden the "suspect" group, is subjected to strict scrutiny. Wechsler's cavalier dismissal of any kind of inquiry into legislative motive underlies his refusal to take seriously various familiar facts of social life—for example, the force of separate-but-equal as a formal mask of racial hatred.[133] Subsequent constitutional developments have shown the Court well able to deal with many of the cases Wechsler regarded as problematic in light of the desegregation decisions.[134] His claim that the constitutional principle of these decisions is the right of association is without foundation in the history of the Fourteenth Amendment, which in any event speaks not in terms of associational liberties (not specifically mentioned anywhere in the Constitution[135]) but of "equal protection of the law." The practice of de jure segregation deprived a group, the traditional object of racial contempt, of fair access to state liberties and opportunities on the basis of a group characteristic which, on the ground of contractarian principles, is or should be irrelevant as a basis for fair distribution of social goods. As such, such state practices were correctly found unconstitutional; and the Court has correctly perceived its constitutional duty to extend the mandate of Brown into all areas in which the state explicitly or implicitly uses or condones the use of racial classifications in comparable circumstances.

Importantly, this conception of the application of the "suspect classification" prong of the strict test does not turn merely on the existence of the fact that the "suspect" group is disadvantaged by a law passed by a group of men having no or few members of the group. Ely's "we–they" analysis is suggestive.[136] But it fails to capture the crucial feature: the existence of widespread social prejudices on the basis of an attribute which is irrelevant to any morally justifiable distinction among individual persons. Suppose blacks had a representation in state and federal legislative bodies at least proportionate to their numbers. That fact alone would not justify no longer finding blacks to be a "suspect" group within the meaning of the strict test. As long as racial prejudice continues to prevail, the use of racial classifications to burden traditionally despised groups, on the basis of morally irrelevant group characteristics, should continue to elicit strict review. Blacks, despite growing electoral power, remain a small minority, whose power may easily be isolated and cabined by obdurate popular prejudices which do not allow the usual interest group accommodations which democratic politics should theoretically facilitate. The strict test, accordingly, remains an important requirement of contractarian principles, which limit majoritarian rule in order better to realize the requirements of individual justice and fair-minded equity.

In similar fashion, this conception of the strict test does not rest simply on the idea of ameliorating the condition of worst-off groups, as Fiss's analysis suggests.[137] "Suspect classifications" may or may not identify groups worst-off according to some economic or social measure; but they do not necessarily do so.[138] Fiss's contrary view, identifying "suspect classification" strict review with helping worst-off groups, would cast off equal protection analysis from its moorings in notions of fair dealing among individual persons as constitutional and moral equals, and replace it with a simple concern with considerations of group redistributive justice—leaving traditional ideas of equal protection fairness to other constitutional guarantees (e.g., due process). There may well be room for such ideas of redistributive justice in equal protection analysis,[139] though the Supreme Court has been traditionally unreceptive to them.[140] But there is no good reason to eviscerate the traditional meaning of equal protection in the interest of an aim which can be accommodated by traditional equal protection or other constitutional analysis, suitably developed. The equal protection clause has been interpreted as the broad vehicle for humanitarian ideas of fair treatment among constitutional and moral equals; if moral ideas of economic and social equality develop in certain directions, the equal protection clause can probably accommodate them.[141] If not, other constitutional provisions can.[142]

c. *The Constitutionality of Reverse Discrimination.* Reverse discrimination has been a classic constitutional conundrum for the theory of equal protection review. Bickel, for example, thought he was able, contra Wechsler, to develop a neutral principle supportive of the desegregation cases; but the cost of his formulation of the neutral principle was that reverse discrimination could not be constitutionally justified. Originally, Bickel urged the exercise of the "passive virtues": programs of reverse discrimination should not be reviewed by courts.[143] Eventually, Bickel urged, in *DeFunis*, that such programs be declared unconstitutional.

The crux of Bickel's analysis is that all racial classifications of *any* kind should trigger the strict test. Preferential programs, of the kind involved in *DeFunis*, used such disfavored racial classifications; as such, they must trigger the strict test, under which they are unconstitutional (being both over- and underinclusive). Bickel's reasons in support of this interpretation of the "suspect classification" strict test rest essentially on the thought that *any* use of racial classifications creates ideas of different racial castes which stigmatizes the individual dignity of both those favored by the preferential classification (skin color or parental origin, being a group for favorable treatment, rather than individual merit)[144] and those disfavored (exclusion from governmental benefits on the basis of race alone).[145]

The moral analysis proposed here suggests that Bickel's analysis is wrong in constitutional and moral principle. The "suspect classification" prong of the strict test rests, not on the use of group classifications *simpliciter*, but on the use of those group classifications which have been the subject of traditional prejudices which rest on characteristics bearing no moral weight and used in the statute to burden or disadvantage that group. Thus, racial classifications, drawn in terms of being black and used to disadvantage that group, have naturally been the original candidate for "suspect classification" status. The use of this group designation, being black, was evidently an important historical element in the development of the most rationally systematized institution of racial degradation and exploitation, slavery (racial distinctions became a natural and appealing way to demarcate the familiar, the masters, from the unknown and alien, the slaves).[146] This institution had a long history in the United States, which, after abolition, took the form of widespread social attitudes of obdurate racial prejudice against blacks as a group; these attitudes led, until quite recently,[147] to patterns of *de jure* segregation by race, which have not yet been completely undone, and continue in the form of widespread patterns of *de facto* segregation by race.[148] Accordingly, classifications in terms of being black, drawn unfavorably to blacks, naturally and correctly call for "suspect classification" review. But the moral policy of "suspect classification" review does not in general apply to *all* forms of classification by race or even *all* forms of classification based on being black. It applies only to those specific kinds of racial or other classifications, the subject of traditional immoral prejudice, which disadvantage such groups. Such classifications are "suspect," and thus subject to exacting judicial scrutiny, because they putatively accord with familiar popular prejudices, which violate fundamental constitutional principles; the protection of such groups from the expression of such prejudices in forms of law is a natural exercise of judicial power justified by the traditional role of the courts in ensuring that the majoritarian political process accords with underlying principles of justice. In contrast, other kinds of classifications not reflecting these considerations do not call for such special judicial protection.

Bickel's case rests completely on his insistence that the neutral principle underlying the desegregation cases, which Wechsler challenged the court to produce, is a basic prohibition on all forms of racial classification. Reverse discrimination is wrong because it violates this principle. But Bickel's formulation of the neutral principle of the desegregation cases is artificially simplistic. Those cases rest on a neutral principle, but it is not the simple one which Bickel proposes. Rather, the principle, as we have suggested, is that the use of a classification, based on characteristics typically associated with familiar stereotyped social prejudices against a certain group, to burden that group is to be subjected to strict scrutiny. This formulation of the principle of "suspect classification" strict scrutiny review does not automatically subject preferential programs to strict review.

Even if preferential programs are not thus automatically subject to and invalid under strict scrutiny review, they may, on further inquiry, be constitutionally suspect. Perhaps, the schemes can be shown to be drawn invidiously to certain groups traditionally the subject of social prejudice (e.g., Jews); or perhaps the schemes can be shown to be constitutionally irrational even under the weak rational basis test of constitutional review. In order to assess these questions, we must examine the grounds for such programs.

Preferential programs may be morally assessed along a number of dimensions, for example, grounds of compensatory justice, redistributive justice, or general utilitarian advantages which eventuate.[149] Insofar as grounds of justice are typically the main thrust of arguments supportive of such programs, we naturally must assess these programs in the light of the principles of justice offered here.

As an initial matter, it seems clear that the strongest arguments for preferential programs are those which invoke claims of compensatory justice. Grounds of redistributive justice, to the effect that money and wealth should be more equally distributed, hardly happily justify the use of preferential programs as a means; rather, such ends of redistributive justice would be better served by direct forms of governmental subsidy. In fact, however, proponents of preferential programs do not necessarily defend such forms of subsidy at least in the same form as they are willing to defend preferential programs (i.e., being limited to blacks or certain other ethnic or racial groups). This suggests that the grounds of justice, on which preferential programs are supposed to rest, relate to different grounds from those of redistributive justice, at least as traditionally conceived.

In the light of the conception of principles of justice here proposed and defended, we naturally turn to the principle of greatest equal liberty and opportunity for a clarification of the moral basis of preferential programs, especially to the equal opportunity aspect of this principle. Equal opportunity, in the form required by this principle, encompasses the entire range of social institutions which relate to the formation of a person's concept of his rational good and his capacity to bring that concept to realization, including, as we have seen, the educational, cultural, and family system, the economic system of jobs, the legal system, and the like. A more narrow concept of opportunity, such as the idea that it only makes careers open to competition on the basis of talent alone, captures only a part of the proper moral scope of the concept of opportunity: namely, the wide range of developmental and personal opportunities subject to human regulation and control which relatively advantage and disadvantage people in fundamental ways without any basis in merit, worthiness, or any other justifying principle or aim.

With the wide range of institutions to be assessed in light of the principle of greatest equal opportunity, the question remains how this principle applies to such institutions. The relationship between equal opportunity and such institutions is not simple; equal opportunity, for example, does not necessarily mean equal educational expenditures even at the basic educational level. Unequal expenditures are justified by special handicaps of children, whether a physical disability such as blindness or the manifold psychological and physical disabilities resulting from morally significant social deprivation; equal opportunity here means that ensuring such children an equal chance of realizing their good requires greater expenditure for them than for other children. The cost of purchasing comparable educational resources also varies from place to place because of differences in the cost of living, school transportation outlays, economies of scale, and the like. It is therefore reasonable to allow for unequal expenditures which correspond to differences in real costs. Indeed, equal opportunity requires such inequalities. In general, it is a reasonable moral position that the principle of equal opportunity requires equal expenditures at the basic educational level, at least through the mandatory ages of school attendance, unless special handicap or cost levels indicate that equality of opportunity requires inequality of expenditures.[150]

The notion of inequalities in institutional opportunities, justified, even required, by the moral concept of equal opportunity, lies at the base of the moral idea of a compensatory justice, which is typically invoked in defense of preferential programs for blacks. The history and present situation of black people in the United States is a clear case of morally unjustifiable unequal opportunity. Historically, blacks lack the usual immigrant history of voluntarily seeking in the United States new opportunities perceived as desirable in the light of highly developed cultural traditions. Rather, forced to come to this country as slaves lacking basic human liberties, blacks were stripped of their native culture and left unprepared to meet opportunities here in anything but the form which slavery as an institution required. After abolition, the deprivation of basic opportunities took a form different in degree but not in kind from those which existed under slavery. Blacks were deprived of the basic cultural opportunity and family training in skills, expectations, and aspirations which would allow them to take advantage of available opportunities. Opportunities, though formally enlarged with abolition, were circumscribed by widespread attitudes of racial prejudice which condemned blacks to inferior basic education, meager higher education, and poor job opportunities. Being black was supposed necessarily to disable a person for anything but the most menial tasks and most limited horizons. Such a crippling social stigma, associated with race, undermined basic self-esteem in personal competence and rendered effort and aspiration stupid because pointless. The damage of such deprivation in basic opportunity, finally, was perpetuated from generation to generation in an infinite circle of despair, desperation, and self-contempt as parent taught child the spiritual script of slavery—docility, acceptance, the appeal of the child for love, not of the adult for fairness and responsibility.

This pattern of unequal opportunity, clearly violative of the principle of equal opportunity, continues today, supported, as it is, by patterns of racial prejudice which, premissed on crude racial stereotypes, condemn blacks to an institutional pattern of inferior opportunity. Such racial prejudice makes the form of unequal opportunity significantly racially specific. Blacks suffer continuing wrongs inflicted on the basis of their race. If the wrongs in question are racially specific, remedies therefore are understandably racially specific also. To deny the appropriateness of such remedies, in the name of some idea of equal treatment, is to disregard the nature of the particular kind of unequal opportunity which pervasively exists and which, in the name of equal opportunity, calls for unequal measures by way of remedy.[151]

This moral analysis thus explains the force of claims of compensatory justice by blacks: they rest, not on general redistributive grounds (of the kind governed by the principle of justified inequality), but on grounds of equal opportunity, which call for specific measures which endeavor to remedy the kind of unequal opportunity from which blacks suffer. These measures include programs designed to ensure special kinds of opportunities which remedy the unequal opportunities, from which blacks as a group suffer, in the direction of ensuring a greater equal opportunity. If, as we now understand, such inferior opportunity crucially turns on early cultural deprivation in the family and on the effects of continuing economic and social isolation, remedial programs naturally include not only additional expenditures on special educational programs for blacks at the basic educational level, but forms of integration in schooling and elsewhere which relieve the effects of social isolation.[152]

Remedial programs at the higher educational and post-educational job level take a somewhat different form. Access to higher education and to many kinds of jobs turns on the existence of certain competences which enable persons to deal with the special demands of higher education and the requirements of certain jobs; people do not in general have a right to higher education or to certain jobs in the same way as they have such a right to basic education. However, educational and job competences are not self-evidently measured by high scores on standardized testing procedures. Such procedures may, for example, reflect not real competence, but the effects of past unequal opportunity (students of equal competence, but from different backgrounds of family and cultural opportunity, may score radically differently). The qualifications for certain kinds of schooling and jobs may include many factors not well measured by standardized tests, including the needs of communities for professionals who understand their problems.

In the case of black people, there is reason to believe that blacks as a group are unjustly deprived of access to higher education and various jobs by an excessive dependence on standardized testing procedures which results in only very small numbers of blacks obtaining such access.[153] Blacks, as we have said, suffer from inferior opportunity derived from the legacy of slavery, poor cultural and family background in basic skills, and the failure to develop the requisite self-esteem which would motivate them, continuing patterns of social and economic isolation by race, and widespread attitudes of racial prejudice which discourage the development of skills required for the "white" world of work. Accordingly, an excessive dependence on standardized tests fails to capture those blacks of real ability but inferior opportunity who could, with requisite help and challenge, perform as well in school and on the job as higher-scoring whites of equal competence but greater opportunity. Similarly, an excessive dependence on standardized tests fails to give reasonable weight to a number of other relevant considerations in deciding who will have access to limited opportunities for higher education and various jobs: for example, considerations of autonomy, co-operativeness on the job, sympathetic understanding of the needs of people served, and the like. An important part of a lawyer's or physician's work turns on client or patient contact; a professional unable to communicate or to be supportive at this basic level may well be a much less effective lawyer or doctor than another, even though on law or medical school tests the latter scored less well than the former. Factors, other than test score results, must reasonably be given weight in deciding on access to such professions and the schooling leading to them. Being of a certain racial group is one of these other relevant factors, ensuring certain kinds of understanding and background which are highly relevant to being a good professional. In law schools, the case for giving weight to racial factors is even stronger: it ensures a kind of law school experience, in and outside class, which better prepares future lawyers to understand the claims and attitudes of various minority groups. Given the political power of the legal profession in the United States, such experience is of exigent public importance.

The idea that race *per se* has a proper role among the factors which should influence the choice of those who have access to advanced education and the jobs to which they lead is, I believe, a modest claim, which should not be confused with other claims, from which it is quite distinct. Thus, the claim is not that racial factors must supplant test criteria, but that they must be given independent weight. No one has suggested that standardized tests be abandoned entirely, but only that they not be regarded as decisive. There is an enormous difference between the proposition that the rank ordering assigned by results on a standardized test must be disregarded entirely and the claim, defended here, that certain ranges of this ordering (above a minimum level of acceptable competence) may be assessed in terms of other factors of choice, including, within limits, race. The implausible view that "qualifications" for schooling and work are self-evidently defined by the top range of the test score ordering is the central idea under attack here. Such an inflated conception of "qualification" fails realistically to measure competences central to certain professions or to give proper weight to considerations of fairness in ensuring equal opportunity to all.

In general, no contention is made that blacks as a group should be guaranteed a place in higher education or the professions proportionate to their numbers in the population. Equal opportunity does not conceptually or factually imply equal results or achievement. To suppose that the failure to ensure equal results is a moral criticism of equal opportunity[154] is to confuse equal opportunity, premissed on strong substantive ideas of equality in the facilitating conditions for rational development, with a notion of exploiting talent for the public good, governed by the principle of justified inequality, or maximizing performance from limited inputs. So far from making or acquiescing in this confusion, we have insisted that the moral grounds justifying preferential programs are not general redistributive considerations calling for more equal achievement, but rather the principle of a greatest equal opportunity. In the present context, this principle does not require blacks in schools and professions proportionate to their numbers, but calls for forms of preferential programs which ensure that a certain group, which has systematically suffered as a group from lesser opportunity, be given the kind of countervailing opportunity which tends to produce the pattern which would have existed had there been equal opportunity in the first place. Such countervailing opportunity takes the form of giving race an independent weight in admissions to schools and jobs. Since unequal opportunity importantly turned on race, race is a natural criterion to use in righting the balance. In this way, the lesser opportunity, which blacks suffer as a group (poor cultural and family background, social and economic isolation by race, racial prejudice leading to low self-esteem and poor motivation), is increased consistent with the requirements of a greatest equal opportunity for all (giving blacks a special opportunity to overcome the effects of their background, combating the effects of isolation by race by promoting the integration of higher education and the professions, expressly disavowing and combatting racial prejudice by producing black role models of self-esteem and success in the white world of work and politics). Perhaps, thus promoting equal opportunity will produce more blacks in the professions than their proportionate representation in the population; perhaps it will produce less. In any event, there is no necessary connection between equal opportunity and proportional representation. The aim of preferential programs, properly conceived, is not proportional representation, but securing the kind of pattern of opportunity which would have existed had there been a greatest equal opportunity for all. Nonetheless, as a temporary matter, proportionate representation may play a just role in the formulation of administrable rules which courts and government agencies use in ensuring that the underlying moral aim of these programs is met.[155] But a temporary practical administrative accommodation must not be confused with the justification of such programs. They rest on the search for a more just distribution of basic opportunities; proportionate representation plays no necessary role in this search, is morally problematic, and will in time, one hopes, be dispensable as an administrative tool.

Are preferential programs, justified by such grounds of justice, constitutional? We have argued in general that the use of racial classifications, in the way used by preferential programs, should not subject those programs to traditional "suspect classification" strict scrutiny review. Given the foregoing analysis of the moral grounds of those programs, we see that these programs are an attempt to remedy the unjust deprivation of basic opportunities, opportunities denied on the basis of race. It would be morally incoherent for a court to apply the "suspect classification" strict test, designed to combat legislative attempts to use morally irrelevant group characteristics to burden a group subject to majoritarian prejudice, to programs precisely designed to undo the effects of such prejudice in the way the principles of justice require. The moral principle underlying the "suspect classification" strict test would indeed be violated by such an unwarranted extension of the strict test beyond its proper moral scope. Equal opportunity calls for inequality in order to remedy inequality. The insistence on strict equality, as a constitutional mandate of "suspect classification" strict review, is a superficial invocation of the forms of equality in violation of its substance, failing to take seriously or responsibly the heritage of unjust inequalities in basic opportunities from which blacks in the United States have suffered and continue to suffer, a heritage which the "suspect classification" test was invented to acknowledge and attack.

The only plausible argument, to subject preferential programs to strict review, is to the effect that such programs somehow invoke other constitutionally suspect classifications in the way the strict test forbids; for example, they may affect Jews who, like blacks, have suffered and still suffer from indignities and deprivations on the basis of morally irrelevant group characteristics, including, for example, quotas limiting their acceptance into schools and entrance into professions.[156] Though it is certainly understandable why Jewish commentators should fear in preferential racial programs a kind of unjust discrimination, now or in the offing, against them as a group,[157] there is no evidence that such programs in fact have that purpose. If programs of such kinds should arise, they should be attacked on the ground of "suspect classification" strict review. But preferential programs at present are not justly subject to this kind of attack and criticism.[158]

Still another form of this argument is to the effect that preferential programs should be regarded not benignly as belated majoritarian solicitude for minority claims, but rather malignly as a form of oppression by one group of advantaged whites against other poor whites.[159] Undoubtedly, the white majority in the United States is not homogeneous in its opinion on any significant political question, and it is certainly not uniform in its view of the acceptability of preferential programs. But this heterogeneity of thought and sentiment hardly justifies the claim that the formulation of preferential programs by certain whites, as a critical response to widespread racial prejudice and consequent unjustly unequal opportunities, is an unjust attack on poor whites. The foregoing consideration of the grounds of preferential programs shows that such programs are justified by the principles of justice as a consistent attempt to remedy certain pervasive wrongs. In any event, the argument proposed here does not depend on the proposition that preferential programs are constitutionally acceptable because the majority is helping the minority; it depends only on the thought that such programs are not subject to "suspect classification" strict scrutiny because they do not use racial classifications to oppress a group, the traditional object of racial prejudice.

More generally, the argument has been made that any kind of racial classification is constitutionally odious, since it stigmatizes those favored by the preferential classification (skin color being a ground for favorable treatment, rather than individual merit) and those disfavored (exclusion from governmental benefits on the basis of race alone). This argument misconstrues both the purpose of the "suspect classification" strict test and the effects of preferential programs. Racial classifications *in certain circumstances* have been found constitutionally suspect, but not in general. It is difficult to see why they should be constitutionally condemned in general. The notion of "individual merit," invoked here, is itself morally and constitutionally dubious. Racial prejudice, which "suspect classification" strict review combats, denied blacks equal treatment on the basis of a morally irrelevant group characteristic. The consequence of this is a pattern of unequal opportunity, the result of which —in terms of conventional achievement indices—is itself morally dubious. The invocation of "individual merit" accordingly lacks moral weight; the appeal is made to a pattern of achievement which is violative of the principle of equal opportunity. "Individual merit" is what racial prejudice ignores; the attempt to rectify this wrong naturally and properly uses race, the ground of the wrong, to define the scope of the rectification. For similar reasons, those disfavored by preferential schemes (the class of persons who, without the preference, would have secured admission) lack just ground of complaint. The appeal to standardized test results, on which their case rests, assumes that those tests fairly secure an equal opportunity to all. But we have seen that this is not so; given the underlying pattern of unequal opportunity, the results of these tests reflect the underlying unjust pattern, and are accordingly, as the sole measure of "qualification," unjust. Preferential programs, properly conceived, thus deprive those disfavored, not of their just deserts, but of what they have no just claim to in the first place.[160]

Finally, granting that "suspect classification" strict scrutiny is not properly applicable to preferential programs, we must inquire whether these programs are constitutionally valid under the weak rational test, which applies to all cases not governed by the strict test. Such schemes, admittedly, are often over- and underinclusive relative to their purposes; if these purposes are to remedy the background of relative deprivation associated with racial prejudices, the groups chosen for preference may include individuals who have encountered no such deprivation (e.g., an advantaged immigrant black from a nation having no racial prejudice) and may fail to include certain racial and ethnic groups who have suffered from such deprivation associated with racial or ethnic prejudice (e.g., a lower caste immigrant from India). It is possible, of course, to argue that preferential programs are precisely tailored to meet the evil aimed at (namely, relieving racial prejudice against blacks). We do not so argue here because preferential programs typically include other minority groups,[161] and in any event it seems a rather disingenuous argumentative ploy to argue this way when the purpose of such schemes can be plausibly construed in a broader way.

Though preferential schemes are often over- and underinclusive, they clearly fall within the boundaries of legislative rationality required by the weak test of equal protection review. Such schemes pursue a constitutionally laudable goal, and do so in a reasonable way. Thus, preferential programs concentrate on the main forms of the evil of unjust deprivation of basic opportunities on the basis of racial prejudice (namely, racial prejudice against blacks, the traditional object of constitutional solicitude under the fourteenth and associated Civil War amendments), and do so in the reasonable way of giving independent weight to race among the factors relevant to admissions to higher education and entrance into the professions. The overinclusive and/or underinclusive features of these schemes are part of a constitutionally rational scheme, designed to afford administrable rules aimed at curing corrigible evils in a sensible way. If preferential schemes gave decisive weight to race in admissions or entrance procedures, or if the preferred classes were drawn in an arbitrary way bearing no relation to the evil aimed at, preferential schemes might not survive constitutional scrutiny even under the rational basis test. But that is not the present case.

CONCLUSIONS

In this essay we have tried to show that contractarian moral theory can play an authoritative role in both the interpretation of structural features of constitutional adjudication in the United States and the explanation of particular constitutional values. In particular, we focused on the constitutional conundrum of reverse discrimination, showing how moral theory may significantly clarify the moral and constitutional issues in dispute. Commentators critical of preferential programs have speculated on the reason why these programs can have been so staunchly upheld by courts and administrators in the face of widespread political unpopularity. The conclusion reached is typically that these programs are taken to involve fundamental moral values which cannot be politically compromised.[162] Agreeing with this explanation, though not with the critique of it, the view proposed here has analyzed the moral force behind these programs as a form of judicial protection and concern justified by countermajoritarian constitutional principles. In particular, the analysis proposed here explains why preferential programs should be assessed under the weak, not the strict test, of equal protection review, and should be upheld under that test as a reasonable way of pursuing a constitutionally laudable goal.

At the beginning of this essay, we noted our common intellectual need to accomplish a satisfying fusion of constitutional and moral theory. The confusion over the issues of reverse discrimination reflects, I believe, our poverty of constitutional and moral theory. But this plight is not the responsibility of the Court alone or of lawyers in general; it reflects a deficiency in moral and political philosophy to which judges and lawyers have looked in vain for guidance. Moral philosophy has until relatively recently been alienated from its sources in the study of practical reason throughout social life, focusing instead on meta-ethical issues at the expense of serious and sustained inquiry into the traditional subject of moral philosophy, practical reason. This view is now under deserved critical re-examination,[163] and its waning clearly has facilitated the revival of a useful interrelationship of law and philosophy. This essay reflects this return of moral philosophy to its sources. The consequence, I believe, is not only a deepening of philosophical inquiry but a bracing realization of its exigent practical role in shaping practice in the light of its insights. Theory and practice are thus shown, as the greatest philosophers have always insisted, to be indissolubly one.[164]

NOTES

1. See his *The Bill of Rights* (New York: Atheneum, 1968), which, from the beginning (at pp. 1–3) eschews the usefulness of moral ideas in understanding constitutional law, and adopts instead the interpretation of the will of the con-

stitutional founders. Cf. with this Hand's indictment of the role of the Court as "Platonic Guardians," at p. 73.

2. Archibald Cox, *The Role of the Supreme Court in American Government* (New York: Oxford University Press, 1976), p. 113.

3. Ronald Dworkin, "The Jurisprudence of Richard Nixon," *The New York Review of Books*, May 4, 1972. See also idem, "Legal Research," *Daedalus*, 102, No. 2 (1973), 53–64, at 63.

4. See David A. J. Richards, "Equal Opportunity and School Financing: Towards a Moral Theory of Constitutional Adjudication," 41 *University of Chicago Law Review* 32, at 32–33, 39–41 (1973).

5. See ibid.; see also Richards, "Free Speech and Obscenity Law: Toward a Moral Theory of the First Amendment," 123 *University of Pennsylvania Law Review* 45 (1974); idem, "Unnatural Acts and the Constitutional Right of Privacy: A Moral Theory," 45 *Fordham Law Review* 1281 (1977). These themes are developed more extensively in idem, *The Moral Criticism of Law* (Encino, Calif.: Dickenson, 1977).

6. *Areopagitica*, in *The Prose of John Milton*, ed. Max Patrick (New York: New York University Press, 1968), pp. 265–334.

7. *Second Treatise*, in *Two Treatises of Government*, ed. P. Laslett, 2nd ed. (Cambridge: Cambridge University Press, 1967), pp. 285–446.

8. Three clauses in the Constitution refer to slaves in a way which contemplates the continued existence of the institution of slavery, though in each case a circumlocution is used, not the word "slave" or a variant thereof. The Slave Trade Clause provides: "The Migration or Importation of such Persons as any of the States now existing shall think proper to admit, shall not be prohibited by the Congress prior to the Year one thousand eight hundred and eight, but a Tax or duty may be imposed on such importation, not exceeding ten dollars for each Person" (art. I, § 9, cl. 1). See also art. I, § 2, cl. 3 ("three-fifths of all other persons") and art. IV, § 2, cl. 3 ("Person held to Service or Labour").

9. Thirteenth Amendment (adopted 1865), Fourteenth Amendment (adopted 1868), Fifteenth Amendment (adopted 1870).

10. For a general account of this development, see *Developments in the Law— Equal Protection*, 82 *Harvard Law Review* 1065 (1969).

11. See, e.g., *Meyer v. Nebraska*, 262 U. S. 390 (1923) (the right of a child to study a foreign language); *Pierce v. Society of Sisters*, 268 U. S. 510 (1925) (the right to educate a child in a school of the parents' choice); *Griswold v. Connecticut*, 381 U. S. 479 (1925) (the right of married couples to use contraceptives).

12. The technical legal history of free speech, for example, in England and America prior to the adoption of the First Amendment obviously renders doubtful any consensus on the specific application of the amendment. See, in general, L. Levy, *Legacy of Suppression: Freedom of Speech and Press in Early American History* (Cambridge: Harvard University Press, 1960).

13. For example, the existence at the time of the adoption of the First Amendment of such laws as that against seditious libel has never been supposed to conclude the question of the constitutionality of such laws. For a discussion of the crime of seditious libel at common law, see ibid. For the view that seditious libel was abolished by the First Amendment, see *Beauharnais v. Illinois*, 343 U. S. 250, 272 (1952) (Black, J., dissenting); *Abrams v. United States*, 250 U. S. 616, 630–31 (1919) (Holmes, J., dissenting). See also *Bridges v. California*, 314 U. S. 252, 264–65 (1941); *Grosjean v. American Press Co.*, 297 U. S. 233, 248–49 (1936)

(the First Amendment prohibits taxes which restrict newspaper circulation, although such taxes were employed in England and America at the time of its adoption).

14. See also works listed at note 1.

15. Joseph Tussman and Jacobus tenBroek, "The Equal Protection of the Laws," 37 *California Law Review* 341, 364 (1949).

16. See, e.g., John Kaplan, "Equal Justice in an Unequal World: Equality for the Negro—The Problem of Special Treatment," 61 *Northwestern Law Review* 363 (1966); Larry M. Lavinsky, "*DeFunis v. Odegaard*: The 'Non-Decision' With a Message," 75 *Columbia Law Review* 520 (1975).

17. See, e.g., Robert O'Neil, "Preferential Admissions: Equalizing the Access of Minority Groups to Higher Education," 80 *Yale Law Journal* 699 (1971); Kenneth L. Karst and Harold W. Horowitz, "Affirmative Action and Equal Protection," 60 *Virginia Law Review* 955 (1964). See also Frank Askin, "The Case for Compensatory Treatment," 24 *Rutgers Law Review* 65 (1969); Graham Hughes, "Reparations for Blacks?" 43 *New York University Law Review* 1063 (1968).

18. 416 U. S. 312 (1974).

19. 416 U. S. at 320–21 (Douglas, J., dissenting).

20. Ibid. at 322–23. The cut-off point was 74.5.

21. DeFunis rated 76.23. Ibid. at 325.

22. Ibid.

23. 416 U. S. 312 (1974), *vacating as moot* 82 Wash. 2d 11, 507 P. 2d 1169 (1973).

24. 416 U. S. at 334.

25. 416 U. S. at 333.

26. *Swann v. Charlotte-Mecklenburg Board of Educ.*, 402 U. S. 1 (1971).

27. "School authorities are traditionally charged with broad powers to formulate and implement educational policy and might well conclude, for example, that in order to prepare students to live in a pluralistic society each school should have a prescribed ratio of Negro to White students reflecting the proportion for the district as a whole." Ibid. at 16.

28. 42 U. S. C. §2000e (1970).

29. See, e.g., *Associated Gen. Contractors of Mass., Inc. v. Altshuler*, 490 F. 2nd 9 (1st Cir. 1973), *cert. denied*, 94 S. Ct. 1971 (1974); *Contractors Ass'n of E. Pa. v. Hodgson*, 442 F. 2d 159 (3d Cir.), *cert. denied*, 404 U. S. 854 (1971).

30. See, e.g., *Bridgeport Guardians, Inc. v. Members of Bridgeport Civil Service Comm'n*, 482 F. 2d 1333 (2d. Cir. 1973); *Carter v. Gallagher*, 452 F. 2d 315 (8th Cir.), *cert. denied*, 406 U. S. 43 (1971).

31. See cases cited at ibid.; cf. *Griggs v. Duke Power Co.*, 401 U. S. 424 (1971).

32. 45 C.F.R. §80.3 (b) (6) (1973). Title VI of the Civil Rights Act of 1964, 42 U. S. C. §2000d (1970), forbids racial discrimination on the part of recipients of federal grants, which include state universities. Though an argument can be made that the language bars preferential admissions policies, the courts have not read similar language in Title VII in that way. See Karst & Horowitz (note 17), at 964–65. For a discussion of fund termination as a sanction compared with an ordinary damage action, see Fiss, "The Fate of An Idea Whose Time Has Come: Anti-Discrimination Law in the Second Decade After *Brown v. Board of Education*," 41 *University of Chicago Law Review* 742, 757–58 (1974).

33. See note 7.

34. See, e.g., Rousseau, *The Social Contract*, in *The Social Contract and Discourses*, trans. G. D. H. Cole (New York: Dutton, 1950); Kant, "Concerning

the Common Saying: This May Be True in Theory, But Does Not Apply in Practice," in *Society, Law, and Morality*, ed. F. Olafson (Englewood Cliffs, N.J.: Prentice-Hall, 1961), pp. 159–72; Kant, *The Metaphysical Elements of Justice*, ed. J. Ladd (Indianapolis: Bobbs-Merrill, 1965).

35. See, e.g., Hand, *Bill of Rights*, pp. 1–3, 33–34.

36. See Alexander M. Bickel, *The Morality of Consent* (New Haven & London: Yale University Press, 1975), esp. chap. 1; Harry H. Wellington, "Common Law Rules and Constitutional Double Standards: Some Notes on Adjudication," 83 *Yale Law Journal* 221, 279–80, 285 (1973).

37. See James B. Thayer, "The Origin and Scope of the American Doctrine of Constitutional Law," 7 *Harvard Law Review* 129 (1893).

38. Hand, *Bill of Rights*. Cf. Alexander Bickel, *The Supreme Court and the Idea of Progress* (New York, Evanston, & London: Harper & Row, 1970), in which a value skepticism similar to Hand's leads to a critique of the idea of moral reform through constitutional adjudication. Moral reflection and reform in the light of principles is to be replaced by unconscious moral historicism; see esp. pp. 174–75. These ideas represent a significant retreat from Bickel's earlier views in *The Least Dangerous Branch* (Indianapolis & New York: Bobbs-Merrill, 1962).

39. See Hand, *Bill of Rights*, pp. 1–3, 33–34; the famous appeal to wash the law in cynical acid derives from Oliver Wendell Holmes, "The Path of the Law," *Collected Legal Papers* (New York: Harcourt, Brace, 1921), pp. 167–202.

40. For an attempt so to view it, see Richards, *A Theory of Reasons for Action* (Oxford University Press, 1971).

41. Cf. the remarks of Alexander Hamilton to the effect that judicial supremacy was intended as a bulwark against "encroachments and oppressions of the representative party" (*Federalist Papers*, ed. Clinton Rossiter [New York: New American Library, 1961], No. 78, p. 462).

42. See note 7.

43. This claim is more extensively defended in chap. 3 of my *Moral Criticism of Law*. See also Dworkin (note 3).

44. See, e.g., Hand, *Bill of Rights*; Thayer (note 37).

45. See Hand, *Bill of Rights*.

46. See Thayer (note 37).

47. See H. Wechsler, "Toward Neutral Principles of Constitutional Law," 73 *Harvard Law Review* 1 (1959).

48. See note 43.

49. See note 6.

50. See note 7.

51. See note 34.

52. See note 34.

53. See part A of the third section, "The Principles of Justice."

54. See John Rawls, *A Theory of Justice* (Cambridge: Harvard University Press, 1971), at pp. 221–28.

55. For court opinions to this effect, see *Baker v. Carr*, 369 U. S. 189 (1962); *Reynolds v. Sims*, 377 U. S. 533 (1964). For supportive commentary, see Anthony Lewis, "Legislative Apportionment and the Federal Courts," 71 *Harvard Law Review* 1057 (1958); Carl A. Auerbach, "The Reapportionment Cases: One Person, One Vote—One Vote, One Value," 1964 *Supreme Court Review* 1. For critical commentary, see Phil C. Neal, "*Baker v. Carr*: Politics in Search of Law," 1962 *Supreme Court Review* 252; Bickel, *Supreme Court and the Idea of Progress*, pp. 151–73.

56. See Richards, *Theory of Reasons for Action*, chap. 7, pp. 92–106.

57. See note 9.

58. See note 8.

59. See note 15.

60. See, in general, H. Flack, *The Adoption of the Fourteenth Amendment* (Gloucester, Mass.: Smith, 1908); F. Frank and L. Munro, "The Original Understanding of 'Equal Protection of the Laws,'" 50 *Columbia Law Review* 131 (1950); J. James, *The Framing of the Fourteenth Amendment* (Urbana: University of Illinois Press, 1956); J. tenBroek, *Equal Under Law* (New York: Macmillan, 1965).

61. See note 15.

62. E.g., *Harper v. Virginia Bd. of Elections*, 383 U. S. (1966) (Virginia poll tax held unconstitutional). See also *Reynolds v. Sims*, 377 U. S. 533 (1964); *Baker v. Carr*, 369 U. S. 186 (1962).

63. *Douglas v. California*, 372 U. S. 353 (1963) (denial to an indigent of counsel on appeal held unconstitutional); *Gideon v. Wainwright*, 372 U. S. 335 (1963) (denial to an indigent of counsel in a criminal case held unconstitutional); *Griffin v. Illinois*, 351 U. S. 12 (1956) (failure to provide stenographic transcript on appeal to defendant unable to afford it held unconstitutional).

64. E.g., *Shapiro v. Thompson*, 394 U. S. 618 (1969) (statutory provisions denying welfare assistance to persons who met all eligibility requirements except that they had not resided within the jurisdiction for at least a year immediately preceding their applications for assistance held unconstitutional). But see *Sosna v. Iowa*, 419 U. S. 393 (1975) (residency requirement for bringing divorce action upheld).

65. E.g., *Skinner v. Oklahoma ex rel. Williamson*, 316 U. S. 535, 541 (1942) (Oklahoma statute providing for compulsory sterilization of habitual criminals held subject to strict scrutiny because it affected "one of the basic civil rights"). For a related decision under the due process clause, see *Roe v. Wade*, 410 U. S. 113 (1973) (Texas abortion statute held unconstitutional as abridging on the right to privacy and the liberty not to have children).

66. For an exception, see the discussion of the Japanese relocation cases in part B of the second section, "The Constitutional Status of Racial Classifications."

67. See *Dunn v. Blumstein*, 405 U. S. 330 (1972).

68. *Railway Express Agency v. New York*, 336 U. S. 106 (1949).

69. 347 U. S. 483 (1954).

70. See, e.g., *Mayor of Baltimore v. Dawson*, 350 U. S. 877 (1955) (beaches); *Gayle v. Browder*, 352 U. S. 903 (1956) (buses); *Holmes v. City of Atlanta*, 350 U. S. (1955) (golf courses); *New Orleans City Park Imp. Ass'n v. Detiege*, 358 U. S. 54 (1958) (parks).

71. See *San Antonio Independent School District v. Rodriguez*, 411 U. S. 1 (1973). For critical commentary thereon, see Richards (note 4).

72. See note 47.

73. *Bill of Rights*.

74. *Plessy v. Ferguson*, 163 U. S. 537, 551 (1896).

75. See note 47, at 33.

76. Ibid. at 34.

77. Ibid.

78. See, e.g., Arthur S. Miller and Ronald F. Howell, "The Myth of Neutrality in Constitutional Adjudication," 27 *University of Chicago Law Review* 661 (1960); Addison Mueller and Murray L. Schwartz, "The Principle of Neutral Principles,"

7 *U.C.L.A. Law Review* 571 (1960). See also Jan G. Deutsch, "Neutrality, Legitimacy and the Supreme Court: Some Intersections Between Law and Political Science," 20 *Stanford Law Review* 169 (1968); Thurman Arnold, "Professor Hart's Theology," 73 *Harvard Law Review* 1298 (1960).

79. See Louis H. Pollak, "Racial Discrimination and Judicial Integrity: A Reply to Professor Wechsler," 108 *University of Pennsylvania Law Review* 1 (1959); Charles L. Black, Jr., "The Lawfulness of the Segregation Decisions," 69 *Yale Law Journal* 421 (1960). See also Ira Michael Heyman, "The Chief Justice, Racial Segregation, and the Friendly Critics," 59 *California Law Review* 194 (1961).

80. See *Least Dangerous Branch*, chaps. 1–2, esp. pp. 49–65.

81. Bickel thus opposed Wechsler's view that the Supreme Court has a mandatory jurisdiction over cases properly before it, having no discretion not to review difficult cases on grounds of unprincipled quasi-legislative expediency. Rather, Bickel argues that such grounds of expediency perform an important role in allowing the Court not to extend necessarily rigid neutral principles to their full logical extent. For a forceful critique of Bickel's doctrine of the "passive virtues," see Gerald Gunther, "The Subtle Vices of the 'Passive Virtues'—A Comment on Principle and Expediency in Judicial Review," 64 *Columbia Law Review* 1 (1964).

82. Brief of Anti-Defamation League of B'nai B'rith as Amicus Curiae, *DeFunis v. Odegaard*, 94 S. Ct. 1704 (1974).

83. *Korematsu v. United States*, 323 U. S. 214 (1944) (relocation); see also *Hirabayashi v. United States*, 320 U. S. 81 (1943) (curfew).

84. See *Katzenbach v. Morgan*, 384 U. S. 641 (1966) (law establishing the completion of certain grade in certain schools as sufficient proof of literacy for purposes of literacy requirements for voting held constitutional, though it under-inclusively fails to include completion of certain grade in other schools).

85. See note 82 at 31.

86. See, e.g., *Swann v. Charlotte-Mecklenburg Board of Educ.* (note 26).

87. See note 83.

88. See Ely, "The Constitutionality of Reverse Racial Discrimination," 41 *University of Chicago Law Review* 723 (1974).

89. See "Groups and the Equal Protection Clause," 5 *Philosophy and Public Affairs* 107 (1976).

90. See "Judicial Scrutiny of 'Benign' Racial Preference in Law School Admissions," 75 *Columbia Law Review* 559 (1975).

91. "Foreword: In Search of Evolving Doctrine on a Changing Court—A Model for a Newer Equal Protection," 86 *Harvard Law Review* 1 (1972).

92. See, e.g., *San Antonio Independent School District v. Rodriguez*, 411 U. S. 1 (1973).

93. See note 86, and accompanying text.

94. See Karst and Horowitz (note 17).

95. See generally Rostow, "The Japanese-American Cases—A Disaster," 54 *Yale Law Journal* 489 (1945).

96. See *Theory of Justice*.

97. This point was developed by David Hume in his remarkable discussion of the conditions of moderate scarcity (*A Treatise of Human Nature*, ed. L. A. Selby-Bigge [Oxford: Clarendon, 1888], pp. 484–501).

98. The notion of rationality considered here is developed in Richards, *Theory of Reasons for Action*, pp. 27–48, 63–71. See also Charles Fried, *An Anatomy of Values* (Cambridge: Harvard University Press, 1970), pp. 87–101; Rawls, *Theory*

of Justice, pp. 407–16. The general view of the good is discussed ibid., pp. 395–452, and in Richards, *Theory of Reasons for Action*, pp. 286–91.

99. Self-respect has its natural basis in our desire to exercise our capacities competently. See ibid., pp. 257, 267–68; R. White, *Ego and Reality in Psychoanalytic Theory: A Proposal Regarding Independent Ego Energies, Psychological Issues* (New York: International University Press, 1963).

100. The notion that property is a general good obviously does not prejudge the morality or justice of private or public ownership of the basic means of production.

101. This category includes the capacity to enter into love and friendship relations whose possibility depends on the special intimacy afforded by being able to waive property rights as to one person but not another. This point seems to underlie the critique of communist systems in Aristotle, *Politics*, Book II, chaps. 3–4. A similar point on privacy is well made in Fried, *Anatomy of Values*.

102. Cf. J. Feinberg, *Social Philosophy* (Englewood Cliffs, N.J.: Prentice-Hall, 1973).

103. See, e.g., C. Crossland, *The Future of Socialism* (Westport, Conn.: Greenwood, 1977), chaps. 8, 10; R. H. Tawney, *Equality* (New York: Barnes & Noble, 1964), pp. 141ff.

104. See Rawls, *Theory of Justice*, pp. 150–61.

105. See note 99. See also Rawls, *Theory of Justice*, pp. 440ff. where self-respect is deemed a primary good.

106. For the notion of rational life plans, see the reference at note 98.

107. See Rawls, *Theory of Justice*, p. 440.

108. The notion of capacity should probably be included with liberty and opportunity. To keep this article on its avowed focus, however, the just treatment of the general capacity problem must be put aside. For a discussion of this point, see Richards, *Theory of Reasons for Action*, pp. 135–38.

109. The validity of this position is unaffected by possible justifications—ignorance, illiteracy, economic underdevelopment—for the lack of voting rights. A different question is whether universal voting rights with different weights may be justified. See Rawls, *Theory of Justice*, pp. 231–34.

110. For example, incentive effects which prompt the more highly gifted to work more will in a reasonable time increase the quality or quantity of property or wealth available to others.

111. This formulation is taken from my *Theory of Reasons for Action*, p. 121. For Rawls's formulation see *Theory of Justice*, pp. 302–303. Rawls's account differs from my formulation in stopping short of my emphasis on the priority of opportunity to the goods governed by the principle of justified inequality; Rawls emphasizes the traditional liberal idea of equal opportunity as access to careers being predicated on talent (see pp. 301, 511–12). I find no defense for Rawls's view other than the intuition that the kind of view here defended would subject certain institutions—the family, for example—to extreme criticism, presumably on the ground that the family, as currently constituted, distributes opportunities unequally (such as the opportunity to have had more loving or concerned parents).

112. *Federalist Papers*, No. 78, p. 462.

113. Ibid., p. 469.

114. See note 8.

115. The incapacity of courts to deal competently with matters of economic and social legislation has been a prominent feature of American constitutional law since the demise of substantive economic due process in *Nebbia v. New York*, 291

U. S. 502 (1934) and *West Coast Hotel Co. v. Parrish*, 300 U. S. 379 (1937).

116. See, e.g., *Lloyd Corp. v. Tanner*, 407 U. S. 551 (1972) (there is no dedication of a privately owned shopping center to the public so as to entitle people to exercise First Amendment rights therein); *Moose Lodge No. 107 v. Irvis*, 407 U. S. 163 (1972) (the fact that a private club has a liquor license does not constitute state action, so that racial discrimination by the club cannot be reached by courts under the Fourteenth Amendment).

117. See the conflicting opinions on this point in *United States v. Guest*, 383 U. S. 745 (1966). There is no comparable problem under the Thirteenth Amendment since that amendment is not limited to "state action." *Jones v. Alfred H. Mayer Co.*, 392 U. S. 409 (1968).

118. This requirement is derived from U. S. Const. art. III, §2.

119. See, e.g., *Muskrat v. United States*, 219 U. S. 346 (1911).

120. See *Baker v. Carr* (note 62); *Luther v. Borden*, 49 U. S. (7 How.) 1 (1849).

121. See note 15 at 349–50.

122. Ibid. at 350.

123. Ibid. at 352.

124. See note 83.

125. For an elaboration of this analysis, see Richards, *Moral Criticism of Law*, chaps. 3–4.

126. *Brown v. Board of Education*, 347 U. S. 483 (1954). The task of implementation of *Brown* has not been completed even after two decades. See, e.g., *Swann v. Charlotte-Mecklenburg Board of Educ.* (note 26).

127. See, e.g., *Graham v. Richardson*, 403 U. S. 365 (1971); *In Re Griffiths*, 413 U. S. 717 (1973); *Sugarman v. Dougall*, 413 U. S. 634 (1973).

128. See *Frontiero v. Richardson*, 411 U. S. 677 (1973). For a similar development regarding illegitimacy, see *Levy v. Louisiana*, 391 U. S. 68 (1968); *Weber v. Aetna Casualty & Surety Co.*, 406 U. S. 164 (1972). But cf. *Labine v. Vincent*, 401 U. S. 532 (1971).

129. See "Mental Illness: A Suspect Classification?" 83 *Yale Law Journal* 1237 (1974).

130. See Frank I. Michelman, "Foreword: On Protecting the Poor Through the Fourteenth Amendment," 83 *Harvard Law Review* 7 (1969).

131. See "The Constitutionality of Laws Forbidding Private Homosexual Conduct," 72 *Michigan Law Review* 1624 (1974).

132. See note 15, and accompanying text.

133. Cf. Pollak, and Black (note 79).

134. For miscegenation, see *Loving v. Virginia*, 388 U. S. 1 (1967). For sex-based discrimination, see *Frontiero v. Richardson* (note 128).

135. Freedom of association is at most a constitutional value inferred in order better to protect explicit constitutional values like freedom of speech and thought. See in general Thomas I. Emerson, "Freedom of Association and Freedom of Expression," 74 *Yale Law Journal* 1 (1964).

136. See note 88.

137. See note 89.

138. Women, who seem on the verge of becoming a "suspect class," clearly are not a worst-off group in this sense.

139. See Michelman (note 130). See also idem, "In Pursuit of Constitutional Welfare Rights: One View of Rawls's Theory of Justice," 121 *University of Pennsylvania Law Review* 962 (1973).

140. See *Dandridge v. Williams*, 397 U. S. 137 (1971); *James v. Valtierra*, 402 U. S. 137 (1971); *Lindsey v. Normet*, 405 U. S. 56 (1972); *Boddie v. Connecticut*, 401 U. S. 371 (1971); *United States v. Kras*, 409 U. S. 434 (1973); *Ortwein v. Schwab*, 410 U. S. 656 (1973).

141. See note 139. But cf. Ralph K. Winter, "Poverty, Economic Equality, and the Equal Protection Clause," 1972 *Supreme Court Review* 41.

142. For example, due process of law could be interpreted to include some kind of minimum insurance rights. See Michelman (note 139), 121 *University of Pennsylvania Law Review* 962. Cf. Richards' critique of Michelman (note 4), at 69–70.

143. See note 80.

144. Justice Douglas emphasized this point in his *DeFunis* dissent, 94 *S. Ct.* at 1719.

145. See note 85, and accompanying text. For a general statement of this position, see Nathan Glazer, *Affirmative Discrimination: Ethnic Inequality and Public Policy* (New York: Basic Books, 1975), esp. pp. 108, 202–203, 220.

146. See M. I. Finley, "A Peculiar Institution?" *Times Literary Supplement*, July 2, 1976 at 819.

147. See note 126.

148. See Owen M. Fiss, "Racial Imbalance in the Public Schools: The Constitutional Concepts," 78 *Harvard Law Review* 564 (1965). On the propriety of abandoning the *de facto–de jure* distinction in constitutional law, see Justice Powell's separate opinion in *Keyes v. School District No. 1, Denver, Colo.*, 413 U. S. 189 (1973).

149. See, in general, James W. Nickel, "Preferential Policies in Hiring and Admissions: A Jurisprudential Approach," 75 *Columbia Law Review* 534 (1975).

150. See Richards (note 4), at 52–60.

151. See Taylor, "Reverse Discrimination and Compensatory Justice," 33 *Analysis* 177 (1973).

152. See J. Coleman, *Equality of Educational Opportunity* (Washington, D.C.: Government Printing Office, 1966); *On Equality of Educational Opportunity*, edd. F. Mosteller and D. Moynihan (New York: Vintage, 1972); C. Jencks, *Inequality: A Reassessment of the Effect of Family and Schooling in America* (New York: Harper & Row, 1973); *The "Inequality" Controversy: Schooling and Distributive Justice*, edd. D. Levine & M. Bane (New York: Basic Books, 1975).

153. See generally O'Neil, "Preferential Admissions: Equalizing the Access of Minority Groups to Higher Education," 80 *Yale Law Journal* 699, 718–25 (1971). On the possible cultural bias of standardized tests, see K. Clark and L. Plotkin, *The Negro Student at Integrated Colleges* (New York: National Scholarship Service and Fund for Negro Students, 1963), pp. 25–26; J. Adler, "Intelligence Testing of the Culturally Disadvantaged: Some Pitfalls," 37 *Journal of Negro Education*, 364 (1968); A. Astin, "Racial Considerations in Admissions," in *The Campus and the Racial Crisis*, edd. D. Nichols and O. Mills (Washington, D.C.: American Council on Education, 1970), p. 113.

154. This is the central pivotal thesis in Jencks, *Inequality*, pp. 209–65. This regrettable confusion aside, Jencks's general egalitarian thesis—that the present degree of wealth inequalities in the United States is unjustified—is plausible and quite possibly true.

155. See notes 31 and 32, and accompanying text.

156. See note 85, and accompanying text, which suggests the concern that quotas favoring blacks may be seen as quotas restricting other groups.

157. See note 81.

158. Cf. Ely (note 88), at 737–41.

159. See Greenawalt (note 90), at 573–74.

160. On the force of the perception of unfairness by "white ethnics," arising from preferential programs for blacks, see Glazer, *Affirmative Discrimination*, pp. 195, 200–201. Although I believe such perceptions of unfairness are in this case unjustified, a different issue is raised when, in the absence of any such preferential program tailored in the ways here suggested, a right is extended to blacks but not to whites. In such cases, a just claim of unfairness would lie. See, e.g., *McDonald v. Santa Fe Trail Transportation Company*, 96 Sup. Ct. 2574 (1976).

161. In *DeFunis*, for example, the preferred group included blacks, Chicanos, American Indians, and Philippine-Americans.

162. See Glazer, *Affirmative Discrimination*, pp. 205–206, 210.

163. For examples of this return to the study of practical reason, see K. Baier, *The Moral Point of View* (New York: Random House, 1966); D. Gauthier, *Practical Reasoning* (Oxford: Clarendon, 1963); G. Grice, *The Grounds of Moral Judgment* (New York: Cambridge University Press, 1967); R. M. Hare, *The Language of Morals* (New York: Oxford University Press, 1952); idem, *Freedom and Reason* (New York: Oxford University Press, 1963); Rawls, *Theory of Justice*; Richards, *Theory of Reasons for Action*.

164. This essay was written in the fall of 1976, and reflects the state of the law and commentary at that time; in particular, it does not address the most recent of the Supreme Court's affirmative action decisions, *Regents of the University of California v. Bakke*, 98 S. Ct. 2733 (1978), announced on June 28, 1978. The consequence of *Bakke* was to disallow arguments of compensatory justice alleged to square affirmative action programs with the equal protection clause of the Fourteenth Amendment, though allowing the possible justifiability of such programs to the extent that they are directed at ensuring the educational advantages of a diverse student body. In the case at hand, Bakke's claim of unconstitutional disadvantage, under a program based on claims of compensatory justice not on educational diversity, was upheld, and his admission to medical school, accordingly, was ordered. The crucial opinion was that of Justice Powell, who invalidates the Davis affirmative action program but allows that other affirmative action programs aimed at securing diversity may be constitutional. Justice Powell bases his opinion on the equal protection clause, but the four justices who join him in his result expressly refuse to base their decision on that clause (claiming instead the *per se* illegality of racial classifications under Title VI of the Civil Rights Act of 1964). The four justices in dissent do base their decision on the equal protection clause, but disagree with Justice Powell in his holding that compensatory justice arguments may not justify affirmative action programs under the clause. The arguments presented in this essay suggest that Justice Powell is in error and that the four dissenters are right in regard to the equal protection justifiability of compensatory justice arguments in support of affirmative action programs. In particular, Justice Powell makes the remarkable argument that the reason affirmative action programs must be subjected to strict scrutiny, and thus invalidated, is that, if they were not, the Court would be compelled to take into account social facts in an illegitimate way. But how can it be plausibly argued that the proper interpretation of the equal protection clause can ignore facts about racial prejudice which may exist in cases of majoritarian oppression of minorities, but not in cases of affirmative action programs designed to benefit minorities? Justice Powell confuses, I believe, the sound requirement that constitutional decisions must rest on the articulation of general

principles with the fallacious idea that principles, as such, cannot be accommodated to the complexities of varying facts. See, in general, my "Rules, Policies, and Neutral Principles: The Search for Legitimacy in Common Law and Constitutional Adjudication," 11 *Georgia Law Review* 1069, 1106–1108 (1977). *Bakke,* accordingly, is, I believe, wrongly decided. For arguments to similar effect with which I agree, see Ronald Dworkin, "Why Bakke Has No Case," *New York Review of Books,* November 10, 1977, at 11; idem, "The Bakke Decision: Did It Decide Anything?" *New York Review of Books,* August 17, 1978, at 20.

7

Justice and Goodness

CHARLES A. KELBLEY

Fordham University

THIS IS AN INQUIRY into the moral quality of the virtue of justice. Its ultimate goal is to interpret the *value* of justice.

The first section presents a variety of viewpoints according to which justice constitutes either a minimal level of morality or a set of practices which it is desirable, if not always possible, to transcend. This conclusion is typically reached from the critical perspective of a theory of goodness (or, alternatively, from the "higher" perspective of altruism, love, generosity, etc.) which allegedly transcends "mere justice" in terms of moral content. What I call the Humean View of justice gives, in the modern period, the best formulation of the idea of the minimal morality of justice, and it is the pervasive influence of the Humean View which this essay, in turn, criticizes.

I discuss in the second section the relation between justice (or rightness) and goodness, and attempt to clarify the grounds for and the significance of a conception of justice which is formulated independently of goodness. Rawls's theory of justice is invoked here as a model.

Finally, in the third section, I present considerations on the nature of human conflict and justice which allow us to overcome the Humean View and to raise significantly the moral value of claims of justice. Justice and goodness, it is argued, are both major and co-equal signs of the moral perfection of human beings. The conclusion that justice is not a moral inferior to goodness is defended.

JUSTICE AND MORALITY

The common tendency to think of justice as a dull and uninspiring virtue with limited moral significance is so entrenched in the habits of public discourse that an alternative view which would argue for the comprehensive and richly moral character of justice now almost borders on patent nonsense.[1] It may be a disconcerting truth, but, with very few exceptions, scattered among widely ignored traditions going back to and stemming from ancient thinkers of the stature of a Plato or an Aristotle, philosophers and legal scholars have themselves generally contributed to this tendency by the way in which they identify and conceptualize the natural and human circumstances which allegedly found the necessity for law and justice in the first place. In the modern period one thinks immediately of the decisive and enduringly influential views of David Hume.[2] Indeed, there is more than a little justification for taking the celebrated opinions of Hume on justice as a summary statement of the conventional wisdom of jurists[3] and philosophers[4] on this subject. For Hume's opinions seemingly provided a quasi-natural explanation why this tendency could have become so deeply rooted in the long and complicated history of justice in philosophical and legal literature—as if Hume had discovered the very quintessence of justice in facts so compelling and so obvious that they were easily and understandably overlooked by previous thinkers of some distinction. Following Hume, what could be more obvious than the deduction that if the world could supply us with an inexhaustible abundance of goods, capable of satisfying all possible human wants and needs, and if human beings were able to transcend their selfishness and were capable of basing their relations with others on love and generosity, then justice would surely become an "idle ceremonial" and never find place in the "catalogue of virtues."[5]

Yet it is important to note that Hume's views did not simply amount to the fanciful idea (which is, nonetheless, a prevalent interpretation) that if the conditions of the world and human nature could be changed, then justice, or the need for it, would quickly disappear. On that understanding of his view, we could just as easily imagine the conditions under which there would be no need for the virtue of temperance (e.g., where conditions of the human body were such that it would be impossible to overindulge in food or drink, etc.) or of courage (e.g., if the body were immune from attack or danger and never in need of rescue, etc.) or, indeed, for any virtue whatsoever. It would even appear quite obvious that love and generosity, or language and thought, could well be dispensed with as well in another world with a different human nature. In the richly imaginative mind of a Hume, the fictive possibilities must have been almost without end.[6] Unfortunately, as we shall see later, such possibilities are also virtually useless for judging the moral value of justice.

More modestly, however, Hume the empiricist was also claiming that human nature is somehow deficient or defective by comparison to an ideal state of affairs which is rooted in and outlined by our actual human nature as we know and experience it now, not merely as it might be thought of in imagination or as it is sometimes portrayed in utopian literature or science fiction.[7] If this is true, and if Hume's views are the linchpin on which modern conceptions of the morality of justice crucially depend, then some examination of them is certainly in order.

I shall undertake this examination in this section in a rather generalized fashion, returning to Hume explicitly only occasionally in the course of focusing on the broader (but still Humean) claim that the morality of justice does not derive from positive factors intrinsic to human nature. I shall call this claim the Humean View, without, however, wishing to imply that everything brought under it below can be traced back to Hume's own explicit thought on justice.[8]

A. *Justice as Minimal Moral Obligation.* The Humean View that human nature is somehow defective, that it usually falls far short of the way we sometimes experience it or want it to be, can be taken as the crucial empirical claim that the modern period has largely resorted to in order to ground the need for justice. How far this view represents a consensus or reflects Hume's best thinking is an unimportant detail in the present context. It is enough that some philosophers and some jurists have based their conception of justice on such a view.[9]

Now, one important effect of this claim is that justice is presented in a frankly negative light. Although it will have much to do with utility and, thus, produce many good results, justice will have almost nothing to do with inherent human goodness. For, according to the Humean View, justice is meant to make up for the defects and deficiencies of human nature; it springs from a lack, not from a positive presence. Thus, one might say that justice, on this view, necessarily has functions analogous to restorative, preventive, punitive, and curative devices. Much like modern medicine's view of the body (which seems to consist primarily in a movement from the conditions of disease back to those of health), theory in this area starts not with the whole person, from which it might *subsequently* understand injustice (or, in medicine, illness); instead, theory's function from the outset is more practical, even technological: the tasks of maintenance, equilibrium, prevention, and repair of damage predominate; in both cases, art must supply what nature or ordinary nurture has failed to provide. Since they lack a theory of the person, one might wonder what more could be expected from either a system of medicine or a system of justice. Although we are obviously limited in the legitimate use which we may make of the analogy between justice and medicine, it is nevertheless suggestive of an important point about the lack of theory in general. Just as medicine, as conventionally practiced, is concerned with a minimal level of health (that is, for the most part ignoring the superior considerations of nutrition and psychosomatic analysis, to cite two extremes, physical and psychic, on the scale of high theory), so too, justice, as conventionally understood and practiced, is concerned with a minimal level of moral obligation—defining and enforcing what is "due" to persons. Disparate as these fields may seem, their minimal concerns stem more from a common theoretical lack than from failings in pedagogy or in their organizational and "delivery" systems.[10]

In any event, the Humean View sets up a fairly identifiable background against which we can better understand the reasons underlying various conceptions of the minimal moral content of justice. Briefly, justice cannot get beyond that minimal content because of its humble origins and the limited nature of its moral task: the need to make good the defects of human nature. Having its origin in a negative, it cannot possibly compete with the positive springs of human action, in whose shadows it always remains inferior and understandably subservient in terms of the larger scheme of human desires and the higher and wider purposes of human life.

One sees a similar attitude toward justice represented routinely and quite clearly in recent work on social theory. It is argued, for example, that the "vicarious affects, and in particular the positive ones [such as sympathy and love], are not preoccupied with mere justice, but with something exceeding it—not with what is 'the just due' of the objects of one's participatory interest, but with their good fortune."[11] Viewed in this light, rendering to another his due may be a matter of justice, but if we can discern the presence of morality therein, it is surely one which is uninspired by deeply humanitarian or substantive moral motives. For, by contrast to the vicarious affects of love and sympathy, what is due another will generally be thought to have its source in merely impersonal forces, in abstract considerations on the nature of equality, or in legally defined and enforced agenda—but surely not in positive personal attitudes of good will or benevolence, and not in the natural emotions of love and feeling or of sympathy and caring, which greatly exceed "mere justice." Quite simply, it is held that justice "aims at no more than establishing certain minima of obligation—whereas morality also recognizes the claims of special relationships in which these minima are greatly transcended."[12]

Obviously, this point of view presents justice as a matter of fundamental, but very minimal, public morality. On the one hand, it stresses the obligatory and, by implication, the enforceable nature of the demands of justice; on the other hand, it offers the vicarious affects, such as sympathy and love, as examples of deeply personal and highly intense expressions of substantive morality, a morality which springs, as it were, from the real but unknown depths of our being.

It may be noted in passing that in certain respects this point of view can actually come very close to the point of contrasting justice with morality, as if justice had either very little or literally nothing to do with morality itself. In this connection, it is certainly the case that the histories of jurisprudence and moral philosophy have offered countless examples of theories which separate justice more or less completely from morality.[13] In every age, it seems, reflective analyses of the subject again and again produce the thesis that justice is empty of serious moral content.[14] But, however interesting those views may be, I shall not consider them here, at least not primarily. I shall concentrate instead on the less extreme and more plausible claim which argues that although justice is certainly a matter of morality it is nonetheless a virtue which lays down only those moral minimums on which civil society must base its desire for peace and security. But in the spirit of the Humean View, there lurks in all this a pervasive attitude which, in effect, tells us: "How much better life would be if we could transcend the need for justice and law."

Before evaluating the adequacy of this view of justice, I shall sketch out several other ways in which this conclusion is typically reached. But, of course, if there are several ways in which this conclusion can be sanely defended, the question to bear in mind is whether they are adequate reflections of the nature of justice, all things considered. Just how one goes about making such an assessment will be discussed in a subsequent part of this essay.

I shall assume, then, that justice (social, economic, legal, criminal, etc.) has real foundations in a correctly conceived moral theory, that justice does not derive principally from considerations of rational prudence or mere efficiency, or, even less, that justice can be derived from maxims such as "might makes right." Once this assumption has been made, the principal issue for examination concerns the degree to which justice partakes of morality, the degree to which we are inclined to ascribe great or small moral importance to it, and the underlying reasons for this inclination. In this way, I am proposing an interpretation of the value of justice.[15]

Now, a central way to account for the minimalistic demands of justice is to lay out its rational foundations and what those foundations must impose on all people, simply in virtue of their human nature. The following conception may not appear initially to fall under the general idea of the Humean View, since it seems to emphasize something positive in human beings. But as we proceed, it will become apparent why it must (or at least how it can) be seen in terms of the Humean View.

To start, I shall say that what is due another is determined, prior to positive law, by quite complex ideals which, although familiar enough, have a tendency to remain abstract. In effect, the exact nature and justification of these ideals normally transcend the thinking and emotions of individual persons, at least insofar as these ideals could be said to have their origin in a rationality which is typically foreign to the average person's conception of "true" morality. What I have in mind are the familiar ideals of equality, social freedom, and fraternity. Now, even though it is common for citizens, at least those living under forms of democracy, to acknowledge these social ideals as true and necessary for social life, they are typically not regarded as ideals expressive of a highly moral life. At most, they are likely to be thought of as the great expressions of "civic" virtue, part of that minimal morality expected of us as *citizens*. This may be seen more clearly if we situate justice in relation to one of these ideals.[16]

In trying to identify the foundation for justice, one is inescapably led to associate justice at some point and to some degree with the concept of *equality*. I shall not argue at length for this relationship here but largely assume that equality is one of the foundational components of justice,[17] more so, perhaps, than is true of liberty or fraternity. If, then, we look upon equality as one of the traditional notes or properties of justice, this might mean that "giving each his due" is ultimately based on some view on the similarity or identity of all persons, however such notions may be interpreted in the concrete.[18] Or, alternatively, to say that all persons are equal entails that all are entitled to certain things; and a system of justice, in the broad sense which embraces law, will be the social means of ensuring that each person is given those things: the same consideration before the law, the same rights and liberties, the same treatment in relevantly similar circumstances, etc.

The view that justice in some sense presupposes and incorporates the concept of equality is an idea which obviously has been more important for some societies than others, depending upon such things as the way in which equality has been interpreted and the degree to which it has been affirmed and implemented by social and political institutions. The point is that some notion of equality is virtually always relevant to a conception of justice; otherwise, we risk a serious distortion of its essential meaning and threaten to dismantle the very foundations of social and minimal moral life. On this much there seems to be a consensus in the literature on justice in virtually every epoch.[19] If human beings were unable to consider each other their equals, the effects on most theories of justice would be literally devastating.

Again, it is doubtless true that the application of the concept of equality has not been evenhanded over the course of time. Because of diverse interpretations of the effects of such things as race, religion, and gender on basic human identity, some people, as we know, have not been treated equally or even been considered to be equal beings. In order to account for how equality can be compatible with apparently substantive inequalities, we must recall that the history of the process of understanding and achieving equality has been characterized by social conflict and contestation. But, of course, a normal and frequent effect of these latter processes (at least when they are successful) is an increase in the number of those people who are considered equal and a diversification of what is thought to be equal.[20] In light of this, we can see that when one complains that there is no justice or equality, such a complaint must normally be understood to mean, not that these concepts fail to be embodied in social policies and practices, but that they have not yet been "extended" to certain persons in ways which those persons believe significant or to aspects of their situation which they consider neglected or deliberately ignored. In spite of the fact that moral philosophy, legal systems, and general culture have not for some reason thought such things to be important, some persons do claim their importance and call for their inclusion under the rubric of equality, to form thenceforth part of the normally expected consequences of justice.[21]

Now, the above considerations, brief as they are, tend, I think, to express a basic truth about just and moral relationships: that they are necessarily founded to some extent on human equality. Nonetheless, I believe that they, so stated, succeed in expressing what is all too apt to be perceived as an extremely minimal account of moral relationship. It is easy to see that, for anyone who takes equality for granted as a matter of course, we have probably isolated only an elemental, perhaps even trivial, content of morality. For even if human beings were to abide by the dictates of justice, rendering to each his due, they could easily remain basically immoral in regard to the very people to whom they render justice. It is all too obvious that one may resent or hate the others to whom one renders their due, or that one may secretly or openly crave much more than is one's due. But all this tells us what we already knew: that there are sound reasons behind the adage that one cannot routinely "legislate morality." Thus, insofar as justice (as embodied in laws, rules, the civil and criminal procedure, etc.) tries to bring about a greater equality, it is not necessarily increasing the morality of citizens, not, at least from their point of view.

In light of the foregoing considerations we may often unwittingly transfer the grief engendered by equality onto justice; for the latter considerations would seem to make it more appropriate to ascribe the greater part of the complaint against justice to equality.[22] Moreover, the complaint against equality, so understood, is not without some basis in fact. For equality can be challenged in countless ways on factual grounds: people are unequal in virtually every measurable respect—in strength and beauty, in intelligence and grace, in performance and ability to give pleasure—such that the assertion that they are equal flies in the face of known facts and must, therefore, border on absurdity. Consequently, to the degree that justice is founded on equality, and to the degree that equality is not reflected in our review of the actual facts characteristic of human beings, to that degree the dictates of justice will strike us as lacking a solid foundation in human nature.

A common remedy is to restrict equality to certain (usually abstract) qualities and to base justice in part on merit, i.e., on the recognition of the distinctions or differences between persons, not exclusively on their identity, sameness, or equality. But outside of a completely meritarian society, merit ordinarily does not override all the claims of equality. In principle, two persons are (or may be) entitled to identical social benefits and civil status, or to the same consideration before the law, in spite of the greatest differences between them in natural or social fortune.

Obviously, at this point, it can be seen that merit must play some foundational role in a conception of justice. It must be recognized, of course, that justice is an exceedingly complex notion, which even a fully defined view of equality can only begin to unravel. But the aim of this essay is to present neither a theory of equality nor a complete analysis of the concept of justice. My only purpose is to locate, as it were, the place of justice within the larger framework of morality. Thus, the only relevant point of these considerations on equality is that even if equality should be a mark which deeply characterizes human beings it is not sufficiently recognized, or experienced, or socially efficacious, or consented to by persons. Consequently, a system of justice is needed to counteract the insufficiencies of human nature. In the spirit of the Humean View, if only people were able to recognize and implement human equality, there would be no need for justice in the "catalogue of virtues." This is, of course, a seductive view, but ultimately we shall have to reject it (see the third section).

B. *Harshness and External Origin of Justice.* In being thought of as a virtue which defines only the minimums of social morality, justice is typically and compatibly perceived as harsh and negative, blind and formal. This is not merely true of criminal justice, where one would most expect it; it is also characteristic of the civil law and of economic and social justice in general. A simple fact of economic justice requires some people (the rich or the middle-class) to pay proportionately higher taxes, often against their will, in conformity with some abstract conception of economic equity. Once again, formal abstract equality seems to be at the root of the just treatment of all individuals. The morality of justice is a matter of heeding certain words and formulas, holding to an identity or equality of persons which it is nevertheless quite difficult for human beings to affirm voluntarily.

Obviously, to speak of justice as negative and harsh, as is often the case, suggests that justice is concerned with a minimal level of morality. One ought to pay one's taxes. But doing such a thing is hardly a major criterion of being a good person, which accounts for why otherwise moral persons can so easily reconcile a bit of legerdemain in such areas.

The symbolism of justice helps to confirm this view by representing justice as blindly weighing both sides of an issue, adjudicating, via legislation or judicial decision, competing claims, and rendering decisions which, unfortunately, can rarely please all parties to a dispute. In some sense, justice seems at times to be much less concerned with the content of what is being weighed than with vindicating principles and rules, with setting things right, correcting the deficiencies of human relations which are normally guided by an extremely fallible human nature.[23]

This helps to explain why justice is also typically perceived as "external." It comes to us, as it were, from outside ourselves, and in many cases, especially those falling under the common law or constitutional amendments, no one can know for certain what is just until learned judges, several courts, or reflective juries make their decisions. But, of course, it is notorious how often we are surprised or angered to learn what justice is said to require in a given case, prompting appeal to a higher court whenever there are knowledge and resources to allow this to be done. Where knowledge and resources are lacking, there may be only resignation.

c. *Justice Separated from Morality.* An extreme example of the near separation of both law and justice from morality is found in Oliver Wendell Holmes's famous lecture on "The Path of the Law."[24] Holmes advised students of the law to make a clear distinction between law and morality if they hoped to become successful lawyers. For although the law may be the "witness and external deposit of our moral life" and "its history the history of the moral development of the race," one can, nevertheless,

> see very plainly that a bad man has as much reason as a good one for wishing to avoid an encounter with the public force, and therefore [one] can see the practical importance of the distinction between morality and law. A man who cares nothing for an ethical rule which is believed and practiced by his neighbors is likely nevertheless to care a good deal to avoid being made to pay money, and will want to keep out of jail if he can.[25]

Holmes therefore advised students to look upon the law from the point of view of the "bad man," whose attitude illuminates the major reason for engaging a lawyer in the first place: to obtain an accurate "prediction" or "prophesy" of what the courts will do if a given action is performed or not performed. Since justice emanates from the courts which use the public force to carry out their judgments, "people want to know under what circumstances and how far they will run the risk of coming against what is so much stronger than themselves, and hence it becomes a business to find out when this danger is to be feared."[26]

The common man's interest in justice is thus a reluctant and often cunning quest for personal rectitude, but only in order to escape the force of public reprobation. Perhaps nothing can better suggest the potential separation of law and justice from morality than Holmes's view of approaching the law with the bad man's attitude.[27]

To summarize the last few sections: it would seem that justice is a virtue which is imposed from without, practiced with resignation, mixed with much grief, reluctance, and cunning, and ultimately unattractive although admittedly quite necessary to social life. Now, these considerations lead us back to the idea that justice does not stem from anything positive in our nature. In accordance with the Humean View, it implies that something is missing from human nature, a deficiency which must be made good by corrective and guiding forces working from the outside. Indeed, following the lead of Hume, one tradition in moral learning theory argues that the aim of moral education is to supply missing motives for the performance of right conduct.[28] This tradition frankly contends that human beings are simply ill-equipped by nature to practice the virtue of justice. And so, we find additional support for the sentiment that justice comes to us from the outside and corrects both the deficiencies of our original nature and the careless way we proceed to use it.

The analogy with the conventional practice of medicine again comes to mind: the purpose of medicine is not to understand health on the basis of a theory of the person, but to treat and, wherever practical, prevent disease on the basis of a multitude of scientific disciplines for which we lack a comprehensive and theoretical unity. Just as medicine works from disease back to health in an experimental way, and not from health to disease on the basis of a theoretical command of the whole person, so too the implementation of social virtue often seems to work more from the conditions of social disease (or injustice) toward a condition of justice which is judged to be so, less for theoretical than for practical reasons (the achievement of peace, social tranquillity, etc.). Being as theory-poor as the art of medicine, it flounders just as often in a sea of confusion and relies on rules-of-thumb just as consistently. Accordingly, there may be more than a little justification for thinking that until theory can exercise its rightful place in these domains, the criminal justice and health-care systems will in all probability continue to expend a growing proportion of scarce social resources only to reap comparatively meager results.[29]

D. *The Waning of Goodness.* The idea of the minimal moral nature of justice can be put in more philosophical terms by utilizing the historically familiar idea that the concept of the good has had sovereignty or primacy over rightness or justice. Generally speaking, and despite contrary tendencies, it has been held throughout the history of ethics that the good should have sovereignty or primacy over the right. This *de jure* primacy notwithstanding, many philosophers and social thinkers would agree that it is unfortunately true that, *de facto,* "the idea of goodness (and of virtue) has been largely superseded in Western moral philosophy by the idea of rightness, supported perhaps by some conception of sincerity. This is to some extent a natural outcome of the disappearance of a permanent background to human activity: a permanent background, whether provided by Good, by Reason, by History, or by the self."[30]

The above criticism deplores the supremacy of rightness over goodness, attributing this supremacy to the lack of a permanent background against which we might judge the morality of human activity, a background which has often been provided by "intelligible essences,"[31] by the teleology of history or reason, but perhaps mainly by the idea (or ideas) of the good (see part B of the second section). It is as if, once supremacy has been given to the right (which is conceived of as setting down one's minimal obligations to other people), the highest morality of content thereafter attainable is the morality of sincerity, which amounts essentially to a private morality.[32] It is as if the concept of rightness could give us, in the public realm, only a morality of form, that is, one concerned almost exclusively with the *formal* relations with other people: impersonal legality, formal equality of opportunity, equal rights, etc. Consequently, public morality has no substantive content, only an impersonal form which is applied anonymously to all people in order to ensure an at least minimal morality.[33]

Now, there is a sense in which this thesis is obviously correct and a not so obvious sense in which it is very probably false. Before turning to the latter sense, I shall discuss its limited but plausible sense over the next few paragraphs.

To the degree that there surely exists a contemporary emphasis on individual or group justice which generally excludes reference to concerns for the common good and social welfare, this thesis has a basis in fact. Indeed, nothing seems more apparent than that individuals and groups in our time are increasingly demanding their rights—the right to equal pay, the right to use their bodies sexually as they so choose, the right to live, the right to abort, the right to die, and so on endlessly. There can be little doubt that in contemporary culture more individuals and groups are not content with their lot, that they are focusing their attention on their rights. Perhaps many critics would consider all this to be merely an emphasis on the superficial aspects of self. This may be true. But, in any event, it is held that the unhappy aspect of this cultural drift is that there is no end, or form of objective good; that this emphasis points to no "permanent background" against which one is to measure the value of the multitude of claims of right and justice. Unfortunately, so the complaint runs, the right takes supremacy because of the absence of the good or, alternatively, because of the lack of consensus on what the good, which should guide the quest for ethical rightness, is. Therefore, lacking the good (or a consensus on it), we inevitably fall back on rightness itself. For this reason, ours is not an age of goodness.[34]

No doubt there is a tendency in every age for people to think that, by contrast to previous ages, their age is unique and truly modern. Of course, we can see that this is an almost unavoidable tendency; after all, what could be more modern than the present. But historians and social thinkers can convince us that forward movements in time are compatible with regression in ideas and morality.[35] Progress does not necessarily occur on all fronts simultaneously. Indeed, it is probably safe to say that in the last quarter-century, since, roughly, the 1954 Supreme Court Decision in *Brown v. Board of Education*,[36] American society has witnessed greater increments, slowly but surely, in the amount of justice and equality available to its citizens than in almost any previous quarter-century in American history.[37] Yet many would contend that we have simultaneously witnessed a greater decline in goodness—a net decrease in the moral goodness of our lives and our society in general in the same time period than in any two previous decades. It is tempting to think that a kind of law may be at work here: the more justice, the less goodness; justice is purchased at the expense of goodness. Moreover, in terms of the particular moral outlook which formulates this relationship between justice and goodness, the primary ingredient of morality is, of course, goodness. In light of this, there follows a more negative, even paradoxical, way to formulate the relationship: the more justice, the less morality (or the more individuals seek their rights, the more they separate themselves from others).

The intuitive idea here is that morality is intrinsically bound up both more intimately and more publicly with positive relationships to other people. Justice, by contrast, is perceived as negative, emphasizing individual rights and liberties, the *freedom from* interference by other people and institutions. Genuine personal relationships, on the other hand, have to be seen on the model of vicarious affects such as sympathy and love.[38] Perhaps it is not too much of an exaggeration to say that goodness is often thought to focus on the needs and welfare of other people, whereas rightness tends to look toward the prerogatives of the self.[39] In this connection, it is interesting to note that even a social contract theory such as Hobbes's arrives at a social morality of "law" on the basis of such emotions as fear and prudentially rational desires for such things as peace and security.[40] But such desires and emotions are ultimately reducible to individual self-interest, and, accordingly, the relative superiority or moral quality of altruism and other positive grounds of interpersonal relationship becomes apparent. One might say that the Hobbesian View, like the Humean View which it resembles in many respects, takes the natural condition of man, the conditions of amorality or immorality (or, more precisely, the conditions of an original social *anomie*) as reasons for building a set of social rules and sanctions. And this it calls morality.[41] But it is open to question whether the pessimistic view of human nature found in Hobbes's work allows for a superior morality, that is, one which gets beyond the legalistic claims of what Hobbes calls "natural law." But of course the very same question is à *propos* of the morality of justice which flows from the Humean View.

Given the above perspectives, it may be thought that an ethic which explicitly espouses the primacy of the right or of justice may be doing so for several reasons, not all of them compatible: the inability to reach agreement on the nature of the good; the consequent subjectivism of the period; the necessity to have some kind of morality, one of formal rightness, even if we cannot have one of substantive goodness, etc. Or, alternatively, quite apart from reasons having to do more with culture than with ethical theory, it might be argued on philosophical grounds that the priority of the right is synonymous with the idea of *its* sovereignty or primacy, much as some philosophers have defended, perhaps on erroneous philosophical grounds, the sovereignty of the good.[42]

Before we embrace the latter conclusion it will be helpful to note that although a deontological theory is typically marked by the priority of the right over the good,[43] this priority is not necessarily synonymous with "sovereignty." What is involved here is the difference between the promptings of life as it is lived and the structure and exigencies of ethical theory. In life as it is lived, sovereignty or primacy (in the sense of overriding *interest*) will doubtless be given to the good. That is, it is difficult to understand the interest in rightness (or duty) for its own sake—unless, of course, we can understand an "upright" life as a way of being good, in which case it is not rightness for its own sake. In any event, human psychology being what it is, goodness may hold a sovereign position with respect to other concepts. But this only tells us what the aims or ends of life are about: the good. On the other hand, ethics being what it is and for reasons peculiar to ethics and quite apart from the teleology of life, priority (in the sense of being defined first and independently) may well belong to the right. The right wins, as it were, an intellectual and moral, but not an existential, victory.[44]

An argument for the priority of the right, therefore, does not necessarily preclude the sovereignty of the good; that is, it does not require us to assign the good to an inferior category in life, although it does rule out its chronological primacy in ethical theory. Thus, instead of rejecting the sovereignty of the good, one can perhaps retain it while defending the priority of the right—as long as we distinguish the two kinds of *prominence* at issue here: on the one hand, the exigencies of an ethical theory, and, on the other, the primary forces which motivate human living. This is simply another way of emphasizing how important it is to distinguish ethics from psychology.

In the last analysis it is a mistake to employ the language of victory and sovereignty in discussing the relative weights of the right and the good. It is a mistake because an ethics which emphasizes either the right or the good at the expense of the other turns out to be a one-sided ethics. In any event, I shall argue in due course that this conclusion flows from our sense of morality when it is duly unfolded. But lest the focus of my above remarks be lost, my intention has been to indicate one other aspect of the origins of the alleged minimal morality of justice, and how this may turn on the way in which we interpret the relation between the right and the good, the priority and/or sovereignty of one over the other.

Our conclusion here must be that if the waning of goodness results in an exaggerated emphasis on justice (or the right), and if justice, absent goodness, provides us with only a minimal morality, this is not because of a doctrine which gives priority to the right over the good. To think so is to confuse priority with sovereignty, the exigencies of an ethical theory with the exigencies of life.

E. *The Need or Wish to Go Beyond Justice.* One view of society invites us to look upon justice as a necessary but regrettable fact stemming from a defective human nature and an imperfect world. Another view looks upon justice as a temporary stage in the evolution of society. According to both views, it is an ideal of society or of the nature of social logic somehow to transcend justice, to get beyond the conditions which make it necessary in the first place. Perhaps this is the most direct way of expressing the idea of the extremely minimal morality in the virtue of justice, which brings us back to our point of departure, the Humean View.

Although it is not concerned with defending either this particular ideal or this form of social logic, one recent work on justice characterizes this ideal such that "a society in which all can achieve their complete good, or in which there are no conflicting demands and the wants of all fit together without coercion into a harmonious plan of activity, is a society in a certain sense beyond justice."[45] The phrase "beyond justice" is a suggestive clue to the pervasive conception of the worth of justice under review in this section: temporary and wholly inferior surrogate for something better, pale reflection of true and complete morality.

Now, an ethic emphasizing the central role of the "vicarious affects"[46] in human dealings may want to argue that this is surely a noble, if not sensible, ideal to try to realize. Even if its realization would require unimaginable efforts or superhuman powers, it will be said that an ethic of altruism and love is not easily discouraged by such factual limitations. With an almost religious fervor, this view will maintain that whatever the difficulties to be surmounted, the ideal remains forever meaningful as an indispensable measure of how far we have come or must go toward realizing relationships which are fully moral and truly expressive of our complete moral nature. Should the factual limitations be definitive, admitting of no change, such that there is no foreseeable time when we can get beyond the need for justice, this, it will be said, does not prevent us from viewing justice as a minimal level of morality. It is our duty to strive for a morality of goodness, using the morality of rightness or justice as a surrogate, temporary or permanent.[47]

In the eighteenth century David Hume gave classic expression to a view which relegates justice to a mere artifice invented by human beings to deal with the defective circumstances of the world and human nature. As we have seen already, Hume argued with some brilliance,

> if every man had a tender regard for another, or if nature supplied abundantly all our wants and desires, that the jealousy of interest, which justice supposes, could no longer have place; nor would there be any occasion for those distinctions and limits of property and possession, which at present are in use among mankind. Encrease to a sufficient degree the benevolence of men, or the bounty of nature, and you render justice useless, by supplying its place with much nobler virtues, and more valuable blessings.[48]

Indeed, it would appear virtually impossible to quarrel with Hume's imaginative hypothesis that "if men were supplied with every thing in the same abundance, or if every one had the same affection and tender regard for every one as for himself, justice and injustice would be equally unknown among mankind."[49] If only "men were endow'd with such a benevolence, these rules [of justice] would never have been dreamed of."[50] But, as I have already suggested, if Hume's reasoning is unassailable, his imagination is perverse. For we could just as easily say: "If only human biology were different, men would never have to eat, sleep, or die." We can in this way, carried far enough, wish away the entire world and the whole of human nature. But, in the end, we shall have to question whether the Humean View overlooked important *positive* factors in human nature, factors which infuse justice with a value beyond his wildest imagination.

Again, Hume did not think that it was really possible to achieve a society beyond justice. Yet this did not prevent him from judging the worth of justice by comparison to what he thought was characteristic of such an idealized society. His standard of judgment for justice is extremely problematic and curious, and possibly absurd. But this is not to say that there is no coherence in his statements on justice. For certainly it seems to make good sense to say that what prevents men from ever achieving a society beyond justice are the circumstances of human nature and the more or less permanent conditions of the world in which we live,[51] conditions which demand resignation to the necessity of justice in any known society in the world as it is. Thus, though his view reflects the ideal of a society beyond justice, Hume thought so little of the possibility of realizing that ideal that he never formulated a practical program to implement it.

With Marxism we encounter a cast of mind which is strikingly different. For Marxism presents us with reasons to believe that a society beyond justice is not a vain hope, and it offers in addition a program designed to lead us toward that colossal achievement. It too criticizes justice, but for reasons totally other than Hume's. Whereas Hume saw the transcendence of justice checked by unalterable natural and human-psychological facts, Marxism sees justice as a temporary necessity (in some societies, at least) which is imposed, not by natural, but by entrenched political and ideological forces.[52]

This presents us with a paradox. For it is commonly thought that Marxism is a caustic critique of an unjust society, capitalistic society, morally condemning what historical forces themselves will eventually punish without fail. This means that although corrective forces spring from the nature of the dialectical processes of history itself, Marxism (or so it has been argued[53]) adds a moral condemnation, in the name of distributive justice, of capitalistic society. But in crucial respects this view is difficult to sustain, especially in light of the ridicule and scorn which Marx and Engels poured on the concept of justice, that bourgeois virtue which elicited from them "a torrent of testimony that the principle of distributive justice is alien to the mental world of Marxism."[54]

How can this paradox be removed? The famous maxim "From each according to his abilities, to each according to his needs," a maxim adopted by Marxism, is often thought to be a principle of distributive justice, i.e., a formula which tells us the way in which the duties and goods of a society are to be justly distributed. Yet, as one Marxist scholar notes, for "Saint-Simon and many later socialists . . . the moral basis of socialism was not the ideal of justice but rather the ideal of human brotherhood or love." And so the famous formula ("From each . . .") should not be looked upon as a formula for distributive justice or equity, "since the needs of individuals may be in inverse proportion to their abilities and to their contribution to society, and in any case they will normally differ from person to person. What the formula expresses is an ethic of brotherhood."[55] Thus a Marxist society, in agreement with the idealized society of the Humean View, does not really esteem a morality of justice. On the contrary, for Marxism such a morality is more nearly a cloak for immorality; similarly, in the Humean View, justice is a technological response to the missing motives for morality in mankind, a response to the deficiencies of human nature.

Contrary to the Humean View, however, Marxism holds that capitalistic societies need an ethic of justice in order to legitimize existing socio-economic relations; and these relations, far from being an expression of mutuality and the brotherhood of all men, serve to establish barriers among men and to introduce conflict into relations which could not long last if they were not authenticated by a powerful system of justice and law.[56] And so the underlying spirit of Marxism is to transcend justice. Although it has much in common with the Humean View, it goes further, boldly to set forth reasons which suggest that getting beyond justice is only a matter of time and the dialectic.

F. *Justice and Love.* The foregoing remarks on Hume and Marxism lead naturally to a final perspective on the minimal morality of justice, the perspective of love. Here I shall merely indicate first the nature of this perspective and, secondly, the reasons which tell against its practicality. In a sense, the morality of love has all along been the tacitly invoked critical perspective from which the morality of justice was judged so inferior and minimal. What follows, in due course, is the beginning of an alternative critical perspective which will enable us to elevate justice to its rightful place in the moral sphere.

It is held that love, in contrast to justice, is not moved primarily by considerations of duty or obligations; it does not act, nor can it be effectively commanded to do so, under the threat of punishment or the public force of the law. It proceeds, let us say, from the heart, which, as Pascal classically expressed it, "has reasons of which reason is ignorant"[57]—which is to say that reason, as conventionally defined, is not in a position to command the workings of love. Or, following a long line of philosophers and psychologists, we could say that love is based on feeling, and feeling, as many moral theorists have argued, is sovereign over reason as far as morality is concerned.[58]

However, if human nature is such that people are largely moved by selfish and self-interested motives, then an ethic which fails to take this into account, presenting instead a moral theory founded primarily on love or altruism, risks the fate of being an ineffective and even foolish ethic. This is not to say that an ethic of love has no place in a moral theory; it means that, human nature being what it is, love is not able to provide a reliable basis for determining the content of morality, not even, let us emphasize, a principle for determining the content of love itself.

One could, of course, argue that it is necessary to decide whether the facts in question, such as those of selfishness and self-interest, are part of a universal human nature or whether they are the result, wholly or in part, of social and cultural influences. If societies generally encourage people to be grasping and acquisitive, it is imperative to know how far these tendencies can be altered and by what means. If love and altruism do not characterize human relations generally but only marginally (e.g., in the private sphere), it is necessary to know how far this is the result of culture and not of human nature, and how much it is open to alteration, if alteration is desirable. Thus, the present facts characteristic of human relations which argue against love as the heart of morality may be only contingent facts and, as such, subject to change. This may or may not be the case. But in any case it is a question for empirical investigation to resolve, not one for philosophical analysis.

Fortunately, it is not only contingent facts which can argue against love as the *heart* of morality. Ironically, love suffers a defect which is the converse of sincerity's weakness. Sincerity, understood as the formal congruence between feeling and the avowal of feeling,[59] is this side of morality; love is on its far side. That is, sincerity does not go far enough to achieve substantive morality; love transcends it and may, in the process, even violate it. In both cases, we confront genuine virtues which inhabit the outer margins of morality. By themselves, neither can specify the heart of morality. Viewing love in this way may, of course, seem somewhat paradoxical insofar as love is often thought to be the very heart and soul of morality. As we shall see, it would be better to say that love is a higher expression of morality, but first presupposes much which precedes it and upon which it must build. At any rate, the argument of this essay will be that justice and goodness make up the heart of morality. Without being clear on these things, love not only may be blind but may constitute a serious form of immorality.[60]

In order to clarify the role of justice as constituting the core of morality, not merely a minimal expression of it, I shall in the next two sections discuss more systematically the relative roles of both justice and goodness in ethical theory. For at the heart of the idea of the minimal moral content of justice lies the claim that goodness alone brings us into the sphere of substantive morality, thus transcending the commands of "mere justice."

THE THEORY OF JUSTICE

An essay on justice and goodness can hardly avoid some reference to John Rawls's *A Theory of Justice*.[61] Indeed, given its importance, future discussions of the subject will virtually be compelled for quite some time to draw upon this work as a necessary background. It is especially pertinent here since one of the principal purposes of this essay is to discuss the issues which make the association of justice and goodness problematic. Whatever else it may contain, Rawls's work presents a theory which illustrates this problematic relation in an original and, I think, appealing way. Thus in this section I shall frequently draw upon some of the key concepts of *A Theory of Justice*. But since the main purpose is not to explicate Rawls's own theory, in all its labyrinthine complexity, I shall make no claim to completeness or accuracy in my discussion of it. Details aside, Rawls's work can at least provide an appropriate point of departure for reorganizing our thinking on justice and goodness.[62]

In the few years which have elapsed since *A Theory of Justice* was first published, innumerable reviews and critical articles have appeared in various journals of philosophy, jurisprudence, and social science in general. This massive reaction alone may serve to foretell that the work is destined to become a classic in the field of moral philosophy, on a par with Sidgwick's *The Methods of Ethics*.[63] Be that as it may, it is noteworthy that, with few exceptions, the articles and critical reviews have been devoted, in a sense, to but half of Rawls's moral theory, his conception of justice, and have for the most part neglected his theory of the good. Even the two book-length studies which have, as of this writing, been devoted exclusively to Rawls's theory omit any sustained discussion of his substantive theory of the good. Indeed, one might gather from the title and table of contents of Brian Barry's monograph that the theory of moral goodness is not one of Rawls's principal doctrines.[64] And in his recent collection of critical essays on Rawls, Norman Daniels has had to restrict the scope of his book such that papers on Rawls's theory of goodness are intentionally excluded.[65]

I do not wish to criticize this lack of attention to the theory of goodness. Indeed, there are several reasons which can help us to view this apparent one-sidedness as entirely natural—or almost so. First and foremost, Rawls's work is obviously about justice. At the very outset, in the first part of the three-part work, Rawls presents an original and highly challenging theory on the nature of justice—so challenging and so provocative that one naturally finds no want of material to probe and question in reviews and articles on the nature of his conception of justice, enough, at least, to subject his vision of the good to benevolent neglect.

There is also the fact that, with one important exception (which I shall comment on later), his view of justice is consciously elaborated without reliance on a theory of the good. Indeed, this is so distinctive a trait of *A Theory of Justice* that one feels entitled, if not bound by the nature of Rawls's own explicit description of his enterprise, to discuss justice while refraining from incorporating concepts of goodness into criticism and evaluation of his work.[66]

It is apparent, then, that a distinctive trait of Rawls's work, perhaps the most important one from a theoretical point of view, is the systematic way in which his theory is committed to the priority of the right (or of justice) over the good. Unless we seek first the nature of justice (or so Rawls seems to be saying), and unless we render ourselves blind, as it were, to the nature of the good, we risk a serious compromise of our eventual view of justice. In effect, Rawls claims that a sound presentation of a theory of justice demands an initial freedom from the good, as if we could be truly free for the good and for our ends only by first being provisionally free and independent of them; free from the good, at least, until the conception of justice is actually securely established.[67]

There is much to be said, then, at least within the context of Rawls's work, for the separation of justice and goodness. But this is not to suggest that *A Theory of Justice* has nothing to say about the good. A full reading of this work clearly shows that one of Rawls's central concerns is to examine the harmony or congruence between justice and goodness. Approximately one-third of *A Theory of Justice* is, in fact, devoted to an account of the nature of goodness. This fact alone suggests that the topic of the good hardly constitutes a minor aspect of Rawls's overall thinking on justice.[68] What we have to account for is how Rawls justifies a theory of justice which relies, in its formulation, so minimally on a theory of goodness and yet, at the same time, presents justice as being far more than a minimal morality.

A. *The Independence of Justice.* We may start by emphasizing that *A Theory of Justice* is concerned both with the separation of justice from goodness and with their congruence or harmony. The idea of their separation may seem puzzling, and we shall have to explain it. But the idea of their congruence or harmony is hardly astonishing if it is true that the concepts of rightness and goodness are the two most fundamental concepts in ethical theory. It is indeed truly hard to conceive of a moral theory which could totally neglect either one of these two concepts.

However, in analyzing one line of criticism which Rawls's work has provoked and which, in a sense, may reflect one of the possible weaknesses of the work, we face a certain irony which bears on the continuing topic of this essay and which will serve to introduce it from another perspective. It consists in this. Although Rawls has taken great pains in the third part of *A Theory of Justice* to show that goodness is congruent with his independently derived notion of justice, it has nevertheless occurred to some critics that Rawls's separate account of justice proper amounts to an extremely rationalistic, perhaps inhuman, theory of justice. The reason for this stems from Rawls's emphasis on impersonal reason and on certain peculiar and impersonal conditions under which principles of justice are "chosen" by theoretically defined persons. (Here we are referring to Rawls's notion of an "original position" in which hypothetical persons deliberate on the content of the principles of justice which are to guide the structuring of the basic institutional complexes of society.[69])

In other words, despite the fact that Rawls has presented a powerful vision of human good in the third part of *A Theory of Justice*, and even though this theory of the good may in fact turn out to be congruent with justice (as this is defined in the first part of his book), his conception of justice (so the criticism would run) is nevertheless defective precisely because it is elaborated and defined without explicit *prior regard* for human good. The fact that justice is ultimately congruent with goodness is therefore held to be of little consequence if justice has been defined independently, in the dark, as it were, about the nature of goodness.

It may be remarked that Rawls himself surely had a premonition of this line of potential criticism when he acknowledged, close to the end of his work, that his account of social values (or of the "good" of sociality) reveals "aspects of the theory of justice which are developed slowly beginning from what looks like an unduly rationalistic conception that makes no provision for social values."[70] It is somewhat ironic that Rawls is criticized for separating justice and goodness when in fact he has taken great pains to show, not their union, to be sure, but at least their congruence and interdependence.

But the irony in this may be partially removed when the critic rejoins that the interdependence or congruence of justice and goodness is irrelevant since no matter what degree of interdependence and congruence Rawls may finally achieve with these basic ethical concepts, the inescapable fact remains that he has elaborated principles of justice without using a concept of goodness as one of his premises, and this (so it is contended) makes all the difference to the resulting conception of justice.

Anyone who is not already familiar with Rawls's work may be somewhat at a loss to understand exactly the nature of the problem here. For example, assuming that the complementarity of justice and goodness is a desideratum, one might think that no problem arises from the fact that Rawls presents separate and independent accounts of justice and goodness as long as he eventually establishes harmony between them. And this he has done, although not necessarily to the satisfaction of his critics. Thus the fact that he defines a conception of justice separately, without recourse to or dependence upon a theory of the good, may be held to be of no consequence; what matters is that he has, according to his own lights, established their harmony. And so, one might think that the problem vanishes.

Unfortunately, this is only an apparent solution to the problem. Lest one think that it makes no difference whether the choice for a conception of justice is or is not made in the light of a theory of goodness, it must be emphasized that the nature and content of ethics turns on this very crucial issue. An ethical theory, such as Rawls's, defines the right and principles of justice prior to and independently of the good; such a theory has distinct qualities and important consequences for ethical behavior. What these qualities and consequences are should be clear, at least in a general way, to anyone who is familiar with Kant's ethical writings or with the notion of deontology in ethics.[71]

On the other hand, an ethical theory which starts with the good and *then* defines the right ends up with a conception of right or justice which is merely adjectival to the good and which therefore makes the right dependent on the good. Briefly, this is the symptomatic drift of teleological and utilitarian theories in ethics. Though the deontological ethics defines moral obligations which are valid whether or not those obligations, when kept, lead to the production of the good, the teleological ethics defines moral obligations of justice only insofar as those obligations do lead to the production and achievement of the good.[72]

In light of the foregoing remarks, we can now understand that our critic who saw no problem must now acknowledge, if due respect is to be paid to the history of ethical theories, that separate accounts of justice and goodness can have, and indeed have had, a significant impact on the nature of justice, even if justice and goodness finally turn out to be congruent and interdependent.

One has to see, however, that the separation of justice from goodness is only provisional; within Rawls's deontology, justice, once it is securely defined, is then related to goodness, thus constituting a relatively complete ethical theory. For since, presumably, any acceptable or intelligible ethical theory needs both these concepts, this association is a necessity. But what is crucial is that the particular way in which they are associated flows from the independent accounts of justice and goodness. For Rawls, this association is summarized in the *priority* of justice (or the right, the broader term) over the good.[73]

Now, the point of the above considerations is that there is a basis in ethical theory for giving a priority in moral reasoning to the concept of rightness and justice. A moral theory which underwrites this priority is, I take it, claiming that rightness or justice is at the heart of a moral point of view, more so than goodness; that justice is *in some sense* independent of goodness, although, to be sure, it is not unrelated to it.

The question to be resolved (eventually) is how this claim of the independence of justice affects the modern period's view of the minimal moral content of justice. Is justice, in the spirit of Hobbes and Hume, merely the artificial groundwork of morality, or does a priority-of-justice doctrine help to rescue justice from such a low estate? This question will be taken up more directly in the third section.

B. *Problems with the Priority of Justice: Rationality, History, and Perfection.* As previously noted, criticism of Rawls's theory has not, generally speaking, focused on his theory of justice in *relation* to his theory of the good. Whatever the justification for such an approach, it would seem that one cannot fully appreciate the impact and significance of this theory or, for that matter, any theory of justice without at the same time considering its bearing on a theory of the good[74] or on goodness *per se*. But it is not only adverse criticism of Rawls, made without due consideration of his theory of the good, which I have in mind. Indeed, even carefully considered praise of this theory of justice may be misplaced if its relation to the theory of the good is not also considered. In this respect, Murdoch's notion of the "sovereignty of good" can be quite relevant.[75] For it is doubtless true that there is a widely shared belief that no theory of justice, however rational and compelling it may be, however much it embodies fairness and other qualities desirable for a conception of justice, is able to command the moral sensitivities of human beings unless it also coheres with their duly considered sense of goodness.[76]

This is not to bring in the priority or sovereignty of the good through the back door, once having questioned its admittance by the front. To imply that considerations about goodness always act as the main criterion of justice would be to allow this covert entrance, clearly running the risk of compromising the priority-of-the-right position. On the contrary, I mean to suggest the possibility of a middle ground between two extremes: one makes the good entirely irrelevant to justice; the other claims that justice must never violate criteria of goodness. Now, Rawls's position seems to inhabit this middle ground, since he defends both the idea that some things are just although not good[77] and, as we have seen,[78] the idea that any theory of justice must be sensitive to, although not ruled by, its practical consequences. These two positions are not inconsistent or contradictory, for the idea of "priority" precisely entails the idea of a *relationship* between the right and the good. The difficult task is so to articulate this middle ground in greater detail that this central problem of relating justice and goodness does not lead to the abject servitude of one or the other concept.[79]

Although we cannot go into detail here, let us at least outline the issue more concretely in terms of some specific problems of "priority" in Rawls's theory. As we have seen, a prevalent reaction to Rawls's work takes the particular critical position that his account of justice is "unduly rationalistic"; that it somehow misconceives the nature of human beings, viewing them, in an almost mechanistic way, as rational and disembodied deliberators who can agree upon the principles of justice only because they have forfeited their traditions, passions, and, in brief, their more particular human nature.

This criticism stems from or is compatible with several different alternatives or solutions, depending upon the origin of the complaint of "undue rationality." Marxism, for example, may reach this conclusion as a reaction to Rawls's alleged neglect of history.[80] On the other hand, a liberal thinker may share this complaint because he senses that Rawls's conception of justice does not allow for sufficient individual liberty.[81] Thus, there are symmetrically opposite reasons for sharing the complaint that Rawls's account of justice is rationalistic:

collectivism and individualism. What unites them is their feeling that reason is operating in Rawls's work at the expense of certain indispensable facts about human beings or human society. This criticism is not exactly based on an unwillingness to accept a theory of justice which owes virtually nothing to an explicit theory of the good. Instead, we see here a desire to reason about justice with a somewhat different set of facts and data as background. Their quarrel with Rawls is only secondarily about the pertinence of the good to justice. First and foremost, the criticism concerns the nature or content of what is allowed into the "original position"—the hypothetical position in which rational deliberators are to choose principles of justice behind a "veil of ignorance." As previously noted,[82] on the subject of the "circumstances of justice," Rawls adopts the views of Hume, views discussed earlier in this essay. That is, he relies on the *facts* of moderate scarcity and limited altruism as a summary statement of the need for a theory of justice.

Clearly, the issue here must be understood in terms of a tension between the reasoning process on justice and the factual circumstances of human existence which should condition that reasoning process—factual circumstances such as human liberty (e.g., liberalism) or human history (e.g., Marxism). The issue might be formulated in the following way: Is justice *prior* (in the sense of enjoying a prior claim on our moral judgment) to *facts* of history or *facts* having to do with the individual's liberty?[83] The location of justice on the scale of morality will in part depend on the way this question is answered. But to do this we will need more of a grounding in moral theory (see the next section).

First, we should mention here another criticism of Rawls's theory, one which shows dissatisfaction with his deontology. In particular, it invokes an explicit concept of the good against Rawls's account of justice. That is, this criticism espouses the admission of an explicit doctrine of human perfection into the thinking which goes into the choice of a conception of justice.[84] In this way, this critique will reject the priority of the right and substitute the priority of the good. This criticism strikes at the very heart of Rawls's theory. If successful, it would undermine the primary intuition at work in *A Theory of Justice*, the priority-of-the-right doctrine.

In sum, the two forms of criticism which I have briefly outlined focus their complaint either on the undue rationality of Rawls's theory or upon the lack of a theory of human perfection in it. Admittedly, these criticisms may seem unanswerable. For all we know, they have a *prima facie* validity equal to Rawls's own position. But in order to answer them, we need to go further into the specific components of moral theory. For offhand, it seems that we are simply confronted with conflicting versions of what takes priority in moral reasoning. Is it history (Marxism)? Is it the good or some particular version of human fulfillment (perfectionism)? Is it the individual's freedom (liberalism)? Or is it justice?

MORAL THEORY AND THE PRIORITY OF JUSTICE

In order to try to resolve the problems which we have encountered in assessing the moral level of justice (the first section) and the associated problems of determining the proper relationship of justice and goodness (the second section), it will be helpful to discuss the nature of moral theory on a more general level in terms of the abstract components which constitute morality itself.

The following considerations can be fruitful in several respects. First, moral theory in general, as well as the kind of moral theory which I shall discuss in particular, is eminently suited to deal with both problems treated in the preceding two sections. Moral theory in general should be able to provide, if anything can, an account of the proper moral dimensions of justice; and it should give much direction on the way, properly and compatibly, to relate the two keystone concepts of ethics, the right and the good. More particularly, if there are reasons to oppose the priority of the good over the right, we should expect to find those reasons within an account of the nature of moral reasoning.

The advantage of the particular kind of moral theory which I shall be emphasizing, however, lies in its unique ability to draw upon moral *experience*, appealing both to common intuition and to the latent process of ordering the data of intuition by means of the deep-seated urge for rational coherence characteristic of human intelligence.

A. *The Constitutive Marks of Morality*. To begin, let us suppose that the facts of comparative anthropology and sociology were quite different from what they are. That is, let us suppose what is surely not the case: that identical moral practices exist in all cultures, allowing us to say that "no known society differs from any other society in its moral practices." Despite the universality of moral practices, such invariance would no more prove the objectivity of morality in these cultures than extreme variability would prove its subjectivity. More fundamental than either subjectivity or objectivity are answers to questions concerning the constitutive marks of morality, the nature of the moral data, so to speak, the way we should understand or represent what occurs in a person who is moral. Instead of mimicking the observational sciences, which seek uniformity and universality as conditions of objective scientific truth, we should apply the Kantian–Copernican Revolution to moral experience in a bolder fashion. First and foremost, we should not fear to face the all too obvious fact that each person is familiar with morality. More than anything else, we are moral creatures who possess the makings of a full theory of morality, hidden, as they are, in the diverse experiences of everyday living.[85] But, like beauty and truth, morality is vulnerable to being confused with other things, precisely because, in its original state, it is confused with other things; this fusion leads us to overlook it.

For one thing, we pass over our own moral activity; we tend to devalue our own reflection and to inhabit a "natural attitude"[86] according to which morality is independent of our thought and experience. And, of course, it is or becomes independent as soon as we leave our experience behind in order to focus on alleged objective morality. In this event, morality becomes alienated, foreign to us; consequently, we have to learn it, to study it in the same way as we approach the calculus which someone else invented with great labor and concentration. Unfortunately, by taking this approach as a start, we find soon enough that what is "out there" exists in the plural. We then have to choose one from among the many possible moralities. The specter of relativism and subjectivism confronts us, and the necessity for sincerity is not long in coming.

But, at this point, our primary question concerns how we can give more substance to the nature of a philosophical basis for justice. It seems obvious that an alternative to empirical foundations is required even in order to have an ethics in the first place. Traditionally, norms of morality have been sought beyond the factual world in order to escape the contingency and arbitrariness of the natural and social worlds, that is, in order to have an *intelligible* basis for ethics. We do not believe, for example, that "might makes right" is a moral principle to be followed in deciding issues of legal, ethical, or political right, even though there are still some vestiges of this principle in use in contemporary societies. But why do we think this? The *historical* answer lies in the gradual evolution of conceptions of rightness and justice, an evolution which is marked by more and more independence of facts. We might say that the Idea of right or justice has gradually revealed itself to historical consciousness, drawing justice away from the facts with which it is originally confused. Likewise, the history of the concept of goodness has progressively revealed a movement away from identification with factual desires. Again, the Idea of the good has gradually taken on a certain autonomy. Although it would obviously be profitable to trace the development and the evolution of non-empirical, normative concepts in law and ethics,[87] my approach here will start with more humble sources: our shared fund of moral knowledge and belief, which, however, is decidedly marked by the historical evolution of ethical consciousness. I am not, of course, claiming that ordinary moral language and concepts are innate, divorced from historical development. My approach, in what follows, relies on common sense, but a common sense which has a history of development and refinement. Instead of starting with a set of allegedly self-evident first principles or with *a priori* truths, I appeal to what is commonly accepted as moral. Obviously, such an appeal is not without danger and needs careful definition if it is not to be misunderstood. First, we must get clear about the rationale for this kind of procedure.

An appeal to common moral experience is not merely an anthropological or sociological enterprise, a survey of what is held and believed by people in general in order, in this way, to determine the contents of morality. This idea must be avoided since it is the route to subjectivism and ethical relativism on the one hand, or to objectivism and ethical absolutism on the other. If we start with the assumption that relativism or absolutism is the necessary backdrop for a discussion of morality, the optimum solution we can expect will be either the morality of sincerity or dogmatic moralism. In other words, if morality is either relative and subjective, or absolute and objective, the searching individual is limited at the outset to falling back, in the last analysis, on what he can believe and embrace for himself or what he must believe and accept because of the authority of the facts. Truth will be limited either to its personal affirmation, made in good faith, or to what must be imposed by dint of the alleged authority of facts. Moral truth will be either subjective or objective. (As we shall see, the major flaw, the fatal weakness, in this approach is the failure to recognize that moral philosophy is irremediably Socratic, a point which I shall emphasize shortly.) But common sense makes no such assumptions; it holds no brief for a particular theory on subjectivism or objectivism; it draws no firm conclusions from the results of anthropology and sociology. Nor is it enlightened, at least not explicitly or consciously, by the history of ethics. Common sense is not a scholarly sense. But if it is not philosophical, it is nonetheless the primary source for philosophical reflection. For, in the last analysis, philosophy does not start anything independently. Philosophy comes on the scene in the midst of an *already constituted moral sense* in order to clarify and order our intuitions and judgments.

Let us now look at how we might isolate morality from the general whole of life as it is lived, using what I have loosely called common sense as a guide. First, the *fact* which we observe in the behavior of someone treating another as an equal is not necessarily a part of what we want to call morality. At most it is that external label, that debased form of the ethical. It is, moreover, only a fact, perhaps one which will not be found in another culture. Second, the verbal formula uttered by that person—for example, that "all men are equal"— is also not what we mean by morality; that, too, is a "fact" which is subject, as we have seen, to objection on other factual grounds (e.g., when equality can be contested in the light of obvious physical or intellectual differences). We begin to get a sense of the morality of that behavior and that utterance only when we determine that the person's behavior flows from one of his deep personal *convictions* about his relations with other people. Moreover, this *conviction* is not based on whim, but is backed up by some tacit or explicit *principle* which can explain that behavior and which, it is important to stress, other people can share, at least potentially.

But two extremes need to be avoided in order to understand the nature of the appeal to common sense. First, we are not saying that morality is absent when no reason or principle can be given for a conviction about how we should behave. Reasons and principles act as guarantors; they provide a rational basis for securing an overall consistency in our moral lives. The intuitive idea is that just as we want to be consistent in our behavior and in our convictions, so too we want our moral reasons and moral principles, to which those convictions relate, to be consistent. Thus, the first extreme to be avoided is the devaluation of our convictions (and this is where the virtue of sincerity comes into its own; by themselves our convictions do not lack moral quality; rather, without the guarantee of their reasonableness, assessed in terms of coherent principles, they are liable to be exaggerated convictions, false perceptions, or misperceptions of our moral sense).

The second extreme to be avoided is the tendency to consider as the linchpin of morality the rational principles which are used to account for our convictions. Morality is not hinged on these principles; to think so is to put the cart before the horse. Morality hinges, rather, on the *experiences* which we have of other people and of ourselves, experiences which are the product not primarily of culture or education but of the free development, in and through culture and education, of our natural powers and capacities.

Understanding morality thusly, we can usefully distinguish three levels in a formal approach to it, keeping in mind that this all depends on experience. First, at the most obvious level, we might say that the *behavior* of "equal treatment" is a mere sign that morality may be present; but in spite of the fact that behavior may be a necessary condition of morality, it is not a sufficient determinant of morality; if it were and if the organism is susceptible in certain circumstances to being conditioned to behave in certain ways, then it is surely conceivable that the achievement of morality is merely a technological problem.[88]

Secondly, we may look upon the *conviction* (assuming there is one) underlying that behavior as the subjective or personal index of a moral person, or at least of a person who aspires to be moral. Of course, if the matter ends there, then we have merely a morality of sincerity; there is at most a congruence between behavior and personal conviction. This level of morality frees one of hypocrisy, and perhaps this is no small achievement.

Thirdly, the reason or *principle* is the ground of the morality of the conviction and of the behavior—ground, not in the sense of origin, but in the sense of *justifying* basis. It is at this third level that we finally begin to attain the highest level of the *formal* grounds of morality—formal, as opposed to existential belief and sentiment—which more often are the chronologically prior data of morality. This level is the most complex of all, perhaps, because it is at this level that conflicts between convictions and forms of behavior must be sorted out and adjusted. All things being equal, a moral person has many reasons and principles to bring together into a coherent whole in order to ground his several convictions and the range of his behavior. This is, needless to say, a great task. For, looked at as a whole, these principles and reasons may be inconsistent at many points. Presumably, everyone's behavior at some time and to some degree is inconsistent, which means, if our budding theory of morality is correct, that the conviction and principles underlying that behavior are also inconsistent. Therefore, something has to give. One of our practices must be abandoned, or one of our principles must be modified or rejected. At least this much seems true if we value consistency. Of course, at some levels, in matters of personal habit, for example, we half-realize our inconsistency yet feel that the effects of the inconsistency are too small or at least sufficiently remote for us to worry over.

One additional comment on sincerity as it bears upon conviction. In our times it often seems that nothing impresses us more in other people than the frank avowal of their firm convictions, and that nothing incites our reproach more readily than their hypocrisy. Because sincerity is the opposite of hypocrisy, it may be tempting to see in it the essence of morality. But the trouble with sincerity is that it can lay no claim to being an ultimate virtue, since it is so clearly compatible with virtually any content whatsoever. Murderers and thieves, as we know, can be as sincere as saints and heroes. They, too, can display that quintessential element of sincerity, a certain "congruence between avowal and actual feeling."[89] More metaphysically, they too can enjoy the status of "being what they are."[90] But obviously we need some criterion to tell us whether what we feel is moral. This means that the morality of sincerity (or conviction) presupposes a material to inform. If that material is the heart of morality, sincerity is merely its outer wrappings.[91]

The complex interplay among behavior, conviction, and principle is a way of denominating the constitutive marks of morality; in a way, these marks establish the content boundaries, the limits, of morality. But it is only when they are taken together that they establish a moral life. (Here I am assuming the argument, to come in the next part, on the way the material or content of morality is established, although the present section has already suggested the crucial role of belief, conviction, sentiment, and judgment.) When we take this conception of a moral theory and apply it to our own lives, we then begin to realize the specific weak points in our principles or the blind spots in our convictions; we may realize, for example, that our firm conviction that racial discrimination is immoral conflicts, say, with our equally firm conviction that minorities should be given preferential treatment over whites in entrance to professional schools or in obtaining employment in certain industries. On their face, these two convictions conflict with each other, and we must, therefore, decide whether we have the resources, in terms of principles, to account for this conflict as only apparent. Until we resolve this conflict one way or another, either by changing our convictions or improving upon our principles, we are bound to live in an unsatisfactory state of moral confusion.

At a more general level, we may often find that our deep convictions about justice conflict with our equally firm beliefs about equality or goodness. And so we must, if we are to retain the value of consistency, examine the principles which support these convictions and undertake revision of them if that seems necessary.

Now, the point of the foregoing remarks on the nature of moral theory is that a moral life in the strict sense is not constituted by merely following rules and conventions (this is only custom) or by conforming one's behavior to received ideas and maxims, not even to the so-called Golden Rule. Nor is it yet fully constituted by translating our firm convictions into congruent behavior. It is true that the latter will yield sincerity, but, as we have seen, sincerity by itself can lay no claim on morality, since it is not able to provide grounds for determining the legitimate content of what we are to be sincere about. Again, the crucial question is: What should one feel and how is that determined? What should one's convictions be? Until these questions are answered satisfactorily, morality is only a possibility. That is, my convictions are only possibly moral. Presumably, everyone has convictions in some abundance; and many of these convictions conflict with other convictions, and, of course, with other people's convictions. Thus, if we wish to have a peaceful, harmonious society, we must examine our reasons and principles to see if we can achieve harmony at this level. For even if we could achieve a complete harmony of our feelings and convictions, this would still not answer the question "Is that moral?" We need to have an assurance which is greater than harmony of feelings and convictions in order to guarantee morality, at least as far as that is possible. Analogously, if all scientists shared the conviction that the world is flat, that would surely say more about scientists than about the world. The objectivity of their convictions is only as good as the reasons, principles, and evidence offered.

The above sketch argues that morality involves three components—behavior, conviction, and principle—such that it is not fully achieved unless all the components are involved. (I have not stressed the point, but in a fuller treatment it would be possible to show that the mere possession of principles which do not correspond to or flow into convictions or behavior—action—cannot properly be called morality. Conversely, behavior alone, or conviction alone, does not merit the name morality. Details aside, morality is triple-stranded, involving thought, feeling, and action.) Nevertheless, it is possible to regard each of these components as separate forms or kinds of morality. I have in fact tended in this direction at times in speaking of the morality of sincerity (or conviction), although I qualify such a morality as being incomplete because it is merely formal. Yet, from a developmental view of the person, it is common to speak of *stages* of morality. These stages are usually distinguished by reference to the diverse *origins* of the morality in question. Thus we can speak of the moralities of authority, of convention, of reward (or reinforcement), and of reciprocity, and, finally, of the morality of principle.[92]

Similarly, it is tempting to regard the three components of morality as actual developmental stages. The morality of behavior would be the first; it is, after all, behavior with which we are most concerned in infants and young children, primarily because they lack both the basis for having any firm convictions of their own and the ability to reason about the corresponding principles. But with age we see definite convictions superseding or even contravening mere behavioral conformity to rules and conventions. And at even later stages children begin to develop rational approaches to their convictions. Obviously, then, one could look upon the components of behavior, conviction, and principle as falling into stages and sequences, even being parallel at times to the moralities of authority and convention.

Yet I prefer not to think of the three components of morality as stages or as having been developed over time more or less naturally within a social setting. This is not because I doubt the alleged facts about development or deny their importance. On the contrary, I believe that the developmental approach to morality is clearly quite important to educational theory and moral training in the family. But I am more concerned with the structure of a moral theory which emphasizes, not the *genesis* of a moral sense as maturation sets in, which is a matter for empirical inquiry, but the structural elements in a fully developed moral creature or, more modestly, in an adult who has undergone a normal development of his intellectual and emotional faculties. This is a philosophical inquiry which social or developmental psychology can never replace.[93]

There is a second reason why I prefer not to regard behavior and conviction as early stages on the way to the morality of principle. Even in mature adults there is a constant dialectic between behavior, conviction, and principle. We frequently conform our behavior to authority and convention not because we are immature or delinquent by comparison to some higher stage of morality, but because we respect custom and tradition in and for themselves. For example, we often do not know the principles which govern our customs and conventions; most often there is simply no occasion to examine our customs, and, in any case, there may be no explanatory principles which are easily accessible. Moreover, many adults sincerely believe that the morality of behavior, which has its source in some authority, contains in itself the principle which explains the grounds for obedience. All this needs to be accounted for.

A third reason is the decisive one for concentrating on structural analysis in moral theory. Without a suitable moral environment to start with, a child will not inevitably pass through the stages of moral development. The reasoning process which slowly moves toward the morality of principle presupposes a context in which distinctions are being made by an adult community according to moral principles which the child is gradually coming to understand. In this sense, a genetic approach to moral development depends upon an already developed moral structure of theory and practice. The model for moral education, therefore, cannot be primarily the developmental facts, but the theoretical structure which pre-exists that development, and upon which that development draws, as upon an invisible environment which silently sustains organic life. This is the arena of moral theory proper. The components of behavior, conviction, and principle are therefore contingently similar to developmental stages, but in fact they are the building blocks of any moral theory for use in structuring moral practice.

This suggests a position on the main dichotomy which has divided the history of Western ethics, the issue over whether reason or feeling should be the proper guide and source of morality. From what has been said already, it would seem that, in terms of the three components of the moral theory advanced, if we associate reason with principle and feeling with conviction, then reason holds primacy over feeling. This would be true if we are thinking of ethics in a formal sense, that is, the abstract principles or reasons which endow feelings or conventions with positive moral worth and, at the same time, serve to justify a certain practice. But if we look upon ethics in a more existential or phenomenological way, that is, if our interest is more in the phenomenon or the experience which gives rise to the moral sense in the first place, then feeling or conviction holds that primary place, since it is clearly closer to experience than reason or principle.

This makes it difficult to take a firm position on the issue. For in the final analysis neither reason nor feeling holds primary place, although we can undoubtedly see how such priorities can be justified in certain historical theories such as stoicism or Epicureanism. But I assume that such theories have acquired their prestige and notoriety because they present the data of ethics from an extreme point of view, one which distorts the comprehensive character of moral experience, which is at once a matter of feeling *and* thought. Even Kant's ethics, in light of at least one prevalent criticism of it, which sees duty as the driving force of the moral life, is noteworthy primarily because it strikes us as failing to do justice to our feelings and convictions about morality. It seems that an ethic which exalts either reason or feeling at the expense of the other is somehow at odds with our experience of their indissoluble union. Showing how and why this is so is perhaps a major task of a sustained and clear focus on justice and goodness in our time. For we have clear examples of tendencies in both directions, tendencies which lead, if left unchecked, either toward an uncaring rationalism or toward a frenetic search for self-satisfaction based on feeling.[94]

B. *Moral Personality and the Priority of Justice.* The theory of morality which I have just sketched out places the burden for deciding the primacy of justice on our actual moral judgments. By itself, no one judgment or principle is decisive in the construction of a moral theory. Instead, it is the totality of judgments and principles, the harmonious relations between all the judgments and all the principles, which gives a moral theory its coherence and truth value. No doubt this totality is never fully achieved, such that we would have a finished ethical system, a moral geometry, which would never be in need of revision. As the world and factual matters change, or as our awareness and comprehension of them increase (or decrease), at least some of our judgments are bound to change as well. Likewise, with time and further experience we more fully appreciate the nature, content, and implications of our moral principles, and we recognize the necessity for change. In this light, then, moral theory, like legal theory—or any theory, for that matter—is a never-finished undertaking. This is only to say that being a moral person is always a *task* for the individual, even, we might say, when all the social conditions for morality are provided by relevant authorities or by just plain luck. It is a peculiarity of being a moral being, a decisive feature of human personhood, that one never gets beyond the need to seek and to practice what Rawls calls "reflective equilibrium."[95] Not that a moral person is always interrogating himself about the kind of judgment a particular practice merits and, in turn, the moral principle which underlies the moral judgment. To think this would be to deprive life of its spontaneity and the habits of mind which normally make thought superfluous to action. Yet being a moral person always involves the *liability* to experience the doubts which make reflection and self-examination a possibility, often a necessity.

The impact of such a conception of moral theory upon the relation between justice and goodness is not straightforwardly obvious, and with good reason. For this conception of a moral theory emphasizes the indispensable role of our actual judgments about moral matters, and this means that reaching a decision on the proper relations between justice and goodness will be initially dependent on people's moral judgments. What are our firm convictions about justice and goodness? Here, however, it must be kept in mind that the answer cannot be given from purely factual information. This would constitute the "anthropological fallacy," the idea that morality is the sum total of people's judgments on goodness and justice. But this is only part of an ethic, at the very most its point of departure, what, in terms of the "constituent marks" of morality just discussed, we could call the morality of behavior. But such a morality is only an abstraction. In reality, neither ethics in general nor justice and goodness in particular originate in anthropology or other factual sciences. The discipline of ethics, the philosophical task, is subsequent,[96] both for the individual and for the group.

We wish to focus here on the nature of moral personality. It is tempting to think, in accordance with the Humean View, that conflict between individuals and groups has its origin in *defects* of the persons involved: ignorance, poor judgment, lack of education, absence of sympathy, etc. According to this view, conflict has its roots in either moral or intellectual failure. Given the existence of conflict, a system of justice is needed in order to mediate, if not to resolve, the manifestations of conflict. But, as Hume might have said, if only human beings had a more extensive sympathy for others, then the need for justice would never have arisen.

At this point we might briefly entertain three questions concerning the idea of a society which is free of conflict. First, is such a society possible? If we assume that behavioral science has the capability of shaping or re-shaping human behavior in accordance with principles of "reinforcement" which systematically extinguish behavior which is antisocial or not in accordance with a certain ideal of human interaction, then a conflict-free society is possible. Achieving such a society is merely a technological problem.

Admittedly, taking such a position will invite much criticism, for it is certainly a highly controversial topic today whether human beings should be subjected to the principles and practices of behavioral engineering. I do not wish to skirt the issue; rather, for the sake of the argument to come, I merely wish to assume that, using such principles, such a society is possible.[97]

The second question is whether such a conflict-free society is desirable. That is, quite apart from the means which might be used to achieve such a society, the question is whether this ideal is desirable. Here, too, I shall merely assume that it is desirable, skirting the vexing issue of the value of individual freedom *vs.* the value of social solidarity and social good in general. I merely assume that, in this classic value-conflict, the value of social cohesion will prevail—not that I necessarily believe that it should prevail.

The third question is the decisive one: and the answer to it reveals, perhaps, the superficiality of the answers to the two previous questions. Is a conflict-free society *conceivable*? By this I mean: given what we know of human nature, of what it means to be a moral creature, is it conceivable that we could ever achieve a conflict-free society? I believe that we must answer this question in the negative. For given what I think we must *mean* by the nature of moral personality, it is not conceivable that we could ever achieve a society in which individuals do not conflict and press claims against one another. And this will result not from defects in the human beings but from the *positive* factors in their makeup. This calls for some explanation.

I assume that by a moral creature we mean a being which is constituted in essence by the capacities or developed abilities to have a sense of justice (i.e., a sense for what is right and wrong) and a sense of goodness (i.e., the ability to live for the achievement of some good). For a being not to have these two abilities (or capacities) is for that being not to belong to the human race.[98]

According to this conception of moral personhood, it is only *natural* for a human being to express and defend his conception of justice on the one hand, and his vision of goodness on the other. Details aside, the inability or incapacity either to have or to express oneself on these matters is an index of inhumanity. For, on the view being presented here, it is not merely a defining property, but the very essence of a moral creature to have these capacities and to *exercise* them.

It is, of course, a fact (as well as a necessity) that societies have a single *concept* of justice, such that justice, always and everywhere, is, to express it most simply, the idea that people are not to be treated on the basis of arbitrary distinctions, that similar cases should be treated similarly, that a proper balance between competing claims to the advantages of social living should be sought. But it is also a fact that in all societies there are different interpretations of the nature and meaning of "arbitrary distinctions," "similar treatment," and a "proper balance." Offhand, there seems to be no way to get beyond these differences in interpretation. The existence of laws and a final court of appeal alone seem to bring disagreement to an end, if then, for obvious practical (if not always moral) considerations.

The essential point is that this continual process of contestation on the nature of justice springs not necessarily from negative factors about individuals or social life, but rather from positive factors in individuals and groups. Conflicts on the meaning of justice are manifestations of the *moral* nature of a human being, and no amount of Humean fantasy can relegate this phenomenon to an inferior, lesser status, as if, given an increase in generosity and "tender regard" for others, the virtue of justice would never have been dreamed of or never have found place in the "catalogue of virtues."

A similar conclusion, with one important difference, can be defended with respect to goodness. Human beings differ on the nature and content of goodness not necessarily because of defects in their judgment, or because of ignorance and other lacks; instead, different conclusions on the nature of goodness spring from the inevitably diverse uses of our rational nature. Moreover, there is no one way to define or conceive of goodness.[99] Thus, unlike justice, there is no one concept of goodness with merely different interpretations of this unique concept.[100] Indeed, though it is imperative to have a unique concept of justice, it is *desirable* to have a heterogeneity of concepts of goodness, for the aims and purposes of the self are themselves heterogeneous.[101]

In light of this last conclusion—namely, the idea that goodness is diversely defined by moral creatures—it becomes evident that we need a prior conception of justice if only to mediate between conceptions of goodness when they conflict. This suggests the priority and independence of justice over goodness. Without this priority and independence, justice would be open to compromise by a single notion of goodness, and this would threaten the free exercise of our moral nature by restricting it *a priori* within arbitrary boundaries.

From this it can be seen that far from being an expression of a minimal level of morality, justice is at least the equal of goodness on the scale of morality. If this is not generally recognized, it is because particular and restricted conceptions of goodness have generally been given a prior place in moral theory and ethical systems, leaving justice either to be viewed as the mere means to achieve or maximize the good, or to be diverted from its true moral path to be degraded into a truncated end in itself. In this connection, it is noteworthy that the general failure in moral theory in the past to *separate* justice and goodness for *logical* purposes has given impetus to the tendency in modern jurisprudence to *divorce* justice from goodness for *practical* purposes, leading to such modern antinomies as those of law and morality, justice and goodness, which were touched on in the first section of this essay. This suggests that if legal theory in modern society is to regain the place it once enjoyed in the classic theories of society and morality, it will have to reforge its links with philosophy and, in particular, understand itself once again as a branch of moral theory.

NOTES

1. As subsequent argument below will show, even works which are very positive in regard to the moral nature or level of justice do not entirely escape this criticism. Indeed, even John Rawls's *A Theory of Justice* (Cambridge: Harvard University Press, 1971) is subject to an at least mild version of this critique of justice in the modern period.
2. See, e.g., *An Enquiry Concerning the Principles of Morals*, ed. L. A. Selby-Bigge (Oxford: Clarendon, 1894).
3. Among jurists, see, e.g., H. L. A. Hart, *The Concept of Law* (Oxford: Clarendon, 1961), pp. 189–95.
4. Among recent and noted philosophers on justice, see, e.g., Rawls, *Theory of Justice*, pp. 126–30.
5. Hume, *Enquiry*, p. 184.
6. Presumably, even the intellectual virtue of truth (or, more properly, the moral virtue of honesty) would be unnecessary if we could imagine, à la Hume, a generosity and a selflessness so extensive in human beings that there would never be occasion to lie or to deceive.
7. See *Enquiry*, pp. 183–89.
8. That Hume did not regard the morality of justice as deriving from positive factors in human nature can be seen in his assertion that it is an artifice, a convention. See *A Treatise of Human Nature*, ed. L. A. Selby-Bigge (Oxford: Clarendon, 1888), pp. 484–501.
9. This is, I take it, the general view of the need for justice defended by Hart, *Concept of Law*, and Rawls, *Theory of Justice*. But, as we shall see, Rawls's position is somewhat ambiguous, perhaps inconsistent.
10. As one example of a treatment of justice founded on a wide-ranging philosophy of the person, see Leonard Feldstein's "Toward Integrity and Wisdom: Justice as Grounding Personal Harmony," chap. 4 of this volume.
11. Nicholas Rescher, *Unselfishness: The Role of the Vicarious Affects in Moral Philosophy and Social Theory* (Pittsburgh: The University of Pittsburgh Press, 1975), p. 26.
12. Ibid., p. 72.
13. My interpretation of Hume tends to this conclusion. In jurisprudence Oliver Wendell Holmes's "The Path of the Law," *Collected Legal Papers* (New York: Harcourt, Brace, 1921), pp. 167–202, did much to set the tone for generations of students of the law. See also Learned Hand, *The Bill of Rights* (New York: Atheneum, 1968) and D. A. J. Richards' comments on Justice Hand in "Reverse Discrimination and Compensatory Justice: Constitutional and Moral Theory," chap. 6 of this volume, note 1 and accompanying text.
14. It may be said with little risk of exaggeration that Thrasymachus' view that justice is simply the interest of the stronger, or the thesis that "might makes right," is defended in some form or another in every age. See Plato, *Republic*, 336B–347E.

15. My assumption is that, in one way or another, all the essays in this volume make a contribution to this vast subject.

16. The idea of justice as a "civic virtue" is another way of expressing the minimal moral content of justice. Thus, divorced as it usually is from substantive moral theory, "civics" is understood as an extensive exercise in detailing what is expected of persons as citizens of a given state, what they owe to each other in public as a matter of constitutional and political policy, or as a matter of cultural practice. According to this view, morality is primarily a matter which concerns a person's private life, and, in any case, is not defined by courts or legislatures.

17. See, e.g., Richard McKeon, "Justice and Equality," in *Nomos VI: Justice*, edd. C. J. Friedrich and J. W. Chapman (New York: Aldine-Atherton, 1963), pp. 44–61.

18. What Rawls says of justice can probably be said just as well of equality. That is, Rawls argues that there is one *concept* of justice, presumably valid for all societies merely by virtue of the nature of the concept itself. At the same time there are many *conceptions* of justice, that is, many different interpretations of the same concept. In this sense, what I am saying of equality could be called a conception of equality, the reason being that, although the concept of equality is pervasive of the concept of justice, a particular conception of equality may not pervade some conceptions of justice. Cf. *Theory of Justice*, pp. 5–6.

19. Nietzsche is an obvious example of an exception. See his criticism of equality in *Beyond Good and Evil* (London: Allen & Unwin, 1911), sec. 44. Exceptions such as Nietzsche are, of course, fascinating precisely because they stand out against a background which is largely taken for granted.

20. McKeon, "Justice and Equality," p. 45.

21. It is evident that current debates on equal racial, sexual, or ethnic representation on, e.g., university faculties, are examples of attempts to extend the boundaries of equality.

22. A conception of justice which bases itself on the maxim "to each the same thing" or on some form of egalitarianism may weaken itself precisely because of an exaggerated reliance on the notion of equality in defining justice. See e.g., Chaim Perelman, *The Idea of Justice and the Problem of Argument*, trans. John Petrie (London: Routledge & Kegan Paul, 1963), pp. 17–18.

23. The seeming formalism of justice, however, does not necessarily support an external origin divorced from the person. See part A of the third section.

24. Holmes, "The Path of the Law."

25. Ibid., p. 170.

26. Ibid., p. 167.

27. It is only fair to point out that Holmes was speaking in this lecture to a group of law students.

28. For a general approach to sociality along these lines, see, for example, Werner Stark, *The Social Bond: An Investigation into the Bases of Law-abidingness. I. Antecedents of the Social Bond: The Phylogeny of Sociality* (New York: Fordham University Press, 1976). See also Rawls, *Theory of Justice*, pp. 458ff.

29. For an example of the kind of philosophy of the person here envisioned, see Leonard Feldstein, *Homo Quaerens: The Seeker and the Sought; Method Become Ontology* (New York: Fordham University Press, 1978).

30. Iris Murdoch, *The Sovereignty of Good* (New York: Schocken, 1971), pp. 47–48, 77ff.

31. For an application of this idea to the theory of law and justice, see, e.g.,

Roberto Mangabeira Unger, *Knowledge and Politics* (New York: Free Press, 1975) and *Law in Modern Society* (New York: Free Press, 1976).

32. See, e.g., Lionel Trilling, *Sincerity and Authenticity* (Cambridge: Harvard University Press, 1972).

33. On the notion of sincerity, see Rawls, *Theory of Justice*, pp. 519ff.

34. See, in general, Murdoch's *Sovereignty of Good*.

35. See Stark, *Social Bond*, for a discussion of the distinction between civilization and culture. Though the latter admits of retrogressions (in morals, ideas, values, etc.), the former, conceived of in terms of things and inventions, generally shows a steady progress.

36. 347 U. S. 483 (1954).

37. One naturally thinks of the continuing efforts to combat not only racism, but also sexism and discrimination in housing, employment, or on account of sexual preference, age, etc.

38. See Rescher, *Unselfishness*.

39. This, of course, is an unbalanced view since individual rights by no means exhaust the concept of the right.

40. See *Leviathan*, Part I, chap. 14.

41. For a contemporary view of sociality along quasi-Hobbesian lines, see Stark, *Social Bond*.

42. Murdock, *Sovereignty of Good*.

43. See Rawls, *Theory of Justice*, pp. 446–52.

44. One might say that properly associating the right and the good was the underlying ethical problem in Jean-Paul Sartre's *Being and Nothingness* (New York: Washington Square, 1966), esp. pp. 795–98.

45. Rawls, *Theory of Justice*, p. 281.

46. Rescher, *Unselfishness*.

47. Justice is more apt to be thought of as a process, a never-ending quest, whereas goodness is conceived as instantaneously experienced substance. There are no courts of goodness complementing the "halls of justice."

48. *Treatise*, pp. 494–95. This is what I call the "science fiction" in Hume's criticism of justice. That is, judged by the standards of another world and a different human nature from the one we know, justice is inferior, a lesser virtue.

49. Ibid., p. 495; emphasis deleted. This is the crucial part of the Humean View which I contest in the third section.

50. Ibid., p. 496.

51. See Rawls's reliance on Hume in his discussion of "the circumstances of justice" in *Theory of Justice*, pp. 126–30.

52. Here I follow Robert Tucker, "Marx and Distributive Justice," in *Nomos VI: Justice*, edd. Friedrich & Chapman, pp. 306–25.

53. Ibid.

54. Ibid., p. 313.

55. Ibid., p. 310.

56. For a critique of Rawls's *Theory of Justice* along these lines, see Milton Fisk, "History and Reason in Rawls' Moral Theory," in *Reading Rawls: Critical Essays on Rawls' A THEORY OF JUSTICE*, ed. Norman Daniels (New York: Basic Books, 1975), pp. 53–80.

57. *Pensées*, no. 277.

58. Cf. Brand Blanshard, *Reason and Goodness* (London: Allen & Unwin, 1961).

59. See Trilling, *Sincerity and Authenticity*, p. 2.

60. See Blanshard, *Reason and Goodness*.

61. Part III, "Ends," is especially relevant to the theory of goodness in relation to justice. See also Rawls, "Fairness to Goodness," *The Philosophical Review*, 84 (1975), 536–54.

62. See my "Freedom from the Good," in *Freedom and Value*, ed. Robert Johann (New York: Fordham University Press, 1976), pp. 161–86.

63. 7th ed. (Chicago: The University of Chicago Press, 1907; reissued 1962).

64. *The Liberal Theory of Justice: A Critical Examination of the Principal Doctrines of* A THEORY OF JUSTICE *by John Rawls* (Oxford: Clarendon, 1973).

65. *Reading Rawls*.

66. See *Theory of Justice*, pp. 446–52.

67. I discuss this theme in "Freedom from the Good."

68. But see the preface to *Theory of Justice*, p. x, where Rawls states that it was only as a result of criticism which he received of a draft version of the book that "it seemed necessary to include a theory of the good."

69. See ibid., pp. 17–22.

70. Ibid., p. 584.

71. For the sense in which Rawls conceives of his theory as deontological, see ibid., p. 30.

72. Rawls, ibid., emphasizes the sense of deontology in which the right does not serve to maximize the good. This expresses his opposition to utilitarianism.

73. See ibid., pp. 446–52.

74. Rawls calls this the problem of "congruence" between independently defined notions of justice and goodness. See ibid., pp. 395ff.

75. *Sovereignty of Good*.

76. See Rawls, *Theory of Justice*, p. 30.

77. See, e.g., ibid., pp. 330–31.

78. Ibid., p. 30.

79. The problem of establishing the proper relationship between the right and the good is a main topic of other articles in this volume, especially chaps. 1, 3, 5, and 6.

80. See, e.g., Fisk, "History and Reason in Rawls' Moral Theory."

81. See Robert Nozick, *Anarchy, State, and Utopia* (New York: Basic Books, 1974).

82. See note 51.

83. See, in general, the position on the priority and sovereignty of liberty in Nozick, *Anarchy, State, and Utopia*.

84. See Rawls's discussion of "the principle of perfection" in *Theory of Justice*, pp. 325–32. But cf. Robert Johann's article, "Rationality, Justice, and Dominant Ends," chap. 1 of this volume.

85. The idea is that morality develops out of actual judgments and the reflective and critical assessment of them. For indications on the nature of Rawls's moral theory, see *Theory of Justice*, pp. 46–53.

86. The reference is to Edmund Husserl's phenomenology. See, for example, his *The Idea of Phenomenology* (The Hague: Nijhoff, 1964).

87. The history of ethics in general is double-stranded. On the one hand, theories emphasize the actual desires and definitions of good which people have typically had. This is the empirical strand. On the other hand, theories emphasize the reasons and principles of morality which are more or less independent of actual desires and conceptions of the good. This is the rationalist strand. In what

follows, I suggest a mean between these extremes, extremes which are also found in the law in the forms of legal positivism and some versions of natural law.

88. See, e.g., B. F. Skinner, *Beyond Freedom and Dignity* (New York: Knopf, 1971).

89. Trilling, *Sincerity and Authenticity*, p. 2.

90. See Sartre, *Being and Nothingness*, pp. 96–112.

91. In Sartre's critique of sincerity, ibid., it is allegedly a virtue of content, an ideal of "being."

92. See, e.g., Rawls, *A Theory of Justice*, pp. 453–79. See also Jean Piaget, *The Moral Judgment of the Child*, trans. Marjorie Gabain (London: Kegan Paul, Trench, Trübner, 1932) and Lawrence Kohlberg, "Stage and Sequence: The Cognitive-Developmental Approach to Socialization," in *Handbook of Socialization Theory and Research*, ed. D. A. Goslin (Chicago: Rand McNally, 1969), pp. 347–480.

93. See Rawls's discussion of some differences between Kohlberg's view and his own position in *Theory of Justice*, pp. 461n8, 490–96.

94. In a certain sense, Part I of ibid. can be interpreted as rationalistic; Part III exhibits a greater concern for sentiment, emotion, and will.

95. See ibid., pp. 46–53. In this respect, what Isaiah Berlin says of freedom can be applied to morality in general: "[o]ne of the things that Dostoevsky's celebrated fable of the Grand Inquisitor in *The Brothers Karamazov* is designed to show is precisely that paternalism can provide the conditions of freedom, yet without freedom itself" (*Four Essays on Liberty* [Oxford: Oxford University Press, 1969], p. lv).

96. This paraphrases what Alexander M. Bickel said of legal reasoning in relation to the political process, for which he had an enormous respect. Cf. *The Morality of Consent* (New Haven & London: Yale University Press, 1975), p. 29: "for in its initial process of law formation the Court is not under the discipline of the political process. Neither the Court nor its principles directly originate there. The discipline is subsequent."

97. See, in general, B. F. Skinner, *Beyond Freedom and Dignity*.

98. I follow Rawls here. See *Theory of Justice*, pp. 504–12.

99. See Kelbley, "Freedom from the Good."

100. See Rawls, *Theory of Justice*, pp. 446–52.

101. Ibid.

III
JUSTICE
AND THE
SCIENCES

8

Sociology and Social Philosophy:
The Special Case of John Rawls's
Theory of Justice

JAMES R. KELLY

Fordham University

SOCIOLOGISTS HAVE CLASSICALLY ARGUED that they should study the "real" and eschew any explicit incorporation of moral theory into their sociological work. The gathering of facts and the evaluating of them are two distinct operations, it is commonly argued. Following Max Weber, a detached objectivity is described as the vocation and special professional calling of the social scientist. Many argue that any blending of sociology and social philosophy would corrupt this professional responsibility. But John Rawls's *A Theory of Justice* challenges this intellectual division of labor into analytic and evaluative roles in two ways. First, Rawls argues that a theory of justice significantly depends on the theories and data of the social sciences. Secondly, his notion of justice as fairness explicitly incorporates as methodological devices the transcultural objectivity and impartiality which is said by sociologists to be at the heart of their own methodological commitment. This essay does not directly argue that social scientists should adopt Rawls's specific moral philosophy but, more weakly, suggests that an explicit acceptance of Rawls's *A Theory of Justice* would not lessen the sociologist's responsibility to be objective and would leave undiminished the social scientist's search for empirical regularities. Because of Rawls's explicitly weak assumptions, his methodological devices which seek to maximize transcultural objectivity, and his incorporation of social science perspectives and data, his work represents a special challenge to social scientists.

SOCIAL SCIENCE AND PHILOSOPHY

Colleges and universities have separate and distinct departments of philosophy and social science. The latter, to concentrate on them in general and on sociology in particular, are generally subdivided among the disciplines of sociology, economics, political science, and history. Each discipline has its distinctive professional organizations, its separate journals, and its yearly convention, and ordinarily there is only sporadic and *ad hoc* contact between the disciplines.[1] When asked by interested outsiders to describe their work, sociologists generally present themselves as gatherers of facts and constructors of models of society which can be empirically validated. Social philosophers in describing their work are likely to explain that they critically reflect on the data yielded by social scientists and others in terms approximating the three ultimate Kantian questions: What can we know? What can we hope for? What should we do? The social philosopher might say that he deals with ultimate questions: the ground of human aspiration and the meaning of community. Indeed, one can make a strong and persuasive case for the existing structural and psychological separation of sociology and social philosophy. Far more than academic inertia accounts for it.

For their part, many sociologists are content with their separation from social philosophy.[2] Some emphasize their intellectual liberation from what all too often seems to them to be the empirically irreconcilable and therefore sterile conflicts of philosophy. Freed from philosophical abstraction, they argue, the sociologist can carefully define and operationalize his terms, formulate his hypotheses, and determine whether, or to what degree, these hypotheses are empirically validated. The test of scientific truth, they are likely to say, lies finally in the data themselves, "when nature, however stretched out on the rack, still has a chance to say 'No' to our hypotheses."[3]

Most sociologists, then, emphasize the criterion of empirical validity and attempt to incorporate in their analyses the value-freedom advocated by Max Weber.[4] As teacher and researcher, the social scientist, Weber insisted, must differentiate the role of scientist from that of advocate and should professionally insist on the distinction between observing and evaluating. To be sure, it is readily conceded that the sociologist is not a man without personal conviction or even bias, but the intent of his scientific work, it is said, must be the discovery of objective generalizations which, ideally, would be similarly discovered and analyzed by another scholar, even one of contrary moral and political convictions, in that scholar's professional role as social scientist. Weber admits, of course, that the attempted value-free stance of the social scientist is a metascientific moral choice, which in turn cannot be justified by science alone. He would also concede that the value-freedom of the sociologist is more a regulative norm than a common achievement in the social sciences.

From the philosophical side, the separation of disciplines can be made to appear equally congenial. The moral philosopher can limit his inquiry to an analysis of the grounds and justifications for knowledge and human purposes. What do we mean, the philosopher might ask, by knowing? By valuing? By doing? Indeed, what do we mean by meaning? The persistent danger, of course, is that while probing ultimate questions philosophy might become exclusively a reflection on philosophical categories themselves. As Karl Popper has observed, when philosophy is isolated from the work of other disciplines it can easily succumb to a trivial formalism.[5]

Still, the moral philosopher can take another tack which, while incorporating the distinction between social science and social philosophy, also guards against a possible formalism. Inspecting the empirical data gathered by the social sciences, the moral philosopher might reflect on the data's significance for human knowledge and for purposive action. He might reflect, for example, on the amount of poverty empirically found to exist in a given society and then critically speculate on the regnant cultural beliefs—perhaps in a Darwin-like efficiency—which legitimate the economic patternings associated with the gathered facts about poverty. At first glance this solution—the moral philosopher's reflecting on social science data—seems to respect the modern division of labor between the disciplines, allowing the sociologist to pursue a value-free objectivity (in the example above, gathering the facts about poverty) and the moral philosopher to analyze critically the legitimating cultural ideas and ideals and their degree of philosophical justification. But the innocent simplicity of this division of labor is misleading and overlooks difficulties deeper than those of mere logistics and interdisciplinary good will. To assess adequately the conclusions of research, the moral philosopher must know something of the methodology of research. Within sociology no sociological study stands unchallenged.[6] Lest the moral philosopher be accused of an arbitrary and self-serving selection from the many streams of social science, he should be able to justify both his selection and his interpretation of data.

Nor in practice does the division of labor between sociology and social philosophy work well for the sociologist. Indeed, the non-sociologist might be surprised by the frequency of explicit moral valuations found even in the works of those social theorists who publicly emphasize both the need and the possibility of objectivity in the social sciences.[7] The foremost American theorist once observed that social theory involves "a kind of involvement in subtle combinations of diagnostic and evaluative judgment which multiplies the difficulties of clear and objective statement."[8]

These difficulties should not be minimized. The blunt fact is that there is no one "orthodox" sociological theory or even a basic social science methodology. And this has been true of sociology for a relatively long time. In 1932 Earle Edward Eubank attempted to find the chief concepts used by the leading theoreticians of his generation.[9] His universe of investigation was eight introductory or general volumes of sociology, ranging in dates from 1896 to 1925 and bearing the names of ten prominent sociologists, nine of them past presidents of the American Sociological Society. "Probably no proportionate group of equally authoritative voices," Eubank observed, "could be found within the present or past ranks of sociology. Here if anywhere we might expect to learn what are the basic concepts of our science."[10] But to his dismay Eubank found a confusion of concepts in the field. Indeed, he thought the fundamental disagreements among the authors so great that he surmised that "a casual reader would be justified in failing to recognize them as dealing with the same subject matter."[11] As others have done, Eubank optimistically attributed this ambiguity of language and concept to the discipline's youth. But some recent commentators have skeptically wondered if "youth" is indeed the core of the problem. Robert W. Friedrichs,[12] for example, has expressed serious doubt whether a discipline so intimately connected with human values could ever achieve any unanimity on basic theoretical models which inevitably involve psychological and teleological assumptions.

The point can be made another way. In his presidential address delivered at the annual meeting of the American Sociological Association in 1975, Lewis Coser criticized some recent emphases in sociology (in particular, ethnomethodology and the primacy of seeking precise measurement even at the risk of losing sight of substantive issues) for ignoring the "centrality of power in social interaction" and for refusing "to undertake research that would indicate the extent to which our lives are affected by the socioeconomic context in which they are embedded."[13] Along similar lines, a recent survey of teachers of sociology found that many were implicitly following President Coser's advice and that, compared to other faculty, sociology teachers were far more likely to adopt as a teaching goal the "critical evaluation of society."[14] The pertinent questions, of course, are: What social philosophy were the sociologists themselves using, and with what critical sophistication were they transmitting it to their students? Obviously, when social science directly confronts questions of power, the line between analysis and evaluation is even more likely to be blurred. When other sociologists are politically upset by the social policy inferences of these studies, they are likely to point out, as Robert Nisbet recently did, that the sociological emperor is not as fully clothed as he thinks. "The blunt fact," Nisbet complained, "is that social scientists know very very little."[15]

Nor can the sociologist entirely escape these difficulties by the simple strategem of making explicit his implicit philosophical and political values, as suggested by the economist Gunnar Myrdal[16] and the sociologists Alvin W. Gouldner[17] and Robert W. Friedrichs.[18] If the social scientist merely explicitly states that he personally favors, for example, "equality" or "liberty" or "justice," he actually contributes very little substantive help to his reader's ability to evaluate his analysis or to judge the policy implications of the data. The simple affirmation of a value cannot help the reader (or the author!) to sort out the pragmatic relationship between conflicting values, such as between the liberty of the employee and the liberty of the entrepreneur, or between economic equality and industrial efficiency.

Clearly, the present separation of sociology and moral philosophy leaves each discipline with grave difficulties. The moral philosopher is vulnerable to the charge of formalism, or if he explicitly uses social science data and interpretations, he can be charged with a tendentious and *ad hoc* selection from divergent social science sources of interpretation and data. Similarly, the sociologist can often be criticized for an uncritical blending of social philosophy with social science theory and for frequently indulging in ungrounded social commentary. I will argue that it will be especially instructive for sociologists and moral philosophers to pay close attention to John Rawls's recent work in moral philosophy in which he consciously draws on the social sciences. The work provides a common intellectual ground for both disciplines. Indeed, in his conception of "justice as fairness" Rawls explicitly links social science and moral philosophy.[19] A theory of justice, he writes, depends on a theory of society.[20] More specifically, the choice of the principles of justice, he writes, presupposes a certain theory of social institutions. By institutions Rawls means the prevailing political, economic, educational, and familial patterns which most directly and powerfully shape a person's life and his or her life chances.[21] More than any other discipline sociology has emphasized the overriding significance of social organization, which, by mediating culture, significantly determines the beliefs, values, and ego-ideals of individuals. When, in his reversal of Hegel, Marx wrote that it was not the consciousness of men which determined their consciousness, he was expressing the emphasis of most sociologists, conservative as well as radical. Nisbet, for example, in his *The Sociological Tradition*[22] argues that sociology, as a self-conscious discipline, emerged as part of the early-nineteenth-century intellectual revolt against an ascendant post-medieval individualistic rationalism in which institutions and traditions were perceived as unnecessary barriers to rational development and authentic self-assertion. Sociology was an intellectual counterpart, Nisbet writes, of "the reaction of traditionalism against analytic reason; of communalism against individualism; and of the non-rational against the purely rational."[23] The moral philosopher Rawls shares this fundamental sociological perspective, which, as we have said, emphasizes the overriding significance of social institutions as crucial determinants of personality and life chances. "The basic structure [of society] is the primary subject of justice," Rawls writes, "because its effects are so profound and present from the start. . . . the institutions of society . . . affect men's initial chances in life."[24] Rawls's work on justice, then, is heavily influenced by the perspective of sociology.[25] Informing his analysis throughout is the conviction common to sociologists that the social environment shapes the individual to a degree which most members of a culture simply do not realize, at least thematically.

Though he is obviously influenced by a sociological perspective, Rawls's purpose is to do moral philosophy.[26] In *A Theory of Justice* he tries to ground philosophically a theory of social justice which orders both sociological data about societal patterns and our (the readers') moral intuitions about how these major institutions *ought* to be patterned if we are appropriately to call them just. Without being too misleading, we can perhaps best understand in a preliminary way Rawls's conception of justice as fairness by simply observing that what many people in American society commonly, but without reflection, call "just" Rawls tries to make us see as morally arbitrary. Personal success and failure are not as neatly linked to moral character as common judgment assumes. Even character, Rawls writes, depends in large part upon fortunate family and social circumstances for which the individual can claim no personal moral credit.[27] Gifts of nature, such as birth into a prosperous and educated family, Rawls writes, are not morally earned. Also morally arbitrary, Rawls says, are the large differentials in wealth and power which are historically associated with both genetic and historical privilege. Genetic differences and historical privilege become moral facts only when they are defined (implicitly or explicitly) in terms of the way the benefits and obligations of society are differentially shared. So, we must ask, what are the legitimate social differentials of wealth and power which are associated with varying genetic endowments and historical good fortune? The question of justice seems at least as difficult as the analogous one asked by Pilate. Minimally, the question of justice comprises two fundamental problems: First, how do we reconcile seemingly contradictory moral principles? For example, how can we objectively decide between the Marxist principle "to each according to his need" and the capitalist "to each according to his merit"? As principles, both seem to have intellectual and moral merit, and there seems to be no objective way of establishing, in the abstract at least, a common agreement between the choice of principles. If the first fundamental difficulty confronting a theory of justice is the choice of principles and their hierarchical arrangement, the second is that of objectivity. Ironically, this difficulty arises from the very sociological perspective which informs Rawls's theory. For example, Marx argued that all regnant conceptions of social justice must inevitably reflect vested class interest. One could not, he taught, mentally escape the economic determinism inherent in class privilege. (According to Marx, the proletariat, the source of surplus value and the class without any singular vested interest, escaped this determinism, as, inconsistently, Marx himself did. But these arguments are convincing only to classical Marxists.) The bourgeoisie and the successful must see the world through bourgeois eyes. Claims of justice are simply intellectualized defenses of privilege. Even a non-Marxist sociology of knowledge strongly suggests that on significant issues, which inevitably involve self-interest, men are extremely unlikely to transcend their own limited social experiences and cultural presuppositions. To be sure, the sociology of knowledge has never been able to suggest an Archimedean point safely anchoring the observer against a massive cultural relativism.[28]

Rawls's attempt to dislodge moral judgment from the likely bias of social privilege involves the mental stratagems of the "original position" and the "veil of ignorance." Like the hypothetical "state of nature" found in earlier social contract theorists such as Hobbes, Rousseau, and Locke, the original position does not exist historically. Intellectually residing in the original position involves our imaginative conception of ourselves as constitutors of both the social institutions and the underlying regulative principles behind the distribution of wealth and power in society. In the original position we choose our institutional patterns. But we choose these patterns and their allocative principles without any personal knowledge about where the genetic, historical, and social lottery will place *us*. We do this hypothetically, of course. But here hypothetically also means with all earnestness. In the original position we mentally constrain ourselves toward disinterestedness and impartiality deliberately assuming what Rawls calls a "veil of ignorance." Behind it we must design a society and settle on the distribution of rewards and duties without knowing where we will be placed within any historical society. In the original position, however, the laws of economics, sociology, and psychology are known, for no viable moral position could rationally be pursued which contradicted the knowledge of man and society contained within the social sciences. But behind the veil of ignorance we would not know ourselves personally, that is, our genetic and historical fate. In such circumstances rational men would, Rawls writes, choose (and here we should adopt in thought the imaginative fictions of the original position and the veil of ignorance) to secure basic liberties and the guarantee of the primary social goods. A few words of explanation about both putative rational choices are necessary.

In the original position, again, we do not know what personal beliefs or convictions we will have. The veil of ignorance withholds any personal knowledge from us. Thus we mentally constrain ourselves to exist in a state of complete impartiality and objectivity. Hypothetically ignorant of what beliefs and convictions they might eventually come to possess, Rawls argues, the first principle which rational men would select in the original position is one which would protect their future convictions by securing the widest possible liberty of conscience and action: "Each person," the first principle of justice as fairness states, "is to have an equal right to the most extensive total system of equal basic liberties compatible with a similar system of liberty for all." By liberty Rawls means freedom of conscience, expression, and assembly. Clearly, these liberties are central to the possibility of anyone's moral development. No matter what particular beliefs or plans we historically come to elect, we would rationally want to ensure the personal freedom to adhere to them. If we are to value our convictions and our beliefs, we would not gamble with them in the original position. Thus, Rawls says that the principle of liberty would be serially fixed in the original position, that is, it would be (and thus *ought* to be in the present) protected in the original position against suspensions of liberty made to advance the prosperity of the many.[29] Rawls explains that in the original position the principle of equal liberty would be ranked serially prior to the principle regulating economic and social inequalities. (A serial or lexical order is an "order which requires us to satisfy the first principle in the ordering before we can move on to the second. . . .") There are two fundamental reasons for this serial ordering of principles, the first of which stems from the perception that these basic freedoms are intrinsic to the possibility of our moral development and the achievement of a personal identity. Without some degree of freedom of conscience, no order of personal commitment is possible. The second reason derives from the cautious wisdom that, in the name of material benevolence, political powers have frequently sought to justify the suppression of "inefficient" liberties.

After they have secured their basic liberties, Rawls says that rational men behind the veil of ignorance would choose the "maximin" principle of economic distribution. Since in the original position no one would know where the genetic and social lottery might place him, rational persons would try to minimize their worst possible outcomes in terms of economic and social patterns. In other words, they would seek to arrange society in such a way that they would minimize the consequences of their being assigned their societal location even by their worst enemies! In justice as fairness the person is maximally protected against the chance results of genetics and history. Rawls writes that in the original position the second principle chosen would be the following:

> Social and economic inequalities are to be arranged so that they are both: (a) to the greatest benefit of the least advantaged, consistent with the just savings principle, and (b) attached to offices and positions open to all under conditions of fair equality of opportunity [p. 302].

As Rawls explains, these principles would rule out the common justification that the hardships of some are always offset by a greater good in the aggregate. It may be expedient, Rawls declares, but it is not just that some should have less in order that others may prosper. But, he argues, there is no injustice in the greater benefits earned by a few provided the situation of other persons not so fortunate is thereby improved. From the vantage point of the original position, differentials in power and income appear rational when they benefit the least advantaged. Rawls argues that in the original position—and whenever we choose to judge from that moral vantage point—rational persons would reject an absolute egalitarianism and would agree to differentials in wealth and power when those differentials are recognized as making society better for all, especially the least favored in terms of socially valued skills or social status. Those differentials in income, power, and status found to be necessary to motivate people to develop difficult skills, to undergo rigorous training, or to accept positions of great and risky responsibility are justified from the perspective of the original position if they redound to the betterment of others, especially the most disadvantaged. But to be justified these social and economic differences would have to be associated empirically with an increase in the primary social goods of all, especially the least advantaged. In justice as fairness, genetic and historical advantages could be justified insofar as they are empirically related to the good of all, and not merely as they redound to the personal benefit of the genetically or historically privileged. This moral intuition, which relates individual talent and privilege to the common good, is formulated by Rawls as the "difference principle," which is, in effect, the second principle cited earlier.

Rawls himself is not specific on the mechanics of the economic redistribution which is inherent in his conception of the difference principle, but, given his serial ordering of liberty in justice as fairness, one can suppose that the mechanics of redistribution should involve as little bureaucratic and political interference as possible. Insofar as they are redistributionist without necessarily interfering with personal liberty, policies such as a negative income tax, guaranteed employment, wage and housing subsidies, and national health insurance are devices congruent with Rawls's conception of justice. Many critics of Rawls too quickly equate his difference principle with an attendant centralization of government, which, it is argued, would endanger personal liberty and initiative. But these are questions of strategies and political imagination. Critics of Rawls should at least discuss the possibility of transfer schemes—such as lower sales tax, a negative income tax, and wage subsidies—which might require no more, and in some cases, less bureaucracy and government growth than currently exists. And, of course, a central question is the moral one: What is a just distribution of primary social goods?[30] Though Rawls's principles would, if followed, lead to more egalitarian patterns of income and power, he does not explicitly adopt any specific political ideology and readily concedes that it is not possible to determine in an *a priori* way whether socialism or a private property system, or what mixture of both, is most congruent with the principles of justice.

Before I relate Rawls's theory of justice and sociology more directly, one pertinent critique of his reworking of social contract theory should be mentioned. Many sociologists have severely criticized the social contract tradition by skeptically wondering how the assumptions of the mental fictions of rational and mutually disinterested individuals (in the state of nature or, in Rawls's terminology, in the original position) could possibly lead to a grounding of the more complex notions of community.[31] But an irony of Rawls's reworking of the social contract tradition is that his difference principle is similar to organicist social theories which emphasize "society" rather than the "individual." The view that social facts—such as role expectations—are not reducible to individual facts is usually called a type of "holism" which, in its extreme forms, relies on biological, organic analogies.[32] Since no account of the individual parts taken discretely would deliver an adequate description of the whole, the organism is said to be "more than the sum of its parts." So too, it is argued analogously, the acts of individuals are suitably intelligible only when viewed as the acts of individuals in their roles which, interrelated, constitute a social system.[33] Holistic organicism vigorously distinguishes the unity of a society from a merely mechanical unity and, in turn, places great stress on history as the proper mode of social explanation. As Benn observes, mechanical wholes can be understood if they are reduced to their smallest constituent parts, which conform in their behavior to general laws from which the varying behavior of the aggregates can be deduced. A social whole, on the contrary, is *sui generis*, to be understood not by analysis but by studying it *as* a developing whole.[34] Thus in the tradition of social holism, history is the legitimate mode of sociological inquiry.[35]

In light of the above criticism of a contract view of society, the fact that the difference principle occupies a key place in Rawls's development of this view is instructive. Initially some might be tempted to dismiss Rawls's conception outright on the ground that it *must* fall victim to the classic objection to contract theory: namely, that mentally to place man in an asocial state of nature in the hope of thereby comprehending better his real purposes in society is a radical philosophical error. Such a construct, it is soundly argued, abstracts "man" from the only context in which he could be human. But these general criticisms of social contract theory do not snugly apply to Rawls's theory of justice. Though his original position is a device calculated to constrain the investigator to emphasize the freedom and autonomy which are associated with the term "human," the difference principle incorporates the moral impulse toward community which is latent in organicist conceptions. Indeed, the theoretical elegance of Rawls's conception is, at least partially, due to his effort to combine the personal autonomy of morality (his first principle) with the insight of organicist assumptions (the difference principle). Regarding these general critiques of any approach resembling the artificial state of nature assumptions of classic social contract theory, two considerations are especially pertinent.

Rawls deliberately chooses a conception of justice which requires the fewest presuppositions in order to minimize likely disputes over the proper nature of the good of individuals and society. By attempting to explicate the rational basis of the difference principle, Rawls demonstrates (if one finds the argument convincing) that rational and, because of the veil of ignorance, equal men in the original position would so structure society that it would be, and appear to be, a *cooperative venture*. In a society ordered by justice as fairness, those who have been most favored by nature would legitimately gain from their good fortune only on terms which improve the situation of those who have lost out in the natural lottery. The difference principle, then, corresponds to the notion of fraternity which is implicit in organicist conceptions of society. The term "fraternity" aptly describes our feelings when we do not want to have greater advantages than others unless these advantages also contribute to the benefit of others who are less well off than we are. By publicly adopting the difference principle, men would, Rawls writes, agree to share one another's fate.

Admittedly, those critiques[36] of social contract which are analytically incisive and morally sensitive vigorously argue that a theory which begins with the ahistorical assumption of rational and disinterested egos can never regain in theoretical logic or in practical application the more arational and morally sustaining notion of societal community. But these objections to contract theory do not properly apply to Rawls's reworking of contract theory in a Kantian mode. Rawls adopts a thin theory of the good so that a conception of justice has a greater likelihood of acceptance. Moreover, the difference principle articulates the confused but compelling strivings for community which characterize much social dissent.

SOCIOLOGY AND A THEORY OF JUSTICE

As James S. Coleman has noted, moral philosophy and sociology, though academically distinct, have nevertheless a shared subject matter, the functioning of society and the relationship of the individual to society.[37] It is difficult for sociologists to ignore John Rawls's *A Theory of Justice* completely. It is too early, of course, to gauge its long-range impact on the social sciences, but it is significant that two recent efforts at social theory—Daniel Bell's *The Coming of Post-Industrial Society* and Robert Nisbet's *The Twilight of Authority*[38] —explicitly analyze and, in fact, directly criticize Rawls's work.[39] But in both cases the sociologists never explicitly formulate *their* conceptions of justice, nor in any publicly accountable way justify the philosophical basis of their critique of justice as fairness. Bell broadly describes Rawls's work as providing the philosophical justification for a "major shift in values." "Instead of the principle 'from each according to his ability, to each according to his ability,' we have the principle 'from each according to his ability, to each according to his need.' "[40]

But in this work Bell surprisingly omits any explication of the key methodological devices of the original position and the veil of ignorance; indeed, he never analyzes the philosophical justification of justice as fairness. He simply observes that notions of justice are derived from pertinent reference groups and that conceptions of justice are related to social expectations and relative deprivation. "Relative deprivation" is the neutral sociological term commonly found in sociological analyses involving peoples' notions of social fairness. People object to their conditions only when they have some standard by which to compare their situation with that of others. Deprivation is relative to what a comparable group has and to what people have learned to expect. It is not the poorest of the poor who revolt against their condition, but those who have experienced some progress and expect more.[41] After noting the influence of reference groups on standards of evaluation, Bell then asks, "What is the measure of fairness? Is it objective or subjective? Often a sense of fairness depends upon expectation and the degree of deprivation . . . [so] are we to accept the subjective evaluations of individuals as the moral norm or an objective standard, and on what basis? The point is not clear."[42] But Rawls does make the point clearly. Objective standards of social justice constituting, he says, an Archimedean point of moral judgment can be recognized when we seriously adopt the vantage point of the original position and the veil of ignorance. The principles which we adopt in the original position, Rawls argues, would be identical with the rational choice of anyone so positioned. The choices would be objective, and thus they would transcend the positivistic notions of reference groups and social expectation. The whole point of the methodological devices of the original position and the veil of ignorance is to neutralize the influence of particular reference groups and merely subjective social expectations. But Bell does not inform his reader that Rawls's methodological tactics are specifically designed to enable the investigator to judge and evaluate the different moral claims arising from the use of different reference groups and from subjective notions of relative deprivation. Albeit inconsistently, Bell also writes that in *his* judgment contemporary "redistributist populism" insists on a complete leveling, and he discerns its true motivation, its "chief psychological fuel," as *resentment* against merited status rather than stemming from a sense of justice.[43] This criticism is offered without any supporting data but, more significantly, without any explicit social philosophy of his own. Ironically, after his critique of Rawls and his critical interpretation of contemporary egalitarianism as motivated by envy, Bell informs the reader that he acknowledges "the priority of the disadvantaged as an axiom of social policy, as long as the opportunity for the best to rise to the top through work and effort is not diminished."[44] This position is indistinguishable from Rawls's explicit theory. But, again, in this case Bell the sociologist offers a policy priority which, since it lacks any explicit grounding in moral theory, can only be described as gratuitous.

   A similar complaint can be lodged against Nisbet's *The Twilight of Authority*. Nisbet places Rawls's work within what he calls the "cult of equality" and writes that Rawls's views will be central for those belonging to a "clerisy of power" which seeks an increasing centralization of political power.[45] Disregarding Rawls's serial ordering of principles, in which liberty precedes equality, Nisbet says that in Rawls's conception "equality is the dominant value,"[46] and that this emphasis would lead to an erosion of cultural excellence,[47] vast bureaucratization, and a centralized state especially prone to military adventures. Thus, the advance of equality, Nisbet soberly reports, follows the trajectory of war.[48] Again, Nisbet offers his personal judgment without making available to his reader any explicit moral theory which consciously informs the author's judgment and which might publicly justify his critical conclusions.

Nisbet's and Bell's analyses of contemporary society are ostensibly works of value-free social theorists, yet both are laced with a social commentary unsupported by any explicit mention of a moral theory which might publicly ground their own evaluations. Ironically, both theorists have criticized colleagues for confounding analysis and advocacy.[49] Yet in their own critiques of Rawls's work on justice, both sociologists unwittingly demonstrate the difficulty of completely separating sociological analyses from social philosophy. In this respect they are merely typical.

SOCIAL SCIENCE AND MORAL PHILOSOPHY

From the point of view of sociology, an examination of Rawls's *A Theory of Justice* yields some obvious and perhaps some controversial reflections. A first and obvious reflection is the cautionary one that because moral philosophy is Socratic the generalities discovered by social scientists cannot be reified or described as possessing the same ontological status as an immutable physical law. Once we analyze our moral judgments in terms of their implicit principles, we might very well want to change our principles and/or our particular judgments about some social patterns. When we take time to think systematically, we are more likely to revise at least some of our particular judgments.[50] Even if the sociologist can reasonably restrict his models and theories to explaining (or trying to explain) what "is" currently the case, he must be careful not to identify these models and theories with absolute or fixed laws. To do so would remove *a priori* the Socratic dimension of moral theory. And, indeed, when men and societies, under the pressures of social conflict or the common recognition of some undesirable consequences resulting from existing social patterns, collectively reflect on the principles underlying their system of resource allocation and distribution, they conceivably can alter these institutional patternings. Nevertheless, while describing their own theories and models as objective, sociologists have often without warrant labeled more directly evaluative knowledge or social criticism as "unscientific" and implicitly of lesser cognitive worth than the sociologists' models.[51] But hard data and empirical models can by definition apply only to the actual present—to what currently is—and by definition the structural rearrangements sought by a moral consciousness cannot be empirically validated but must be at least partially perceived in imagination. The future cannot be empirically documented. Clearly, then, it is unwarranted for the social scientist to suggest to his students or readers that his data, models, or theories, which purportedly explain existing patterns of society, are also completely determinative of possible future patterns, which will at least partially result from some exercise of social choice. Although several of the earlier sociologists,[52] such as Herbert Spencer, explicitly deduced ethics from determinate social laws, some later theorists, such as Pareto, disparaged *any* moral philosophy by attempting to show how unscientific all moral theories were. By reserving the notion of "rational" and "empirically validated" to their own theories, theorists such as Pareto and Spencer implicitly debunk notions of social justice by making moral philosophy appear to be arational and sentimental. One conclusion is manifest: social science and social philosophy must at a minimum join in mutual criticism. Social philosophy must challenge the tendency of social science to reify existing empirical patterns and the moral conceptions which they institutionally embody. Social science, on the other hand, can inform moral philosophy of the actual difficulties of molding social patterns according to moral theory. But the problem remains. How should social science and moral philosophy be critically related? Let us review the more common positions.

With a directness uncommon in the social sciences Gunnar Myrdal once suggested what appeared to be an obvious solution to the value problem for the social scientist: the social scientist should make his or her value assumptions explicit so that the student and reader would be directly aware of the political and moral implications of the scholar's analytical categories. Myrdal argued that in all likelihood these values impregnate the social scientist's concepts and analyses. Not only does it apparently minimize the possibility of objectivity as a regulative norm for the social scientist, but, at the level formulated by Myrdal, it actually fails to solve the problem of *critically* relating social science and moral philosophy. If, for example, the author informs the reader that *he*, the author, personally favors "equality," or "liberty," or "fraternity," he is not giving his reader much useful information. Indeed, most of his fellow-citizens might be expected to agree with the author's most general and most abstract values. Critical disagreement usually involves the weighing of several values and the adjudication of moral claims based on these different weighings. The reader, for example, would wonder how the author might decide between conflicts generated by differing emphases on equality *vs.* liberty, or the other way around. The simple affirmation of the value of equality or liberty does not unambiguously allow one to choose between social policies which maximize either income redistribution or the differential rewards based on special merit or uncommon risk. Myrdal's suggestion could be considerably strengthened by having the social scientist explicitly present not merely his value preferences but also his ordering of values and the moral theory which guides it. For the social scientist, Rawls's work should prove unusually appealing because Rawls specifically grounds his notion of justice as fairness in *detached reason*. This grounding of justice on detached reason is of enormous significance for the social scientist. Most social scientists have eschewed the adoption of any explicit moral philosophy as a framework for their data and theoretical models precisely because it has generally seemed to them that moral philosophy inevitably reflects a relativistic and partial world view and, they have argued, such views are hardly a fit partner for scientific theory. Historically, schools of philosophy have been divided among themselves, and the attempt by social scientists to extricate theory and research from these particularistic influences have animated, perhaps naïvely, the social scientists' pursuit of objectivity. But the case of Rawls's theory of justice is different. For the methodological tactic of the original position assumes only a "thin theory of the good." Behind the veil of ignorance there is a hypothetical ignorance of personal philosophical and religious beliefs. It must be emphasized that this "thin theory of the good" is not adopted because Rawls finds religious indifferentism or moral relativism to be appropriate philosophical positions. The contrary is the case. He argues that an individual would choose liberty as a first principle—rather than the institutionalization of a substantive creed or a principle of perfection—precisely to ensure that he or she might be able to choose, or appropriate, his or her beliefs with the suitable freedom, whatever the individual's historical or sociological fate. Clearly, then, the shedding of philosophical and religious beliefs in the original position is not because of any desire to minimize the importance of beliefs and convictions but precisely because of the high regard for the freedom of conscience which the authentic adherence to these beliefs requires.[53]

Besides arguing that rational persons in the original position would first protect their freedom of conscience, Rawls also cogently argues that a viable theory of justice must be based on the fewest possible assumptions. Framers of a theory of justice would seek a conception which might adjudicate competing moral claims from many different groups operating from many different philosophical and religious premises. In justice as fairness Rawls "thinly" assumes only rationality and disinterestedness. His disavowal of perfectionism and his thin assumption of the good undercut most of the classic objections to a closer joining of social science and moral philosophy. As argued by Rawls, justice as fairness involves a transcultural[54] rationality stripped of explicit particularistic metaphysical or religious assumptions. For sociologists this, of course, is the key point. Rationality which transcends any cultural particularity, as in the paradigmatic case of mathematics, has been a methodological goal within sociology since Auguste Comte.[55] But if Rawls's theory contains principles which would indeed be rationally chosen in the original position, and if the social scientist personally recognizes a need for some explicit moral theory to order his implicit intuitive judgments about the justice of institutional patterns,[56] then, we might ask, what blocks the adoption of *A Theory of Justice* as an articulate and publicly accountable framework for social theory and research?

Many things, including the training and socialization of most sociologists by which they internalize a professional identity which requires them to restrict their scholarly attention to the empirically given. A theory of justice, on the other hand, provides a standard by which to judge how the major political and economic institutions ought to be. The "ought" of the theory of justice is not empirically given but is, rather, the standard by which empirical distributional patterns are judged. Rawls himself notes that in justice as fairness the investigator does not take men's present propensities and inclinations as definitively given. The influence of institutions on men's conduct is so pervasive that it would be unwarranted to take existing patterns of conduct as indicative of men's final capacity for justice. "Men's propensity to injustice," Rawls writes, "is not a permanent aspect of community life: it is greater or less depending in large part on social institutions, and in particular on whether they are just or unjust."[57]

Let us suppose for a moment that the claims advanced for social science as "value-free" are well grounded, and let us consider from that vantage point the partial but fruitful contributions which social science could make to a theory of justice. Next, we shall look at the relationship between sociology and moral philosophy with more skepticism about the claims of sociology to be value-free.

(a) First, the social scientist could investigate the extent to which societies embody the principles of justice outlined by Rawls. He could ask: "How many people, and under what psychological and social circumstances, perceive the Rawlsian principles as reasonable?" Lawrence Kohlberg, for example, finds strong empirical evidence for contending that there is, in fact, an invariant transcultural sequential development of moral categories which involves six broad stages: "The scientific facts," he writes, "are that there is a universal moral form successively emerging in development and centering on principles of justice."[58] It might be mentioned that Kohlberg thinks that any significant statement about moral education requires "our being simultaneously a social psychologist and a philosopher."[59]

(b) Besides empirically investigating the stages of moral development and the commonly held perceptions of justice, the social scientist can empirically investigate the extent to which the principles of justice are embedded in major social institutions. Investigations of income distribution over time are an obvious example of a strictly empirical contribution to a theory of justice.[60]

(c) Besides empirical investigations of income distribution and rates of social mobility, an interpretative examination of predominant themes in a nation's culture can also be considered as empirical. For example, Bellah describes the social costs of the cultural emphasis on individualism, competition, upward mobility, and economic success in American life, and contrasts these empirical tendencies with the collective self-understandings of American society expressed in the nation's constitutional and religious documents. He then describes various ways of reappropriating the nation's authentic tradition without, again, explicitly justifying the moral codes which he finds within the tradition which he describes.[61]

(d) The sociologist can investigate the plausibility of Rawls's conception by studying the degree of congruence between his schema and emerging trends in

American society. The sociologist can (I think) make a strong empirical case for the plausibility of major tenets of Rawls's conception of justice. These principles can be seen as consistent with commonly held social sentiments. For example, in American society few people currently consider their lives morally arbitrary or completely subject to impersonal laws operating outside man's technological and political control. Few accept unemployment and inflation as "naturally inevitable"; both are increasingly seen as the result of policy decisions (or non-decisions) of government. In eras of slow technological advance and mass illiteracy, there was more likely to be a general acceptance of fate or accident as determinative of the shape of personal life. In modern societies there is less willingness to accept one's social fate as inevitable, and the major components of social life—employment, health care, education, and housing, for example—seem to many to result from political decisions concerning societal priorities and patterns of distribution. The question of legitimacy is commonly raised. Who makes the rules? And for whose advantage? A basic question of modernity is the question of legitimacy and social fairness.

In more summary fashion, then, even an empirical social science can contribute to a conception of justice such as Rawls's in the following five ways. It can investigate

(a) the psychological and sociological development of moral categories;
(b) the principles of justice which are embedded in major social institutions;
(c) the conceptions of justice contained in the major cultural documents which ground a society's collective self-understanding, comparing these "authentic" conceptions with present trends;
(d) the historical and present distribution of economic and political resources in a society; and
(e) the changing cultural context of a society to determine the congruence between the principles of a theory of justice and the general expectations of the populace in order to ascertain the degree of plausibility which a conception of justice such as Rawls's might be expected to evoke.

Although all these contributions can be described as at least potentially objective, the more interesting observation is that it is, in fact, the theory of justice which provokes the research questions, indicates the types of data to be collected, and might provide the standard by which the data are interpreted. This priority of the evaluative in forming the hypothesis and in providing the standard of judgment is undoubtedly at the heart of W. G. Runciman's seemingly harsh observation that sociology is a consumer of laws, not a producer of them.[62] Indeed, even apart from Rawls, several sociological perspectives consciously incorporate the normative and the empirical, arguing that an observer cannot even know the "empirically given" unless he has a notion of the potential of the human person and society. These perspectives, often loosely identified as varieties of Marxist humanism, have argued that the "given" will offer itself up only to the view which regards it from a perspective of value or interest—the perspective, for example, of a free society, a just state, or the full development of the human person. In their preface to *Aspects of Sociology*,[63] Max Horkheimer and Theodor W. Adorno, representatives of the Frankfurt Institute for Social Research, write that "Whoever does not measure human things by what they themselves are supposed to signify will not merely see superficially but falsely." But Adorno and Horkheimer never make their theory of justice explicit and, as a result, they cannot responsibly defend their systematic values against competing moral traditions. Pertinent also is the fact of the suppression of dissent in Communist nations. It is highly unlikely that a sociology explicitly informed by Marxism would obtain a fair hearing in American society.[64] From a moral point of view it could also be held that the ultimate claims of Marxism are not explicitly grounded in man's universal nature as a free and equal being, as argued in Rawls's original position.

What, then, can we conclude about the relationship between sociology and moral philosophy? Quite obviously, that sociological theory and moral theory cannot be conceived of as entirely separate and mutually autonomous endeavors. Rawls is right in his insistence that an adequate theory of justice requires a general knowledge of the social sciences and of much contingent data. To be sure, the moral philosopher must work closely with the sociologist and read carefully the research dealing with the distributive shares of wealth and power within society. Conversely, the sociologist must either work closely with the moral philosopher or, after proper training and reflection, explicitly identify the theory of justice which informs his sociological work. At least a few more words of explanation are needed on this point.

Most sociologists presumably have a theory of justice. We would expect as much from reflective and thoughtful intellectuals. "Justice is the first virtue of social institutions, as truth is of systems of thought," Rawls writes.[65] The important question is the amount of intellectual control and systematic scrutiny which the social scientist applies to his conception of social justice. In many cases, perhaps, the conception of social justice held by the social scientist is unfocused and unexamined and, thus, his evaluative judgments often surface in an *ad hoc* and ungrounded fashion (as we saw, for example, in recent analyses by Bell and Nisbet). Our final point is the perhaps surprising one that the empirical work of the social sciences would suffer not a whit by an explicit placing of the data and the theoretical concepts of social science within the framework of a theory of justice. The social scientist must always obtain, as best and as honestly as he can, information about the actual workings of society. No one doubts the need for empirical accuracy. But what *is* frequently in doubt is the significance of the data and their implications for human action and social policy. By explicitly considering the data and conceptualizations from the point of view of an articulate theory of justice the social scientist, while still seeking empirical validity, would be more responsible to his readers and to his scholarly calling.

What remains hidden from the reader and unfocused in the scholar's mind can never become a matter of critical dialogue and public accountability. Rawls's work might not constitute the articulate theory of justice adopted by the sociologist. It could not, of course, if the theory did not correspond to the sociologist's critical reflections on morality and justice. But Rawls's thin assumptions about the nature of the good, his reliance on disinterested rationality in the original position, and his emphases on the significance of institutional patterns on character as well as opportunity make his conception of justice as fairness a particularly apt moral framework for social scientists. Justice as fairness does not explicitly rest on particular cultural propositions (although it would certainly *appear* to be more plausible to persons in a culture which honored dispassionate reason). He assumes no special metaphysics or epistemology and appeals only to reason.[66] If social scientists would explicitly adopt justice as fairness as a larger framework for their work (or reject it and then replace it with an alternative conception), the following beneficent consequences would result from such directness:

(*a*) By making explicit his own moral theory the social scientist would be more responsible to his readers and to himself.

(*b*) If data and concepts were considered from the point of view of a theory of justice, the significance of the findings of social science would be more evident.

(*c*) If social science work were informed by an explicit theory of justice, the need for accurata data and unbiased research would not be diminished.

A standard for judging social policy requires accurate information about a nation's distribution of wealth and power, its rates of mobility, and the types and amounts of social and economic differences separating occupational strata. Adapting the perspective of justice as fairness does not diminish at all the classic sociological insistence on the need for an unbiased ascertainment of the "real." The principles of justice as fairness do not replace but give direction to the gathering of data and provide a rational moral standard by which to evaluate the real. In the best sense of the word, *A Theory of Justice* presents an important challenge to social scientists, and it is hard to see how they can avoid responding to it. It is my opinion that, because of its emphasis on disinterested rationality and its thin theory of the good, Rawls's work represents a challenge which is significantly different from that classically posed by religion and philosophy to the separation within social sciences of questions of fact from questions of value.

NOTES

1. There are conspicuous exceptions to this generalization. For example, see Max Black's contribution to the Cornell University symposium on the thought of Talcott Parsons, "Some Questions About Parsons' Theories" (*The Social Theories*

of Talcott Parsons, ed. Max Black [Englewood Cliffs, N.J.: Prentice-Hall, 1961], pp. 268–88).

2. See, for example, Talcott Parsons' essay "Value-freedom and Objectivity" in *Max Weber and Sociology Today,* ed. Otto Stammer (New York: Harper Torchbooks, 1971), pp. 27–50.

3. George C. Homans, *The Nature of Social Science* (New York: Harcourt, Brace, & World, 1967), p. 4.

4. See the essay "Science As a Vocation" in *From Max Weber,* edd. Hans Gerth and C. Wright Mills (New York: Oxford University Press, 1946).

5. See his *The Poverty of Historicism* (London: Routledge & Kegan Paul, 1957), introduction.

6. George Homans once remarked that one question persistently bothered him about the rigorous and putatively scientific laboratory controls proudly used by some colleagues, who, in turn, were skeptical about his more qualitative and therefore less "scientific" methodology: namely, "Why had not methods apparently so rigorous produced more in the way of cumulative results?" Homans observed that "pretty nearly every (social) psychologist had his own theory—at least he used his own words" (*Sentiments and Activities* [Glencoe, Ill.: Free Press, 1962], p. 41).

7. For example, in his *Exchange and Power in Social Life* (New York: Wiley, 1964) Peter Blau purports to offer an objective and deductive analysis of social organization based on "exchange theory," that is, the analysis of actions which are contingent on rewarding reactions. But the homiletic impulse is strong, as evidenced by the following passage: "It is the duty of those citizens of a democratic society who are not immediately involved in particular power struggles to help safeguard equality of opportunity and political tolerance, since the involvement of the participants makes them incapable of doing so" (p. 142).

8. Talcott Parsons, *The Systems of Modern Societies* (Englewood Cliffs, N.J.: Prentice-Hall, 1971), p. v.

9. *The Concepts of Sociology* (New York: Heath, 1932).

10. Ibid., p. 43.

11. Ibid.

12. *A Sociology of Sociology* (New York: Free Press, 1972).

13. "Two Methods in Search of a Substance," *American Sociological Review,* 40, No. 6 (December 1975), 696, 698.

14. Roland J. Liebert and Alan E. Bayer, "Goals in Teaching Undergraduates," *The American Sociologist,* 10 (1975), 195–205.

15. *The Twilight of Authority* (New York: Oxford University Press, 1975), p. 122.

16. *Value in Social Theory* (London: Routledge & Kegan Paul, 1958).

17. *The Coming Crisis in Western Sociology* (New York: Basic Books, 1970).

18. *A Sociology of Sociology.*

19. Most of the remaining essay will deal with the challenge of *A Theory of Justice* for sociologists, rather than with the equally appropriate challenge of sociology for social philosophy. The challenge of moral philosophy to the social sciences seems especially pertinent because of the unwitting tendency of social scientists to take on the role of the moral philosopher. For example, without a trace of irony, James S. Coleman, while reviewing Rawls's book for the *American Journal of Sociology* ("Inequality, Sociology, and Moral Philosophy," 80, No. 3 [November 1974], 739–64), not only criticizes Rawls's conception but offers his own version of social contract theory. The important point here is not so much

Coleman's conception of justice as his own quick assertion of an alternative moral theory; this is merely asserted not defended, although he promises a fuller justification in later work.

20. *Theory of Justice*, p. 62.

21. In his presidential address to the Eastern Division of The American Philosophical Association Rawls expresses this insight with a special emphasis on the social roots of the ego-ideal: "A moral conception incorporates a conception of the person and of the relations between persons. Those who are raised in a particular conception become in due course a certain kind of person and they express this conception in their actions and in their relations with one another. Thus a basic form of moral motivation is the desire to be and to be recognized by others as being a certain kind of person. . . . Then, given our dependence on society, we could not be this sort of person unless institutions developed and encouraged our capacity so to act and others publicly to acknowledge its realization" ("The Independence of Moral Theory," *Proceedings and Addresses of The American Philosophical Association*, 48 [1975], 13).

22. (New York: Basic Books, 1966).

23. Ibid., p. 8.

24. Rawls, *Theory of Justice*, p. 7.

25. James S. Coleman notes that sociology and moral philosophy have remained "wholly apart," with little interchange of ideas ("Inequality, Sociology, and Moral Philosophy," 739). It is true that Rawls's work contains but a handful of references to specific sociological works (but many to economic theory and data)—but the Rawlsian perspective—the overriding importance of the institutional—is decidedly sociological.

26. Rawls locates the heart of moral theory in the investigations of the substantive moral conceptions which people hold. "One thinks," he writes, "of the moral theorist as an observer, so to speak, who seeks to set out the structure of other people's moral conceptions and attitudes" ("Independence of Moral Theory," 7). In this statement Rawls seems to be simply the sociologist explicating the moral beliefs of members of a society. (At this point the social scientist might simply become exasperated. "Who is tending to the normative," he might cry.) But Rawls carefully observes that a theory of justice should embody a scheme of principles which match people's *considered* judgments and convictions in *reflective equilibrium*: "That is," Rawls suggests, "adopting the role of observing moral theorists, we investigate what principles people would acknowledge and accept the consequences of when they have had an opportunity to consider other plausible conceptions and to assess their supporting grounds" (ibid., 8). Rawls wants to do moral theory, not a survey of moral attitudes. Still, he hopes his thin assumptions will lead reflection on to an acknowledgment that his schema does properly order our own moral intuitions. But more of this later.

27. *Theory of Justice*, p. 104.

28. See the discussion by Werner Stark in his article on Karl Mannheim in *The Encyclopedia of Philosophy*, ed. Paul Edwards, 8 vols. (New York: Macmillan-Free Press, 1967), v 151–52.

29. Rawls's deontological critique of teleological doctrines such as those embodied in classic utilitarianism or perfectionism (defining the "right" in terms of realizing the "good") is based on the historically grounded fear that there is in principle no reason why, under legitimating utilitarian or perfectionist principles, the greater gains of some, often material gains, should not be said to compensate for the "lesser" losses of liberties of others. Under teleological or perfectionist

principles there is always the danger that the violations of essential liberties of some will be claimed as "just" because of the promise of a greater good delivered in time to the many.

30. Cf. Arthur M. Okun, *Equality and Efficiency: The Big Trade-Off* (Washington, D.C.: The Brookings Institution, 1975). Okun's notion of "the leaky bucket" metaphorically captures his analytic attempt to balance morally and practically the values of economic productivity and economic assistance to those who for one reason or another lose out in the economic race.

31. See Talcott Parsons, *The Structure of Social Action* (New York: Free Press, 1968), pp. 51–60; Nisbet, *The Sociological Tradition*, p. 8; and *The Social Philosophers* (New York: Crowell, 1973), pp. 1–9.

32. For a good example of the moral and spiritual impulse which can motivate an organicist conception, read 1 Cor. 12:20, 21.

33. See Talcott Parsons, *The Social System* (Glencoe, Ill.: Free Press, 1951).

34. Arguing against a "Durkheimian" social realism, some sociologists emphasize that individuals "constitute" society and attempt (unsuccessfully) to reduce all sociological explanations to psychological ones. See, for example, George C. Homans, *Social Behavior: Its Elementary Forms* (New York: Harcourt, Brace, Jovanovich, 1974).

35. Stanley I. Benn, "Society," *Encyclopedia of Philosophy*, ed. Edwards, VII 470–74.

36. Werner Stark's *The Fundamental Forms of Social Thought* (New York: Fordham University Press, 1963) is a general exploration of the organicist-mechanistic dichotomy.

37. "Inequality, Sociology, and Moral Philosophy," 739.

38. Bell, *The Coming of Post-Industrial Society* (New York: Basic Books, 1973), esp. pp. 440–44; Nisbet, *The Twilight of Authority*, esp. pp. 215–16.

39. As noted previously, the prominent sociologist James S. Coleman reviewed Rawls's work and offered his own theory of justice. But, significantly, Coleman does not philosophically ground his own conception in which, briefly, he partially removes the veil of ignorance and places corporate actors (e.g., families, corporations, states) in the original position. Coleman also concedes that his conception "does not address the problems of inequality, or more generally the distributional problems that arise in a market society, as Rawls's theory does" ("Inequality, Sociology, and Moral Philosophy," 760). In other words, this ungrounded conception, which is offered as a substitute for Rawls's, does not address a key problem of justice. Similarly, "Justice: A Spectrum of Responses to John Rawls's Theory," *American Political Science Review*, 69 No. 2 (June 1975), 588–674, contains several symposium essays by political scientists dealing with Rawls's theory. Allan Bloom ("Justice: John Rawls vs. the Tradition of Political Philosophy," ibid., 648–62) notes that this work has attracted more attention in the Anglo-Saxon world than any work of its kind in a generation. But all the essays are critical. Many object to Rawls's lack of any explicit notion of perfection and human nature. Indeed, Rawls never asks the question "Why be moral?" Rather, he attempts to order our moral sensibilities (which he assumes) in a systematic fashion. On this point, I agree that abstract reason, disembodied from the images and symbols of communal life, might not be the direct source of what most of us would describe as our "moral behavior." But in a pluralistic society, with a need for a conception of justice which is more general than the competing visions of the good, Rawls's conception deserves special consideration. For a good treatment of these difficult matters from a specifically religious point of view, James M. Gustafson's

Can Ethics Be Christian? (Chicago: The University of Chicago Press, 1975) is especially useful. "The Christian theologian's ethical task," he writes, "is engaged in for the sake of the community that shares a set of common experiences and beliefs. . . . But the Christian community is not, however, the exclusive audience. They will be persuasive to others, however, on the basis of supporting reasons different from those that Christians might respond to" (p. 163). Pertinent to Rawls's thin theory of the good, Gustafson suggests that it would be extremely rare that "members of the Christian community would act under any circumstances in a way that could not be justified by principles on which presumably all rational persons could agree" (p. 166).

40. *Coming of Post-Industrial Society*, p. 444.

41. For a general discussion of the concept of relative deprivation, see "Justice, Satisfaction, and the Choice of Comparisons," in Homans, *Social Behavior*, pp. 252–57. The notion of relative deprivation is clearly adumbrated in Alexis de Tocqueville's *The Old Régime and the French Revolution* (New York: Doubleday Anchor Books, 1955).

42. *Coming of Post-Industrial Society*, p. 446.

43. Ibid., p. 453.

44. Ibid., p. 454.

45. P. 215.

46. Ibid., p. 216.

47. Nisbet is unmindful of the *adagium* of that earlier man of letters and guardian of standards, Matthew Arnold, who, in *Culture and Anarchy*, wrote that "The men of culture are the true apostles of equality." In the entry on Matthew Arnold in the *Encyclopedia of Philosophy* (ed. Edwards, I 166–68), Raymond Williams observes that Arnold was critical of the liberal thought of his day, which in the name of abstract freedom opposed any human intervention of the state on behalf of the disadvantaged.

48. *Twilight of Authority*, p. 220.

49. See Nisbet, "Project Camelot: An Autopsy" in *On Intellectuals*, ed. Philip Rieff (New York: Doubleday, 1970), pp. 382–83, and Daniel Bell's comments on the "ethos of science" in *Coming of Post-Industrial Society*.

50. If we have an accurate account, Rawls writes, of the motions of the heavenly bodies which we do not find appealing, we cannot alter these physical motions to conform to what we might think a more aesthetically attractive theory. But, again, once we analyze our moral judgments in terms of their implicit principles, we might want to change our particular judgments or our principles. Moral judgment is Socratic.

51. On a similar issue see the interesting essay by Robert N. Bellah, "Christianity and Symbolic Realism," *Journal for the Scientific Study of Religion*, 9, No. 2 (Summer 1970), 89–96.

52. See *Herbert Spencer*, ed. Stanislav Andreski (New York: Scribner's, 1975) and *Karl Marx*, ed. Z. A. Jordan (New York: Scribner's, 1975). The introductions to both volumes are useful on the question of ethics and social laws.

53. It should be evident that Rawls's adoption of the thin theory of the good in the hypothetical original position—in which individuals will not know the content of their beliefs and convictions—stems from his sense of the overriding importance of such beliefs and convictions, and thus the requirement of freedom of conscience to pursue them. Clearly his position is congruent with philosophical and religious commitment. For example, justice as fairness is compatible with the position adopted by the Roman Catholic Church's Second Vatican Council in its

"Declaration on Religious Freedom": "Inherent in the dignity of man as a moral subject is the exigence to act on his own initiative and on his own personal responsibility, especially in that vital area in which the sense of his own existence and his necessary pursuit of it, are at stake—that is to say, especially in matters religious. This exigence is a thing of the objective order; it is rooted in the given reality of man as man. Therefore, this exigence is permanent and ineradicable and altogether stringent. . . . [Man] asserts his right to immunity from coercion, especially in matters religious. This is man's fundamental moral claim on others" (John Courtney Murray, s.j., "The Declaration on Religious Freedom: A Moment in Its Legislative History," in *Religious Liberty: An End and Beginning*, ed. John Courtney Murray, s.j. [New York: Macmillan, 1966], pp. 40, 41). In this religious passage liberty is based on a principle of perfection. Rawls's assumptions are thinner. But the point remains: a thin theory of the good does not stem from relativism. True convictions require freedom. Rational persons in the original position would recognize this and thus would not institutionalize any principle of perfection.

54. It is probably the case that an elaborate theory such as justice as fairness, which seeks to protect liberty and to a significant degree attempts to equalize social resources, could only be systematically formulated after the historical experience of modern democratic and industrialized societies. As Rawls says, he is trying to help us order our moral intuitions.

55. Comte's final recourse to a "cult of humanity" as an affective counterpart to positivism can be used to illustrate the fact that, since sociology's inception, the self-conscious goal of a detached objectivity modeled on the natural sciences has been more a regulative ideal than a common achievement.

56. A conception of social justice provides a standard by which the distributive aspects of the basic structures of society are to be assessed. It provides, Rawls writes, the only basis for the systematic grasp of more pressing problems characteristic of existing societies. "The point to keep in mind is that a conception of justice for the basic structure of society is worth having for its own sake" (*Theory of Justice*, p. 9).

57. Ibid., p. 31. Ironically, many sociologists are unmindful of this point. Homans, for example, in his *Social Behavior*, explains power and authority by the principle of the differential capacities of individuals to reward others: "When A's net reward—compared, that is, with his alternatives—in taking action that will reward B is less, at least as perceived by B, than B's net reward in taking action that will reward A, and B as a result changes his behavior in a way favorable to A, then A has exerted power over B" (p. 83). After mentioning this "empirical law," Rawls simply remarks that those subject to A's exercise of authority will surely regard him differently depending upon whether the whole arrangement is just and well designed to advance what they take to be their legitimate interests. See *Theory of Justice*, p. 492.

58. Stage I, for example, is described as the pre-ethical orientation of punishment and obedience involving an unquestioning deference to power. Stage VI describes a universal ethical-principle orientation in which "right" is defined by a decision of conscience in accord with self-chosen ethical principles appealing to logical comprehensiveness, universality, and consistency. See Lawrence Kohlberg, "Stages of Moral Development as a Basis for Moral Education," in *Moral Education*, edd. C. M. Beck, B. S. Crittenden, and E. V. Sullivan (New York: Newman, 1971), p. 69.

59. Ibid., p. 24.

60. See, for example, "Income Inequality," in Christopher Jencks et al., *Inequality* (New York: Basic Books, 1972), pp. 209–46. The authors explicitly adopt a utilitarian perspective, agreeing that society should be organized so as to provide the greatest good for the greatest number (p. 9). But they offer no justification for this ethical principle; nor, unlike Rawls, do they discuss principles which would serve to mediate between the social conflicts stemming from this principle.

61. *The Broken Covenant* (New York: Seabury, 1975).

62. For Runciman, sociology is a "residual" term: "If we are puzzled how it happens that certain sorts of research into human behavior are typically called 'sociology' by practicioners and laymen alike, we shall discover on investigation that it tends to be for one or other of five broad and sometimes overlapping reasons: first, because there is not (or not yet) a specialized social science to which it can be assigned; second, because it is too nearly contemporary, or contains too little narrative, to be easily called 'history'; third, because it contains too large and highly developed a community or society for the 'anthropological' method of participant-observation to be appropriate to it; fourth, because it is formulated at so high a level of generality that its empirical content is in doubt; fifth, because it is 'applied' in the still further sense of being concerned with the diagnosis and if possible the cure of some recognized social ill" (*Sociology in Its Place* [Cambridge: Cambridge University Press, 1970], p. 15.

63. Trans. John Viertel (Boston: Beacon, 1974).

64. See, for example, "The American Taboo on Socialism," in Bellah, *Broken Covenant*, pp. 112–38.

65. *Theory of Justice*, p. 3.

66. On this point, see in particular Rawls's "Independence of Moral Theory."

9

International Justice and the World Hunger Problem

MARTIN C. FERGUS

Fordham University

POLITICAL SCIENCE AND THE QUESTION OF JUSTICE

THE TOPIC OF INTERNATIONAL JUSTICE appears, at first glance, to be an unusual subject for contemporary political scientists to examine. In the earliest days of the discipline, of course, questions of what constituted a "just society" were at the center of concern, but over time, the discipline moved farther and farther away from exploring questions of what "ought" to be and concentrated on examining questions of what "is." In recent times, this trend has culminated in the rise of behavioralism as the dominant approach of the discipline.[1]

The triumph of behavioralism had several important implications for the study of politics. Most immediately, it meant that political scientists would be focusing less on legal and constitutional descriptions of governments and more on the behavior of political actors, both inside and outside governmental institutions. A central concern now became the operation, and more particularly the maintenance, of political systems.[2] Coupled with this shift was a movement away from what were regarded as "impressionistic" studies of politics toward the more rigorously scientific approach of "empirical" analysis. Together, these changes culminated in an explicit commitment to a neutral, value-free science of politics. Political science, with the emphasis on science, had come of age.

But this view of the discipline has not remained unchallenged. David Easton, one of the founders of behavioralism, has observed that we are undergoing the beginnings of a new movement, a "post-behavioral revolution."[3] Political scientists representing this new trend disagree with the behavioralists on at least two counts. First, they reject the possibility of *any* value-free science of politics. Any model of politics, they argue, contains value assumptions. In particular, behavioralism is seen as a model of politics which is inherently conservative, and those who use this model, it is asserted, have a strong tendency to equate what "is" with what "ought" to be.[4] Secondly, this new group contests the *desirability* of a value-free science of politics, even if one were possible. The political scientist, they contend, is obligated not only to seek knowledge, but to use the knowledge which he gains to reshape society.[5] Though Easton is highly critical of this new movement, other political scientists have adopted and expanded upon many of its arguments.[6]

Although this debate is not something which can be resolved here, its existence itself indicates that even contemporary political science cannot escape from a concern with values. Furthermore, there are some guidelines for political analysis which one can follow without necessarily opting for one side of the debate or the other. One need not decide whether behavioralism is at all times and in all places a conservative tool in order to draw conclusions about the appropriateness of this approach in particular cases. Thus one lesson of the debate is that it makes sense to look at a specific case to see if, in this instance, the behavioral tools are appropriate.[7] Furthermore, using new and different analytical approaches does not necessarily mean that older tools must be rejected. New ways of examining political questions can be used to supplement and not merely supplant other methods.[8] Finally, although it can be argued that one is exercising a value judgment whenever one selects any theory for analysis,[9] every theory does imply hypotheses which are, more or less, testable.[10] Therefore the presence of value biases does not eliminate the possibility of scientific rigor.

It is within this context that we shall examine the problem of hunger, but before we proceed with the analysis, one final step remains: to specify the particular assumptions which underlie our analysis and to indicate how they differ from those usually associated with the behavioral school. The first difference is the most fundamental. We accept the dictum that, as one author describes it, analysts "should not only seek to describe or explain the world, they must want to change it."[11] This orientation seems particularly relevant to an examination of the world hunger situation, where malnutrition, death, and blatant injustices abound. Secondly, the central question of our analysis will not be the central question occupying much of the behavioralist literature.[12] Rather than focusing on the question of the way a political system maintains itself, this analysis will adopt as its central question "Who benefits and who loses from the existing economic and political structure?" Concentrating on this question does not, by itself, make such an analysis more change-oriented than behavioralism would; but it does bring into focus a different set of "facts" which, in combination with our other assumptions, can move us from the "is" question of politics to the "ought." Our third assumption is that politics cannot be understood apart from economics. The analysis which follows will rely more heavily upon concepts developed in the growing field of political economy than upon the more exclusively political approaches usually associated with the behavioral school.

A final assumption relates to the values which underlie the approach used in this essay. Hugh Stretton has observed that values play a dual role in political analysis.[13] In the first instance, our values direct us to the questions which we choose to examine and to the kinds of tools which we feel are most useful for such an examination. Once these choices have been made, the next phase of our analysis can be more or less objective and scientific. At the end, we return to values, as we draw conclusions from the completed research. This outline closely parallels the process which this writer went through in analyzing the hunger problem: his underlying values brought him to the study of the hunger problem in the first place, guided him in the selection of tools for analysis, and colored the conclusions which appear in the final section. What are these values? Specifically, a belief in the concept of justice as expressed in the Bible. The Old and the New Testaments are quite clear in their condemnation of those who oppress the poor; both reveal a God who demands justice; and both provide examples of the way things could be in a just world.[14] We read in the Book of Acts (2:44–45), for example, "And all who believed were together and had all things in common; and they sold their possessions and goods and distributed them to all, as any had need." It is a commitment to such values which underlies the focus of the following analysis.[15]

Let us turn now to the question of international justice and world hunger, a topic which will help us explore some of the issues raised by the behavioralist/post-behavioralist debate while shedding some light on the hunger problem itself. Following the guidelines outlined above, and using this specific case, we shall examine the appropriateness of various hypotheses for dealing with it, and in the process, supplement, and occasionally supplant, existing explanations.

SOME COMMON HYPOTHESES ABOUT THE CAUSES OF WORLD HUNGER

Let us begin by asking the question "Why is there hunger in the world?" To this question there are a number of possible answers, but four seem to be emphasized more than most. One is that there is a limit to world resources and that there simply is not enough to go around. The problem of hunger is thus a problem of scarcity. A second, related answer is that world hunger is a product of the population explosion, that there are just too many mouths to feed. A third frequently given answer is that hunger is the result of technological underdevelopment. Finally, a fourth explanation is that hunger is caused by the existing political and economic system.

In this section we shall explore the validity of the first three hypotheses—each of which accepts, at least implicitly, the inevitability and legitimacy of existing political and economic institutions—and what we shall find is that each of these hypotheses falls short of providing a satisfactory explanation for world hunger. In the next section, we shall examine the fourth hypothesis, using the perspective of a change-oriented political science, and, as we shall see, this hypothesis seems to provide the most powerful explanation of world hunger. But first let us examine the validity of the other major hypotheses.

The scarcity hypothesis has raised many issues relevant to the question of justice. A major one which has emerged among those who share a belief in this explanation of world hunger is a debate over who should be allowed to live and who should be allowed to die. This has resulted in the touted "lifeboat" analogy, which compares the world to a lifeboat with a limited capacity. If everyone is allowed to climb into the lifeboat, it is argued, the boat will become so overcrowded that it will sink and everyone will perish. Therefore, some must be sacrificed so that others may survive.[16] A very similar theory has been developed comparing the hunger problem to the problem which medics have in dealing with wounded on a battlefield. This is known as the "triage" theory, after the French practice, developed during World War I, of dividing the wounded into three groups. The first group consisted of those who would probably survive without immediate medical attention; the second, of those who probably would not survive even if they should receive medical attention. The third group, which received immediate help, were those who probably could not survive without medical attention but who probably would survive with it. Thus a scarce resource was allocated in a way which maximized the benefit to the wounded. Proponents of this analogy argue that the hungry should similarly be divided into three groups, the implication being, of course, that some persons in one of these groups should be allowed to suffer malnutrition and even death in order to ensure that the other two groups survive.

What can political science contribute to resolving the ethical questions raised by such analogies? A great deal, for what our analysis reveals is that the world hunger problem is not a problem of scarcity at all. Thus one need not consider either of the options outlined above, for neither the "lifeboat" analogy nor the "triage" analogy is appropriate.

The invalidity of the scarcity explanation of hunger can be demonstrated on a number of different levels. First, the recent declines in international grain reserves, which stimulated most of the fears about mass starvation, were the result of certain short-run, temporary conditions and do not appear to be the portent of things to come.[17] Thus the notion of a world of increasing scarcity is currently an inaccurate one. Secondly, although a certain minimum level of resources is necessary to support a given population, there is no absolute relationship between the possession of abundant resources and the eradication of hunger. In China, which has only .37 acres of arable land per capita, hunger seems by and large to have been eliminated. Yet in neighboring India, with .69 acres of arable land per capita, the hunger problem has worsened over the last fifteen years, in spite of a per capita increase in grain production. Even in the United States, with 2.25 acres of arable land per capita, hunger is still a problem.[18] There is also no absolute relationship between the possession of large amounts of other agricultural resources—such as water and fertilizer—and the lack of hunger, as the example of the United States should make clear. Lastly, even when production is increased in proportion to the population, the result in many countries—because of the existing economic and political institutions —is an *increase* in the number of people who are hungry.[19] The simple equation of hunger with scarcity, therefore, just does not hold up under serious scrutiny.

One conclusion which emerges from this analysis is that hunger has more to do with the question of distribution than with the question of scarcity. Worldwide, less than 7% of the world's population uses more than 40% of the world's non-renewable resources, while 61% of the world's population consumes only 20% of these resources. Furthermore, within nations, the gap between the rich and the poor seems to be getting larger, not smaller. In some cases not only are the poor less well-off relatively, they are less well-off in absolute terms. What is the explanation for this unequal distribution? We shall turn to this question when we explore our fourth hypothesis.

Having challenged the scarcity explanation of world hunger, we turn now to our second hypothesis—that world hunger is a result of the problem of over-population. Certainly, a rapidly growing population increases demands for food within nations and in the world as a whole, and future increases in population could theoretically, if only temporarily, outrun the capacity for food production. Yet, for at least two reasons, the overpopulation hypothesis also falls short as an explanation for world hunger. First, as was noted in our discussion of the scarcity hypothesis, there has been an increase in hunger in spite of the increase in per capita food production. The population explosion hypothesis cannot account for this.

Of even greater importance is the fact that the overpopulation hypothesis confuses cause and effect. Advocates of this hypothesis suggest that overpopulation can be dealt with through the introduction of birth control techniques and, when necessary, forced sterilization. The resulting decline in population growth, they argue, will reduce the demand for food and thereby end the hunger problem.[20] Yet the causal relationship is more complex than this. Not only can an excess of mouths to feed lead to hunger, but hunger and poverty can lead to an *increase* in the number of mouths to feed. In poor areas, large families provide parents a form of "old age insurance"—although infant mortality rates are high, at least some children will survive to take care of their parents in the latter's old age. Furthermore, incentives which might encourage small families (e.g. career goals, increased standard of living) are seldom included in the aspirations of the poor. But once poverty is dealt with by providing basic needs such as adequate nutrition, health services, and education, population growth rates actually decline.[21]

Thus the overpopulation hypothesis, too, fails to provide an adequate explanation for the existence of world hunger. On the one hand, the relative reduction of population growth levels would not necessarily result in less hunger.

On the other, attacking the problem of hunger and poverty directly—with better nutrition, health care, and education—would not only increase the immediate well-being of the people involved, but should also, if past experience is any guide, reduce population pressures. The numerous complexities involved[22] notwithstanding, it is nevertheless possible to conclude that overpopulation is more the result of world hunger and poverty than it is the cause.

Our third hypothesis, that hunger is the result of technological underdevelopment, is closely related to the two which we have just examined, for it, too, assumes that the basic problem is one of scarcity. Rather than accepting this condition as fixed, as advocates of our first hypothesis do, or favoring a reduction in population to make food relatively less scarce, as advocates of our second hypothesis do, advocates of the technological underdevelopment hypothesis seek a solution to the scarcity problem through technical advances which will lead to an increase in the food supply. One would not want to dismiss this hypothesis out of hand, for it is certainly true that technological advances, particularly in relation to the development of new genetic strains of plants, have increased the food supply. Furthermore, even those societies, such as China, which have solved their hunger problems have done so only after making technological breakthroughs in agriculture.[23]

Yet technology is not the complete solution which many would have us believe. Suggestions that what is termed the "miracle of American agriculture" be adopted as a model for the underdeveloped world are particularly misleading. One problem with this "solution" is that the American "miracle" is much less of a miracle than most have assumed. Nothing is really obtained cost free, and the cost in American agriculture is energy—energy to run tractors, energy to make fertilizer, energy to package and transport agricultural products, energy for storage, and energy for retailing. As a result, although American agriculture has become more efficient in terms of output per laborer, "Since 1910, United States agricultural efficiency, as measured in energy, has *decreased* 10-fold."[24] Granted: (*a*) that not all this energy is consumed at the level of the farm, and (*b*) that such calculations normally fail to take into account the amount of energy necessary to support the greater number of farm workers required in a labor-intensive farm system, the American farm system, nonetheless, uses particularly energy-intensive technologies. In an energy-short world, the difficulty of adopting the American model of agriculture should thus be obvious.[25] Furthermore, even in the technologically sophisticated United States, the hunger problem has not been solved. But even if technology were a solution to the production problem, United States–style agriculture has dire consequences for the environment, consequences which may be undermining the viability of the agricultural ecosystem itself. As Catherine Lerza points out, fertilizer run-off is polluting water supplies; soil structure and soil fertility are being allowed to deteriorate because, with the availability of fertilizers, they no longer seem important; and fertile topsoil itself is disappearing (the United States has already lost about one-third of this resource).[26] Similar effects have been observed in other countries where American agricultural techniques have been adopted.[27] Add to this the consequences of the use of agricultural pesticides, consequences which include not only damage to the ecosystem but also medical problems for farm workers,[28] and one must seriously challenge technology as the panacea which will solve the hunger problem.

Although some of the difficulties which we have noted are inherent in technological solutions themselves, there is another, perhaps more important limitation to technology. Contrary to many people's assumption, technology is not a "neutral" force which dictates the best, most scientifically sound solution to problems. The choice of which technologies are to be developed and applied is a question as much of political economy as of "scientific objectivity." How is it determined, for example, whether farmers should use large tractors on large plots of land, or more "primitive" techniques on smaller plots? Some would have us believe that this decision is reached exclusively on the basis of technological efficiency. Yet in spite of the fact that in the Third World "small, intensively worked farms actually produce *more* per acre than large farms,"[29] the United States has often promoted the export of farm equipment which can be used only on large farms. Why? Obviously, someone must benefit from such a decision, and in this case, the beneficiaries are clear—the exporters of American farm machinery.

It is apparent, therefore, that the choice of a technology is at least partially dependent upon political and economic priorities. This fact has important implications for world hunger. Keith Griffin argues, for example, that a distinction can be made between "landlord-biased technical change" and "peasant-biased technical change" and that the choice between these approaches to agricultural innovation is entirely dependent upon the goals of the policy-maker. The former has "a large impact on production," but it will also "perpetuate the status quo" and actually "accentuate income inequality and could . . . increase the poverty of non-innovating producers."[30] The latter will "contribute relatively less to raising production." yet it will also have a "great impact on increasing the welfare of rural inhabitants" and "would tend to reduce income inequalities in the countryside and . . . [thus] undermine the status quo."[31] The techniques of the "Green Revolution"—the use of high-yielding plants, fertilizers, pesticides, and irrigation—which are an oft-proclaimed salvation for the hungry world (and which, not coincidentally, are highly profitable for the foreign exporters of this technology) turn out to be landlord-biased technical change; to the extent that benefits could be more widespread,[32] this outcome is prevented by the existing economic and political structures. As a result, one would expect that where Green Revolution technologies are adopted, hunger will actually increase, and this is exactly what happens. One recent study of seven non-socialist countries in Asia which have adopted Green Revolution technology found that in each one, though total production had increased, nutrition and well-being for the vast majority of the population *declined*.[33] The same effect has also been observed in a number of Latin American and African countries.[34]

The incompleteness of the technological change hypothesis is further evidenced by the fact that even some of its strongest advocates find themselves caught up in the political dimensions of the issue. Lester R. Brown, who has been associated with the Overseas Development Council, a group which puts a very strong emphasis on technological solutions to the hunger problem, is a typical example. His book *By Bread Alone*[35] devotes most of its pages to exploring the technological problems of agricultural development. Yet, in his chapter on hunger and unemployment, he notes that modernization will require not only technical changes, but also "profound changes in national development strategies and political and social changes."[36] Spending priorities in health and education will have to be shifted from urban areas to the countryside, expanded credit provided for the small farmer, and land reform instituted. For this to occur, Brown concludes, there must be "major changes in the way power is exercised."[37]

In the final analysis, therefore, even for an advocate of technological development, the necessary condition for solving the hunger problem is a change in political, economic, and social structures.

Inevitably, we are led to the fourth answer to the question "Why is there hunger in the world?" We have seen that scarcity is not the real cause of hunger; that overpopulation is more the result of hunger and poverty than their cause; and that technological development is inseparable from the impact of political and economic power. Let us now turn, therefore, to the hypothesis that world hunger is caused by the existing political and economic system.

CHANGE-ORIENTED POLITICAL SCIENCE AND THE QUESTION OF HUNGER

In examining our fourth hypothesis, we shall follow the outline suggested in the initial section of this article. First, we shall be guided by the idea that, to reduce the extent of world hunger, some changes are necessary. Second, to identify the areas in which change is needed, the major focus of this section will be to answer the question "Who benefits and who loses from existing economic and political structures?" Finally, in answering this question, we shall rely not only upon traditional political explanations of hunger, but also upon concepts drawn from the growing field of political economy.

Let us begin by identifying some of the winners and some of the losers under existing institutional structures. As we shall see, the winners tend to be the more affluent farmers, money lenders, and traditional elites, international agribusiness, multinational corporations engaged in farm machinery and fertilizer sales, banks which finance agricultural development, and consumers who have the greatest amount of buying power. Among the losers are farmers with few financial resources and those with small plots of land, landless peasants, farm workers, and rural and urban consumers with little buying power. What factors in the existing economic and political system are operative here?

The case of the farmers is instructive. For example, when the Green Revolution is introduced into an area, farmers need certain resources in order to be able to take advantage of the new technology: land, large amounts of water, chemical fertilizers, insecticides, and special seed and capital equipment (whether a tractor or an ox). In order for them to make such investments, considerable credit is necessary. But in countries in which credit is controlled by traditional rural elites, interest rates are very high. One example from the Philippines which Griffin cites showed that of the 224 rice farmers in his sample, over one-fifth were paying an interest rate of between 30% and 100% per year; another fifth were paying rates between 100% and 199%; and nearly one-sixth were paying an interest rate of more than 200%.[38] Another example, from Indonesia, indicates that the rates tend to vary with farm size—the larger the farm, the lower the rate.[39] Given this credit structure, the major impact of the Green Revolution has been to make the wealthy farmer wealthier, the poor farmer poorer. Sometimes this is only in comparative terms; but often the larger farmers, through their control of marketing mechanisms, force the small farmers out of business entirely, thereby increasing the number of landless peasants.

One of the most striking examples of this trend is to be found in Mexico, where the "miracle grains" which led to the Green Revolution were first developed. In the 1930s the Mexican government pursued a policy of land reform in an effort to break up the "latifundia system," in which large blocks of land were owned by a select few. These efforts were relatively successful, and by 1940 the number of landless peasants had been reduced from 68% to 36% of the rural population. Another group which benefited were the commercial farmers. Where profits had once been made through the control of land and labor, the new commercial farmers were now required to have "access to capital—especially irrigation facilities, tractors and combine harvesters";[40] the government, which wished to increase agricultural production, "channeled capital to the large, commercial farms."[41] One of the results of this was that between 1940 and 1960, the number of landless peasants *increased* from 36% to 53% of the rural population.[42] To make matters worse, greater mechanization on farms led to higher rates of unemployment among the growing number of landless peasants—a process which continues today with the support of foreign investments from the United States.[43] What occurred in Mexico has been repeated in many other countries of the underdeveloped world.[44]

The problem of an increasingly impoverished peasantry is compounded by a decrease in the availability of crops which make up the traditional diets of these groups. The new, large farms turn to cash crops which can produce the maximum return on investment, and in many cases, this means the growth of crops for export to countries where consumers have more money to spend on food. In Brazil, for example, there is now a shortage of black beans, one of the staples of the Brazilian diet, because crop land has been shifted to the production of soybeans for export. Not only do unemployed farm workers thus have less money for food, but, because of the shortage, the price of black beans has skyrocketed.[45] The situation is similar in Costa Rica, where from 1960 to 1970 meat production increased by 92%, but per capita meat consumption there over the same period *decreased* by 26%. Where did this additional production go? To the numerous, fast-food, franchise restaurants in the United States.[46] Similarly, Peru exports fishmeal to feed poultry and pigs in the United States[47] while many Peruvians suffer from protein deficiency.

The desire on the part of private producers to maximize profits by developing export crops is reinforced by the concern which Third World governments have with the balance of payments problem. These countries need capital goods to "modernize," and often the only source of such goods is the already industrialized world. But to buy these imports, a country must first acquire foreign currency through the sale of exports. Unfortunately, since few of the poorer countries produce goods which are in demand in the wealthier countries, many countries in the Third World have an inadequate supply of foreign exchange.[48] Given the current international market structure, therefore, there are pressures to produce cash crops for export (to gain foreign exchange) even when the immediate impact is an increase in domestic hunger.

The growth of profit-oriented agriculture in the Third World has also made investment in this area attractive to outside interests, as we saw in the case of Mexico. International agribusiness firms have been purchasing land and converting it to cash crops, including sugar, coffee, asparagus, strawberries, and such non-edibles as carnations.[49] Fertilizer and agricultural machinery firms also do their part to promote Green Revolution technology and to sell the idea of the "large, efficient American agricultural system." Banks as well see an opportunity to make money for their stockholders and thus have lent more than $45 billion to the less developed countries.[50] In the process of approving loans, banks demand that certain economic policies be followed by the recipient nations and that others be excluded. For example, the borrowing country may be "encouraged" to allow the private sector to perform the functions of agriculture as soon as possible, to produce agricultural goods for the market and not for government purchase, and to refrain from a policy of government control over industry.[51] The policies of the banks are reinforced by the requirements of international agencies. The International Monetary Fund, for example, demands policies which limit public expenditures, reduce inflationary pressures, and strengthen the balance of payments positions of recipient nations—all of which may produce a stability good for investment and growth, but lead to higher levels of unemployment and an increase in hunger and malnutrition.[52]

Often outside investors will cooperate with domestic actors in the host country, who provide their assistance because of the opportunity for personal gain or the need for foreign exchange, or, perhaps, for both reasons. One analyst cites an example from Senegal, where a European investment group interested in growing vegetables for export prompted the government to throw the peasants off the land and the Peace Corps to assist in building the irrigation network which would make the project feasible.[53] In Brazil the government has been pushing for the development of large farms and the use of mechanized equipment and, as we have seen, the result has been increased production, yet increased hunger. In the Philippines, the government land redistribution and credit program requires recipients to adopt Green Revolution technology in order to participate. Profits for the manufacturers of fertilizer, pesticides, and high-yielding–variety seeds are up. Yet the nutritional levels of significant segments of the Philippine people have declined.[54] Existing legal institutions in India, Pakistan, and many Latin American countries also preserve a system of unequal distribution of land, with greater hunger the result.[55]

Yet the powers of the multinationals and their local allies are not unlimited. Since there are some groups in the host countries which are nationally oriented, and prepared to resist the demands of multinational corporations, more often than not, the relations between multinationals and host governments take the form of a "bargaining game" in which both the multinationals (with their local allies) and the nationalists in the host country have their own political and economic weapons.[56] Nevertheless, even at a time when some evidence would suggest that multinational corporations are having to compromise more often than in the past,[57] there continue to be cases of blatant interference from the outside, a particularly egregious example of which is the activity of International Telephone and Telegraph in Chile.[58]

The kinds of relationships between corporations and governments which we have just described also pervade those government programs which were designed ostensibly to feed the hungry. To illustrate this, we shall briefly examine two aid programs of the United States, since their size makes their potential for worldwide impact great. Many have characterized the first of these, the "Food for Peace" program, which was set up under Public Law 480, as one more indication of the generosity of Americans in dealing with the needs of other people. However, though this program has served the needs of various interests in the United States very well, its benefits for the poor abroad have been somewhat mixed. In the United States, one of the major purposes of Food for Peace was to reduce the vast agricultural surpluses which accumulated after the end of the Second World War. As one author notes, "During the 1950s . . . PL 480 was primarily an instrument of domestic policy, and the pet of the farm lobby."[59] As a result, the "food" for peace program exports not only surplus wheat, but surplus cotton and tobacco as well.[60] Furthermore, when surpluses have not been a problem in the United States, food aid under this program has declined. Between 1966, when surpluses were a problem, and 1974, when there was an international grain shortage, exports under the program fell from 18 million tons of grain to just 3.3 million tons[61]—at the very time the need for food abroad was at its highest. As United States surpluses increased after 1975, so did Food for Peace aid; yet the kind of grains being sent abroad reflects more what the United States has in surplus at the time than what foreign nations have requested.[62]

But the fact that United States interests have benefited from PL 480 does not prove that the poor abroad could not also have benefited, yet evidence suggests that they have not often been beneficiaries. Since the program was founded, the major recipients of aid under PL 480 have been the military allies of the United States rather than those countries with the greatest hunger problem.[63] Even when food aid was directed to countries where it was most needed, it tended to reach the wrong people. Wheat, one of the major exports under the program, went mainly to the non-poor, since the staple used by most poor people abroad was rice.[64] Furthermore, aid received under PL 480 tended to discourage agricultural development abroad, driving poorer farmers out of business and reinforcing the bias of many Third World governments toward the development of heavy industry at the expense of agriculture.[65] Even when agricultural development did occur, it tended to be highly dependent on the importing of American feed grains and American technology.[66] Though the benefits of the Food for Peace Program for United States farmers and exporters of American farm technology are clear, the benefits for the poor abroad are harder to identify.

Another major thrust of United States policy is the foreign aid program, operated by the Agency for International Development (AID). As with Food for Peace, AID's programs clearly benefit United States interests. In fiscal year 1971, for example, of the $975 million worth of commodities purchased for overseas distribution, 99% were purchased in the United States. In addition, $632 million of the AID budget that same year was spent for the "technical service contracts with U.S. companies, consulting firms, and institutions."[67] It is understandable, therefore, that the foreign aid program is often sold to a reluctant Congress as an "aid package" for the United States.

Abroad, the benefits are again mixed. AID, for example, is one of the major promoters of Green Revolution technology. As we have seen, although such technology does increase agricultural production, it also, given existing political and economic structures, tends to benefit the already affluent at the expense of the poor. AID, too, has been an active supporter of international agribusiness. An October 27, 1976 cable, for example, instructs AID's mission directors to follow policies which increase private business and any opportunities for United States agribusiness investment. The primary example of a good program cited in the cable is that of the Latin American Agribusiness Development Corporation[68]—the firm responsible for the growing of carnations in Costa Rica, thereby contributing to the hunger problem in that country. Thus, the AID program, as the Food for Peace program, benefits some at the expense of others.

When such programs have failed to protect United States interests sufficiently, the United States government has often resorted to political coercion. For example, when Green Revolution technology was adopted in India in the early 1960s, the need for fertilizer increased. The Indian government decided to develop fertilizer plants and, following established policies, tried to ensure that at least a majority interest in these factories would be under domestic control. When foreign firms, whose technological assistance the Indians needed, hesitated to get involved, President Johnson put pressure on the Indians to modify their laws by refusing to appropriate any PL 480 funds for India. Johnson relented "in 1965, [only] when the Indian government finally allowed private foreign fertilizer companies full control over product pricing and distribution."[69] On other occasions, the United States has used its dominant influence over such international agencies as the International Monetary Fund and the World Bank to force recipient nations to change their economic policies in favor of the development of private ownership and the market system of distribution. Such policies have had an impact on, among other countries, Egypt, Burma, Ceylon (now Sri Lanka), Iraq, Indonesia, Brazil, Bolivia, Costa Rica, and Guatemala.[70]

But when economic coercion fails, the United States has often used other means. Chile, of course, is the classic example. There the United States government and American-based multinational corporations, fearing what they correctly termed "an experiment in socialism," worked hand in hand to help to effect the downfall of Salvador Allende, using techniques running the gamut from attempts to "destabilize" the economy to interference in the Chilean electoral process.[71] Similarly, when Brazil seemed to be moving too far to the left in 1964, the Brazilian military took over "with obvious approval from the United States."[72] Recently it has been revealed that, for a brief period in 1964, the United States was prepared "to intervene in Brazil with naval and airborne units . . . to prevent leftist forces from seizing power. . . ."[73] Numerous examples of similar actions could be cited—from Guatemala in 1954 to the Dominican Republic in 1965 to Angola in 1976—to show that such incidents, far from being aberrations,[74] represent a long-term policy of the United States government.

The United States also provides both aid and training to help to strengthen the very kind of social structures which we have found to be a major cause of hunger. Once Allende was overthrown in Chile, for example, support from the United States and various international agencies influenced by the United

States again began to flow. There has also been a good deal of support for the Brazilian government since 1964. Assistance involves not only economic and military aid, but also special training programs to help such regimes prevent radical changes in political, social, and economic institutions. AID's "Public Safety" program has trained or provided supplies to more than one million policemen throughout the world, and according to former AID administrator David Bell, the program is designed to help to "establish and maintain the environment of stability and security so essential to economic, social and political progress. . . ."[75] It hardly seems necessary to point out that the kind of "progress" promoted by this program looks more toward increased production and profits than toward a more equitable distribution of available resources.

At this point it seems safe to conclude that we have found strong support for our fourth hypothesis about the causes of world hunger. It is more than evident that hunger is perpetuated by the world economic and political structure. This brings us, also, to a second conclusion. Since the United States government is one of the major supporters and sustainers of this system, the policies of the United States are a major cause of world hunger. This is a very difficult conclusion, since it runs counter to the common notion of the American people that their country has done more than any other nation in the world to relieve the hunger problem, and counter to the notions of a number of contemporary political analysts.[76] By choosing to focus on the question "Who gains and who loses?" and by choosing to examine the political economy of hunger, we have thus come up with a startling picture of political "reality."

What does this tell us about solutions to the hunger problem? What does it tell us about the capacity of political science to deal with questions of justice? We now turn to these two issues.

POLITICAL SCIENCE, JUSTICE, AND SOLUTIONS TO THE WORLD HUNGER PROBLEM

The preceding analysis has followed the pattern which was indicated in the first part of this essay: it began with values in its selection of issues to study and the tools to use for this analysis; it then examined available evidence; now, once again, the question of values arises—in light of the analysis, what should be done? Before we answer that question it would be useful to ask what kind of solutions a more maintenance-oriented analysis might have offered. Had we pursued that kind of analysis, we might have concluded with Brown that, although some changes may be needed, they can be brought about through existing political and economic institutions, and we could then have called for family planning services, for simplifying diets (for reasons of both health and morality), for a "people-oriented development strategy," agrarian reform, and rural public works projects.[77] And we could have said with Brown that:

Whether or not the great food producing potential of the developing world is tapped will depend on both the extent to which the developing-country governments are *willing* to adopt the policies necessary to maximize rural development and the extent to which the economically advanced nations and international aid agencies are *willing* and able to provide appropriate financial and technical assistance.[78]

Brown's reasoning is both faultless and fallible: faultless because these are precisely the kinds of changes which must come about if the hunger problem is to be solved by the existing political and economic institutions; and fallible because, as our analysis illustrates, it requires those who are the beneficiaries of the current system so to change it that the benefits are more widely distributed. Although such actions are impossible, they are extremely unlikely.

Using a change-oriented form of political science leads us in another direction. It causes us (*a*) to challenge, with Griffin, the assumptions "first, that we live in a self-equilibrating system and, second, that there is a basic harmony of interests among the individuals and groups who comprise the system";[79] and (*b*) to accept an alternative picture of what the world may be like. In Griffin's words:

> Our view of the world is quite different. It is akin to that of Karl Marx, who saw class conflict where others imagined harmony, of Thomas Malthus, who feared a cumulative downward spiral as a result of the tendency of population to expand faster than food production, and of David Ricardo, who foresaw that mechanization could create unemployment and hardship.[80]

Although our analysis would dispute the conclusiveness of Malthus' hypothesis, it would certainly tend to support the world-view offered by Karl Marx and David Ricardo. To the extent that this picture is an accurate one, it throws into question the kinds of solutions to the hunger problem which are offered by a maintenance-oriented science of politics.

What kinds of solutions does this lead us to? Inescapably, again, it seems to suggest the need for fundamental changes in the political and economic systems of the underdeveloped nations. That is, power must pass from the groups which currently possess it to groups which are more representative of the people as a whole. Thus, as Joseph Collins concludes, the right question is not "How can more food be produced?" but "How do we remove the obstacles preventing people from taking control of the production process and feeding themselves?"[81] History would seem to teach us that this is much more likely to come about through a violent social upheaval, as in China or Cuba, than through the kinds of reformist efforts which are occurring in countries such as India.

In terms of United States policy, this strongly suggests that the kinds of social revolutions which have been resisted in the past should no longer be opposed. More than likely, though, fundamental changes will have to occur in the United States itself before such policies could be adopted. In terms of individual involvement, the above analysis suggests that persons should resist, wherever and whenever possible, the actions of those who are contributing to the hunger problem. Such resistance might take the form of efforts to influence national legislation or of campaigns to boycott United States firms which are compounding the hunger problem abroad. A full discussion of such options, however, is beyond the scope of the current essay.[82]

Finally, what does our examination of the hunger issue tell us about the behavioralist/post-behavioralist debate? It seems to suggest that, at least in this case, the post-behavioralists have the better part of the argument. Maintenance-oriented analysis of the hunger issue leads to conservative conclusions; to a plea for marginal adjustments in a system which, by its very nature, compounds the hunger problem; to conclusions which fail to take into consideration the full dynamics of the political economy of hunger. In contrast, change-oriented political science recognizes injustice for what it is and calls for basic changes in political and economic structures. Ironically, by admitting the legitimacy of value questions, change-oriented political science also produces a more accurate picture of the empirical world than does behavioralism. Therefore, at least in the case of world hunger, it would be wise for political scientists to recognize that their discipline rests not only upon the "scientific" foundations of a Hobbes or a Machiavelli, but also upon the kinds of "philosophical" questions asked by an Aristotle or a Plato. To do otherwise would be to maintain a dangerous illusion.[83]

NOTES

1. On this point see Eugene F. Miller, "Positivism, Historicism, and Political Enquiry," *American Political Science Review*, 66, No. 3 (September 1972), 796–817.

2. See, for example, David Easton, *The Political System* (New York: Knopf, 1953).

3. "The New Revolution in Political Science," *American Political Science Review*, 63, No. 4 (December 1969), 1051–1061.

4. As an example of this tendency, see Aaron Wildavsky, *The Politics of the Budgetary Process*, 2nd ed. (Boston: Little, Brown, 1974).

5. Easton, "New Revolution," 1052.

6. See, for example, *The Post-Behavioral Era: Perspectives on Political Science*, edd. George J. Graham, Jr. and George W. Carey (New York: McKay, 1972). Note particularly chaps. 2, 3, 9, and 11.

7. A point made in David Braybrooke and Alexander Rosenberg, "Comment: Getting the War News Straight—The Actual Situation in the Philosophy of Science," *American Political Science Review*, 66, No. 3 (September 1972), 818–26, at 824–25.

8. Ibid., 824.

9. Miller, "Political Enquiry," 809.

10. Martin Landau, "Comment: On Objectivity," *American Political Science Review*, 66, No. 3 (September 1972), 846–56, at 853–54.

11. This is Karl Marx's dictum, as cited in Eugene J. Meehan, "What Should Political Scientists Be Doing," in *Post-Behavioral Era*, edd. Graham & Carey, p. 58.

12. That is, it will not focus on the question of system maintenance. To cite just a few examples of maintenance-type models of politics from several different areas of the discipline: Richard F. Fenno, Jr., *Congressmen in Committees* (Boston: Little, Brown, 1973); Graham T. Allison, *The Essence of Decision* (Boston: Little, Brown, 1971); Gabriel A. Almond and G. Bingham Powell, *Comparative Politics: A Developmental Approach* (Boston: Little, Brown, 1966); and Morton Kaplan, *System and Process in International Politics* (New York: Basic Books, 1957).

13. See *The Political Sciences* (New York: Basic Books, 1969), esp. the section on "Scientific Selection," pp. 161–74 and the comments on p. 236.

14. For an excellent commentary on the meaning of justice as expressed in the Bible, see Richard K. Taylor, *Economics and the Gospel* (Philadelphia: United Church Press, 1973).

15. The author is very aware of the distinction which Karl Deutsch makes between values (our patterns of actions over time) and value images (what most people call values, i.e., our aspirations, or what we think we believe in). To a certain extent the use of the term "values" in the text refers to patterns of actions; but it also refers to what are as yet unfulfilled aspirations. For a discussion of values and value images, see Deutsch's *The Nerves of Government* (New York: Free Press, 1966).

16. This is the kind of argument which is developed in Garrett Hardin, *Exploring New Ethics for Survival* (New York: Viking, 1972).

17. This argument is well-documented in F. H. Sanderson, "The Great Food Fumble," *Science*, 188, No. 4188 (May 9, 1975), 503–509.

18. These figures for arable land are taken from J. D. Gavan and J. A. Dixon, "India: A Perspective on the Food Situation," ibid., 541–49, at 545. I have converted the figures from hectares to acres. This article also indicates that India has not solved the hunger problem for her people and explores some of the reasons why. Regarding the lack of hunger in China, see G. F. Sprague, "Agriculture in China," ibid., 549–55. See also Sterling Wortman, "Agriculture in China," *Scientific American*, 232, No. 6 (June 1975), 14–21. On the existence of hunger in the United States, see *Food for People Not for Profit*, edd. Catherine Lerza and Michael Jacobson (New York: Ballantine, 1975), part 5.

19. See Frances Moore Lappé and Joseph Collins, "More Food Means More Hunger," *Development Forum*, 4 (November 1976), 1–2.

20. See, for example, Hardin, *New Ethics*.

21. Lester R. Brown, *By Bread Alone* (New York: Praeger, 1974), pp. 183–88.

22. See, for example, Edward J. Woodhouse, "Re-Visioning the Future of the Third World: An Ecological Perspective on Development," *World Politics*, 25, No. 1 (October 1972), 1–33, at 15–21.

23. Unpublished lecture on agriculture in China given by Dr. Anne Thurston, Fordham University (November 1, 1977).

24. Catherine Lerza, "Emptying the Cornucopia," in *Food for People*, edd. Lerza & Jacobson, pp. 45–57, at p. 48; emphasis added.

25. See, for example, Woodhouse, "Re-Visioning the Future," 10–15.

26. "Emptying the Cornucopia," pp. 49–51.

27. For some examples of the impact of the use of fertilizer and pesticides abroad, see Brown, *By Bread Alone*, pp. 49–55.

28. See Daniel Zwerdling, "The New Pesticide Threat," in *Food for People*, edd. Lerza & Jacobson, pp. 93–98.

29. Brown, *By Bread Alone*, p. 214.

30. *The Political Economy of Agrarian Change* (Cambridge: Harvard University Press, 1974), p. 51.

31. Ibid. For a discussion of the links between land ownership and political power, see Barrington Moore, Jr., *Social Origins of Dictatorship and Democracy* (Boston: Beacon, 1970), passim.

32. Griffin suggests that Green Revolution technology tends "either to be landlord-biased or ultra-superior." He defines "ultra-superior" to mean that the technological innovation would be profitable for all producers to adopt. What prevents the adoption of such a technology by the poorer farmers, however, is the existing political and economic structure (*Agrarian Change*, pp. 49, 51).

33. This study, which was then soon to be published, was referred to by Dr. Joseph Collins during a conference on "Increasing Food Production in Developing Countries: Government Policy and the Commercial Sector," Columbia University, November 19, 1976. The study was done by Keith Griffin and Azizur Khan for the International Labor Organization. Parts of the study are summarized in Francis Moore Lappé and Joseph Collins, *Food First* (Boston: Houghton Mifflin, 1977), pp. 132–33.
One set of studies which seems to dispute the notion that Green Revolution technology leads to more hunger is cited in Victor K. McElheny, "Rice and the Green Revolution, Los Banos, Philippines: The Poor Didn't Get Poorer," in The Staff of The New York Times, *Give Us This Day* . . . (New York: Arno, 1975), pp. 204–208. The flaw in these studies relates to the sites which were selected for analysis. McElheny notes: "Because the study was looking for effects of the Green Revolution, it focused on villages that were ready for change. They tended to be more prosperous than average and to have become accustomed to fertilizers and pesticides and, in some cases, machinery" (p. 207). Such sites, of course, are *least likely* to reveal the negative effects of the Green Revolution. On this point, see Harry Cleaver, "Will the Green Revolution Turn Red?" in *The Trojan Horse: A Radical Look at Foreign Aid*, edd. Steve Weissman, et al. (San Francisco: Ramparts, 1974), pp. 171–200, at pp. 182–88.

34. See William C. Thiesenhusen, "Green Revolution in Latin America: Income Effects, Policy Decisions," *Monthly Labor Review*, 95, No. 3 (March 1972), 20–27. See also Robin Dennis and Ruthanne Landness, "Economics of Hunger," *Science for the People*, 7 (March 1975), 17–20.

35. See note 21.

36. Ibid., p. 216.

37. Ibid., p. 225.

38. *Agrarian Change*, p. 28.

39. Ibid., p. 29.

40. Ibid., p. 93.

41. Ibid., p. 94.

42. Ibid., p. 93.

43. See, for example, Jack Anderson and Les Whitten, "Mexico, U. S. United by More Than Border," *The Reporter Dispatch* of Westchester County, New York, 61 (December 21, 1977), A 12.

44. See Cleaver, "Green Revolution."

45. See Jonathan Kandell, " 'Miracle' of Brazil Makes a Staple Scarce," *The New York Times*, 126 (December 14, 1976), 3.

46. Richard Barnet and Ronald Müller, "How Global Corporations Compound World Hunger," in *Food for People*, edd. Lerza & Jacobson, pp. 248–52, at p. 248.

47. Brown, *By Bread Alone*, pp. 155–56.

48. The discussion in the paragraph is based largely upon Richard J. Barnet and Ronald E. Müller, *Global Reach* (New York: Simon & Schuster, 1974), p. 156.

49. The latter three items are mentioned in Barnet and Müller, "World Hunger," p. 250.

50. This figure was cited by Ernest C. Charron of the Chase Manhattan Bank at the Food Conference at Columbia University (see note 33).

51. These examples were cited ibid.

52. See, for example, Alan Riding, "Austerity Aids Mexican Economy But Imposes Hardships on Many," *The New York Times*, 127 (November 17, 1977), A 14. International Monetary Fund policies can also cause hardships even in the developed countries. See, for example, Peter T. Kilborn, "Britain to Ask I.M.F. for $3.9 Billion Loan, Its Borrowing Limit," *The New York Times*, 126 (September 30, 1976), 1. For a thorough analysis of the origin and impact of the policies of the International Monetary Fund and the World Bank, see Cheryl Payer, "The IMF and the Third World," and Bruce Nissen, "Building the World Bank," in *The Trojan Horse*, edd. Weissman, et al., pp. 61–72, 35–60, respectively. It should be pointed out that, although the above observations apply to the underdeveloped world, many of the same factors are at work in the United States. Small farmers have been driven off the land; there has been an increase in the number of unemployed in farm areas, many of whom have migrated to the cities; agricultural production is being increasingly controlled by agribusiness corporations; pesticides are being used even when they threaten the health of farm workers; products are being produced more with an eye to profit than with a concern for quality or nutrition; prices are manipulated by retail outlets, and advertising increasingly shapes our buying patterns in ways which add to the problem of hunger. On these points see: *Food for People*, edd. Lerza & Jacobson, parts 1–2, and pp. 372–80; Nick Kotz, *Let Them Eat Promises: The Politics of Hunger in America* (Garden City, N.Y.: Doubleday Anchor, 1969), p. 48; Weldon V. Barton, "Food, Agriculture, and Administrative Adaptation to Political Change," *Public Administration Review*, 36 (March/April 1976), 148–54, at 152. It should be noted that many of the comments about United States efforts to feed the poor abroad also apply to United States domestic food programs. On this point, see Kotz, *Let Them Eat Promises*, pp. 45, 48–49, 67–68; Judith A. Segal, *Food for the Hungry: The Reluctant Society* (Baltimore: The Johns Hopkins University Press, 1970), pp. 44–46, 48. Finally, just as United States foreign policy often involves coercion, so, too, does United States domestic policy. On this, see Kotz, *Let Them Eat Promises*, pp. 23, 49; and Segal, *Food for the Hungry*, p. 57.

53. This example was cited by Dr. Joseph Collins at the Food Conference at Columbia University (see note 33). See also Lappé & Collins, *Food First*, pp. 259–60.

54. This example was cited by Dr. Joseph Collins at the Food Conference at Columbia University (see note 33).

55. Griffin, *Agrarian Change*, pp. 18–22.

56. This notion is developed in Theodore H. Moran, *Multinational Corporations and the Politics of Dependence* (Princeton: Princeton University Press,

1974), chap. 6. See also Raymond Vernon and Louis T. Wells, Jr., *Economic Environment of International Business*, 2nd ed. (Englewood Cliffs, N.J.: Prentice-Hall, 1976), chap. 5. For some examples of these relationships, see Richard S. Newfarmer and Willard F. Mueller, *Multinational Corporations in Brazil and Mexico: Structural Sources of Economic and Noneconomic Power* (Washington, D.C.: Government Printing Office, 1975), the report to the Subcommittee on Multinational Corporations of the Senate Committee on Foreign Relations, 94th Congress, 1st Session. For a theoretical examination of how governments and economic elites interact in a capitalist state, see Theda Skocpol, "A Critical Review of Barrington Moore's Social Origins of Dictatorship and Democracy," *Politics and Society*, 4, No. 1 (Fall 1973), 1–34.

57. Moran, *Multinational Corporations*, pp. 157–69.

58. For an account of these actions, see *Multinational Corporations and United States Foreign Policy* (Washington, D.C.: Government Printing Office, 1973), parts 1–2; this is a report of hearings before the Subcommittee on Multinational Corporations of the Senate Committee on Foreign Relations, 83rd Congress, 1st Session. Even the testimony and accompanying documents found here, which paint a disturbing picture, may have covered up worse actions. See Seymour M. Hersh, "C.I.A.–I.T.T. Conspiracy Charged at Hearing," *The New York Times*, 126 (December 23, 1976), 1ff.

59. Israel Yost, "The Food for Peace Arsenal," in *The Trojan Horse*, edd. Weissman, et al., pp. 157–69, at p. 159.

60. Arthur Simon, *Bread for the World* (New York: Paulist Press, 1975), p. 117.

61. Emma Rothschild, "Is It Time to End Food for Peace?" *The New York Times Magazine* (March 13, 1977), 15ff, at 46.

62. Ibid., 47.

63. Daniel Balz, "Food for Peace—or Politics," in *Food for People*, edd. Lerza & Jacobson, pp. 273–78, at p. 277. See also Rothschild, "Food for Peace," 44.

64. Rothschild, "Food for peace," 45.

65. Ibid.

66. See, for example, ibid.

67. Appendix A in *Food for People*, edd. Lerza & Jacobson, pp. 237–40, at p. 238.

68. This cable was summarized by Dr. Joseph Collins at the Food Conference at Columbia University (see note 33).

69. Mary Roodkowsky, "PL 480: Aid for Arms and Agribusiness," *Self-Education Packet* (Cambridge, Mass.: Committee for Self Education, 1976), p. 3.

70. Nissen, "Building the World Bank," p. 57n. See also Payer, "The IMF and the Third World."

71. See *Multinational Corporations and United States Foreign Policy.*

72. Payer, "The IMF and the Third World," p. 70.

73. David Binder, "U.S. Assembled a Force in 1964 for Possible Use in Brazil Coup," *The New York Times*, 126 (December 30, 1976), 7.

74. Arthur Simon is in error when he sees such incidents as aberrations in what has traditionally been a policy of American benevolence (*Bread for the World*, chap. 7). In contrast, see William A. Williams, *The Tragedy of American Diplomacy* (New York: Dell, 1970).

75. Cited in Nancy Stein and Mike Klare, "Police Aid for Tyrants," in *Trojan Horse*, edd. Weissman, et al., pp. 221–35. For an example of this policy in action,

see Jack Shepherd, *The Politics of Starvation* (New York: Carnegie Endowment for International Peace, 1975).

76. See, for example, Brown, *By Bread Alone*; Hardin, *New Ethics*; and Simon, *Bread for the World*.

77. Brown, *By Bread Alone*, pp. 181–83, 197–208, 214–17, 219–24.

78. Ibid., p. 215; emphasis added.

79. Griffin, *Agrarian Change*, 248.

80. Ibid.

81. Lappé & Collins, "More Food," 2.

82. For examples of some options, see the following: Simon, *Bread for the World*, pp. 133–59; *Food for People*, edd. Lerza & Jacobson, pp. 407–27; Taylor, *Economics and the Gospel*, passim; and "Around the Country," *Food Monitor*, 1 (1977), 11.

83. This essay has benefited from the insights of three individuals whom the author wishes to acknowledge. I wish to thank William C. Baumgarth, my colleague in Political Science at Fordham, for referring me to a number of sources which were very useful in the development of the ideas contained in part 1 of this essay. I also wish to thank Bruce Andrews, another colleague in Political Science at Fordham, and Donald P. Evenson, Associate of the Sloan Kettering Institute and Assistant Professor in Cornell's Graduate School of Medical Science. Both these individuals read an early draft of the essay and contributed valuable comments and suggestions. Dr. Andrews was most helpful in the areas of international politics and international political economy. Dr. Evenson, who pursues an avocation in agricultural policy with the intensity of a vocation, helped me avoid a number of errors. Needless to say, each of these three individuals would disagree with some of the points made in this essay and therefore, as is both customary and proper, I absolve them from blame for any weaknesses in the analysis.

10

Science, Technology, and Justice

RICHARD W. ROZETT, S.J.

Fordham University

THE AMERICAN CHILD is introduced to the evil scientist on afternoon television. Dr. Chang threatens the very fabric of Western civilization with his fiendish laser death ray. Our mythology is peopled with characters such as Dr. Jekyll and Mr. Hyde, Dr. Frankenstein and his monster. The evil scientist is a stock character of the popular imagination, but not, I think, of the imagination of the practicing scientist. The self-image of the scientist is a personal amalgam of several different roles. Perhaps it is one part the white-coated, antiseptic, objective observer on the television commercial, who says, "Science has shown that. . . ." And the other part is the image of the keeper of the cornucopia, that source of jets and cars, food and clothing, detergents, plastics, medicines, electronics—all those good things which make up modern life. The scientist typically views himself as a source of information and evidence, as a systematic and objective analyst, as an adventurous discoverer, as the creator and provider.

Recent decades have not been kind to this self-complacent view of science. The atom bomb and the intercontinental ballistic missile had something to do with it. Nazi scientists experimenting with V-2's and with people contributed to it. Communist sputniks and American napalm reinforced the impression. Science is not merely an objective arbitrator, not merely a benevolent millionaire scattering gifts. It has dark, threatening aspects. There is such a thing as malevolent science and, therefore, presumably, there are evil scientists.

Misgivings about science are not new. Humanists were convinced long ago that science depersonalized men and transformed the warm, living cosmos into an ugly, empty machine. Religiously-oriented people believed that science was materialist and atheist in tendency, and destructive of faith, morality, and love. Many claim that the reductionist tunnel-vision of the scientific method robs man of his uniqueness and freedom, and teaches him to forget God. Opposition is not new. What is new is the scientific evidence supporting the opposition. It is true that some of the evidence is circumstantial, and appears to support a case of guilt by association. Scientists detect and report that smoking is injurious to your health, that the burning of coal pollutes the atmosphere, that cholesterol intake may be excessive. Science did not invent coal, tobacco, milk or eggs. But it has blackened the reputation of wholesome things, and tarred itself in the process.

Some of the evidence is more damaging. The food additives created by scientists have driven millions away from the public food supply. The scientists' detergents have polluted our rivers, scientists' freon has damaged our ozone umbrella, scientists' DDT has killed our wildlife, PCB's created by scientists have closed down fishing in the Hudson River. The list seems endless. Of the 30,000 commercial chemicals, one estimate makes 1,500 of them carcinogenic in animals. Mutagens, radioactive wastes, the plutonium economy; chemicals in the air, chemicals in our drinking water, chemicals in our food. You have polluted our world; you threaten to destroy us all. On your own testimony we convict you.

This is the issue I should like to address. Has our technological society become dangerous to our health? Are its creators irresponsible, unjust? Is science really a neutral, intellectual game? What are the moral aspects of the practice of science, and where does responsibility lie?

It is helpful, first of all, to define some terms. By "science" in the present context I mean that body of knowledge, that practice of observation and mathematical elaboration, that art of discovery, that method of validation, and that art of application, which is practiced by physicists, chemists, geologists, oceanographers, meteorologists, and similar people. The appropriate engineers are included, and biologists insofar as they use comparable techniques. This is very far indeed these days.

Knowledge is not of itself moral or immoral, just or unjust. In all probability, the widespread opinion among scientists that science in itself is not just or unjust is based upon this experience of it as a cognitive effort. But a cognitive enterprise can be just or unjust in at least three ways. Knowledge may not be moral, but the *search* for knowledge, the process of learning, can be moral or immoral. Secondly, scientific knowledge is essentially social in character, and inherently requires communication. Now, the process of *communicating* science can be just or unjust. Finally, physical science is inherently related to invention and application. Technology is a part of science. Now, this *use* of science may be just or unjust. This discussion of the moral aspects of the practice of science will be divided into three parts: the first will be concerned with the moral aspects of acquiring scientific knowledge or research, the second considers the moral aspects of communicating scientific knowledge, and the final section discusses ethical aspects of the use of scientific knowledge.

MORAL ASPECTS OF RESEARCH

The process of acquiring new scientific knowledge, or research, has a number of different component strands. Four of them seem pertinent to the present concern.

Objectivity. In the popular mind the scientific ideal is almost synonymous with freedom from prejudice and from the distortion of evidence by personal concerns or beliefs. For scientists generally, I believe, the most prominent moral demand experienced during the scientific effort is the need to sacrifice a favored interpretation in the face of the facts, and the demand to accept the unexpected. This objectivity and detachment may be misunderstood. In fact, it is often misinterpreted as political, moral, or religious neutrality. As we shall see in the fourth aspect of research, this is not an accurate formulation. Nonetheless, freedom from interior, private motives which determine the acceptance of scientific conclusions is a primary ideal and moral demand for scientists. Furthermore, objectivity, freedom *from*, is merely the negative aspect of freedom *for*. The positive aspect is an openness to experience, a willingness to learn. A scientist is a learner, a listener. Many other professionals would claim as much, but the material reality to which the scientist listens speaks in an unusually simple, clear, and even repetitious fashion. This stance of impartial empiricism is reinforced by frequent success. Lapses in this attitude on the part of the scientist are punished by quick, detectible, even explosive, sanctions. Objective empiricism is a prominent feature of science.

Impartial empiricism is not merely an intellectual prerequisite of research. It is also experienced, at least on occasion, as a moral demand. There are a number of threats to this moral attitude of scientists. One of the more highly publicized currently is the distortion of scientific judgment by the advocacy of socially popular causes. A much deeper source of distortion is the force of the egoism and ambition of the individual scientist. But in my judgment the primary distorting influence in this country at this time are the commercial interests of scientists and their employers. Research has been commercialized in a number of different senses. First of all, it has become expensive. Almost without exception research projects require instrumentation and materials. Funds must be acquired from some source to support these needs. Secondly, industrial science is very big business indeed. The marketing of products produced by science and technology means that large sums of money are at stake on the outcome of research. The buying of scientists and the selling of scientific conclusions in various forms are not unknown. Finally, the rise of the commercial research institute, private consulting of academic scientists by industry, and the importance of patents on processes or devices have all added a commercial flavor to the conduct of research. The economic aspects of research are a perfectly natural and good thing. The distortion of objectivity by those economic forces is an immoral thing.

The positive, empirical aspect of science also can be just or unjust. Some knowledge is morally required. In some sort of hypothetical sense, this is true of the basic knowledge demanded by the practice of any profession. In a research project honesty demands that one not deliberately avoid embarrassing evidence. In a laboratory or in a factory, crass ignorance about safety procedures, such as in the recent Kepone incident, has a moral dimension. In the research supporting the marketing of a pharmaceutical or other product, deliberate ignorance about side-effects and long-term consequences is an unethical option.

Rigor. The scientific attitude is not merely impartial and empirical. It is also characterized by a critical attitude and by high standards of proof. To the novice the scientist may seem skeptical and overly suspicious. But this attitude is based upon the experience that reality has no mercy on the hasty and the gullible. A house built with a single weak beam can collapse suddenly. This rigorous critical attitude is shown in the process of observation by a cautious empiricism, methodical observation, quantitative measurement. In the process of validation it manifests itself as a step-by-step testing of hypotheses based on publicly available, quantitative observations. In the elaboration and interpretation of the observed information, this rigor shows itself in cautious and qualified conclusions, in the use of mathematical tools, and in the construction of verifiable hypotheses. This rigorous, quantitative, analytic aspect of the scientific method makes it unacceptable to many free spirits. Exact measurement, mathematical elaboration, order, and restraint are not currently popular traits.

Scientists no less than the rest of mortals are subject to the moral failings of the short cut, the sloppy observation, the ready conclusion. But there are some peculiarly scientific moral failures of rigor. The widespread use of sophisticated instrumentation has provided an opportunity for the use of instruments as "black boxes," devices used ignorantly, devices misapplied, devices misused. Under the guise of quantitative measurement, qualitatively incorrect observations are conducted. Another peculiarly scientific failure of rigor is the misuse of mathematics. Algebraic flights of fancy, statistical lies, are considerably more common than most would believe. Both these failures are combined in the irresponsible use of the computer. The availability of the digital computer and program libraries allows almost anyone to perform extensive calculations despite ignorance of the mathematical techniques, their valid range of application, and their limitations. There is no more guarantee of valid results in such a procedure than there would be if one should attempt to produce a chosen chemical compound by applying a random cookbook recipe to an arbitrary selection of chemicals. The erroneous and not infrequently immoral use of the computer is destined to become a serious concern for scientists.

Creativity. Creativity separates the scientist from the technician. The scientist in his own way is a poet. There are no recipes by which new scientific knowledge can be produced. One can give directions for objective observation, and set down procedures for the rigorous analysis of measurements. But there are only sketchy and inadequate indications which point toward insight, inventiveness, new hypotheses, novel analysis and interpretation. Of its very nature the creative process is obscure, but some aspects of scientific creativity can be discussed.

First of all, creativity is not creation out of nothing. The mind of a scientist is not a blank tablet in any intellectual sense. There is a context, prior information, a state of the question. There are available tools, both mental and instrumental. Research is the art of the soluble, and the context defines the soluble. It is not unexpected, therefore, that simultaneous, independent discoveries of the same novelty occur rather frequently.

In fact, a common and pedestrian example of scientific creativity is the decision to begin or to end a project. The insight into a ripe context, ready tools, a soluble problem, is crucial. Equally crucial is the assessment that a vein of investigation has been played out. It is time to look elsewhere. In a more global sense, every scientist is faced with these same decisions with respect to his own career. The rapid advance of the scientific question carries with it rapid obsolescence. Information, skills, instruments and questions which were pertinent a decade ago may very well be inadequate today. Continual re-education, retooling, the sabbatical, or a change of career, are the price of continued creativity.

Some advances are flashes of insight which are currently unavailable to further analysis. Some are occasioned by definable accidents and serendipitous observations. But there are some tools for discovery which can be used consciously and systematically. First of all, the systematic search pattern can be used to determine the lay of the land and to eliminate possibilities. Second, analogy from other fields, or from previous work, can be a powerful guide. Third, more often than one might like to admit, aesthetic considerations provide the vehicle to novel suggestions. Simplicity, elegance, beauty can characterize an initial hypothesis.

The creative aspect of the scientific method points above all to the active role of the scientist. Routine observation is rarely productive. The scientific process is a dialogue, not a monologue. The scientist listens but also speaks, creates as well as reports. There is an active interior direction to his empiricism. He seeks out selected, pertinent, crucial experience. Manipulative experimentation, focused hypotheses, and model creation are fecund, not rote observation, or quantitative rigor.

A common moral failing related to creativity is the lapse into repetition and triviality. Thoughtless, costly research is a constant threat. On the other hand, the overactive imagination, the facile, hasty fantasy is also known, though it is less common than the pedestrian imagination. The moral demand on the scientist is to be creative but empirical, daring yet rigorous. Science has prospered on the disciplined, reality-oriented imagination, on creativity in the service of empiricism, creativity in the service of rigor. This incredibly powerful and fecund attitude has remade the world.

Commitment. The three strands of empiricism, rigor, and creativity are major aspects of the scientific method. A fourth characteristic of the scientist at work, commitment, lies on a different level, the level of motivation. Scientists are often highly motivated and dedicated to the scientific task. Some scientists, such as M. Curie, show an almost monastic conception of scientific dedication. Previously I spoke of objectivity, here of passionate attachment and commitment. The contradiction is only apparent. Scientists not infrequently show a passionate attachment to objectivity, a driving curiosity, a personal commitment to the search for information and understanding. Objectivity is a tool in the hands of subjectivity.

Science is often said to be value-free. Indeed values do not appear in the publicly available observations and measurements which are the starting point of science. Nonetheless the exercise of the scientific method presupposes and demands values. The significance of, the commitment to, knowledge and learning is presupposed and experienced in the scientific process. Intellectual values such as objectivity, rigor, and creativity are clearly perceived and consciously pursued by the researcher at work. Non-intellectual values such as courage, persistence, altruism, and commitment to a variety of persons and causes accompany and drive the practice of the scientific method. In this sense science is clearly not value-free.

The primary commitment of the scientist may be harmed by some other accompanying commitment when it distorts scientific objectivity, destroys empirical openness, or bends critical judgment in a serious way. Yet non-distorting accompanying commitments are not only tolerable, but even required. If all the personal, economic, social, political, military, medical, moral, and religious motives were removed from scientists, one wonders how much science would be done.

A second moral deformation is an excessive commitment to science. Science is one part of life, and limited in scope. It is not an ultimate concern; it is not a philosophy; it is not a religion. Science cannot support a total commitment. The limits of science are clear from the many things for which science can offer no account. The scientific method, first of all, cannot account for the scientific method itself. Objectivity, rigor, and creativity are not part of the publicly measureable phenomena about which science concerns itself. Creative intelligence is the presupposition, not the product, of science.

Secondly, the scientific method does not account for the experiences which accompany the practice of the scientific method: such as complacency in the elegance of things, and in the elegance of our formulation of things; such as the courage, daring, persistence, and moral demands experienced during the scientific effort; such as the social interactions, affections, fellowships in a common enterprise, and concern for the good and safety of others.

Finally, the scientist himself, the creator of the scientific method, is not accounted for by the scientific method. His dedication and commitment, his freedom to create and pursue knowledge, his free organization of reality in creative technology and invention are not accounted for. His freedom, his responsibility, his uniqueness, and his dignity are not part of the scientific product, but accompany, vivify, and ground the scientific effort.

If there are limits to science, then there are restrictions on science and technology from outside. There are other concerns. Not everything which is good for science is good for the scientist. Not every scientific avenue may be pursued; not every project which is technically feasible may be undertaken. Consequences must be calculated.

One significant concern, one area in which consequences must be taken into account, is the realm of human persons. One must show a moral concern for the manipulation of persons for scientific purposes. The scientist and other humans cannot be treated as the objects of experimentation with as little thought as a piece of coal tar. Graduate students, the workers in chemical and electronic factories, the customers of scientific produce may not be manipulated for the advance of science. The objectification of persons is a temptation which the moral scientist resists. Or he risks becoming such an object himself.

MORAL ASPECTS OF SCIENTIFIC COMMUNICATION

Science is social in character. This is partly due to the magnitude of the scientific task. *Chemical Abstracts*, a journal which carries a few sentences for many of the articles published, printed 62,710 pages in 1975. About 1% of the population in the United States are now called scientists or engineers. Science is also social in the sense that the acceptance and validation of new scientific knowledge is social in character. It is accomplished by the judgment, criticism, and corroboration of one's peers. Not only is science a dialogue with nature, it is a dialogue with other scientists.

Communication is inherent in the social character of the scientific enterprise. The major formal, public, and permanent means of communication is the scientific journal. The rise of the journal is the mark and the condition of the advent of modern science. An important moral aspect of science is the use of the scientific journal. The journal is the major means of access to a significant part of the scientific community. The editor and the referees of articles are the guardians of access to this community. Their fairness, and their tolerance of the unorthodox, the unusual, and the unpopular are of great moral significance. But equally important is the protection of the community from the eccentric, the emotionally-disturbed, from unqualified authors, and sloppy and premature work.

From the point of view of the author, truthfulness and appropriate quality are the most pertinent moral demands. Faked and stolen research occurs. Ulterior motives, such as the "publish or perish" policy of some universities, produce a considerable supply of insignificant, confused, and misleading communication. Scientific publication by means of the newspaper is a more recent and widespread practice. Sensational publication of inchoative, premature work circumvents the validation procedures demanded by ordinary scientific behavior. False expectations, misinformation, and confusion are only some of the evil social consequences which result.

Other moral issues concerned with scientific communication of interest lately are the legitimacy of large-scale, free copying of published materials, and the legitimacy of initiating new journals with no regard for the effect upon the profession.

The issue of secrecy is a sensitive one because the scientific effort feeds on free communication. But there is such a thing as privileged information. The professional secrets of the reviewer and editor, the trade secrets of the industrial chemist are some examples of such information. There is also such a thing as dangerous publication. Responsible men do not give loaded guns to children. But what of the scientists who recently reported a laser-activated method of isotope separation which may allow almost anyone to make his own atom bomb? What about the recent RAND study on alcoholism which in the opinion of some may cause hundreds of deaths by its perhaps unverified conclusions? Should the synthetic organic chemist publish a new synthesis for heroin in such detail that even the technologically inexpert can prepare heroin in his kitchen? Knowledge has consequences, and the consequences of his communication of knowledge places a moral burden on the scientist who publishes.

Industrial secrecy is widespread. The trade secret, scientific information concerning the details of a production process, has often been developed at great cost. To dispense this knowledge freely is unfair and unwise since it destroys the motive for generating such information. We will all be the poorer for it. On the other hand, unshared information also makes us poorer. Patent law and the prosecution of industrial spies and industrial pirates can promote sharing with equitable economic arrangements. Unfortunately, the problem has international political overtones. Since the trade secret can be used as a political weapon, national regulation and international agreements are not yet adequate solutions. The minimization of secrecy is desirable, but until adequate international patent laws and industrial courts are developed, this will not occur.

Scientific secrecy is dangerous. Some of the military secrecy of the past seems to have excluded our own scientific community from information, while the nominal target of the secrecy already possessed the information. Governmental science organizations offer special issues for scientific communication. The governmental scientist often is completely supported by public funds for public projects, and yet retains the information during the pre-publication period in very much the way he would if he were privately supported. The Freedom of Information Act, the personal rights of the scientist to his own efforts, and the rights of the public have not yet been reconciled in a way which is satisfactory.

A final moral issue concerned with scientific communication is the question of scientific protest. Recently a nuclear safety engineer in New York resigned in protest over the safety precautions at the power-producing facility in which he worked. Scientists often uniquely possess specialized information which has public pertinence. This places a special moral responsibility on the scientist to protect the public against economic motives which exert pressure in other directions. Nuclear safety, the plutonium economy, the ABM, pharmaceutical hazards—all represent areas of such responsibility. Of course, public protest is not the first weapon at hand. Internal channels of argument should be preferred. But the leak and public protest may be the only resort in the long run. Public issues are rightly debated in public; public hazards are such public issues.

MORAL ASPECTS OF TECHNOLOGY

That science is power is not a new idea. That power implies moral responsibility for the exercise of that power has not been prominently featured by scientists. Any use of scientific knowledge to manipulate nature may have moral overtones. The simple laboratory hazards such as danger to the eyes, poisoning, fire, explosion, and electrocution are such incidents. But in any discussion of the use of science, the question of the scale of the application assumes unusual importance. A distinction between two kinds of science, public and private, will clarify the discussion. The difference is not precisely that between pure and applied science, between science and engineering, or between academic science and industrial technology, although it is related to all these distinctions. One can define *public* science as that practice of science which is widespread, of prolonged and frequent occurrence, and employing large quantities of materials, such as that practiced in agriculture and industry, and in the military.

Everything else can be called *private* or laboratory science. The distinction is based only on the scope and scale of the application of the science; the two kinds of science differ in a purely factual and extrinsic way.

Any application of science may have moral implications, but public science almost inevitably has a moral dimension because of the large-scale human repercussions. The introduction of gunpowder revolutionized feudal society. Fertilizers, insecticides, and the tractor have made world-wide industrialization and urbanization possible. The internal combustion engine has sharply changed styles of life and warfare, and created suburbanization. The printing press, telephone, radio, television, tape recorder and photocopier have revolutionized the intellectual life, education, and consciousness of the entire world.

Modern public technology has three prominent aspects: the production of new materials; the utilization of new sources of energy and their transformation; and the creation of new devices, instruments, and machines. On this base agriculture and the food industry have been transformed. Insecticides, fertilizers, the tractor, the truck, irrigation methods, and the Green Revolution are one side of it. Nutrition, the large-scale production of proteins, vitamins, and minerals, and the development of refrigeration and packaging techniques, are another. Food additives for the sake of aesthetics, such as Red Dye Number 2, or for the sake of preservation, such as nitrites, are a third. The moral dimension of the world hunger crisis is a related factor.

The medical and pharmaceutical industry is a second aspect of the application of public technology. On the one hand, there are antibiotics and new surgical techniques; on the other, barbiturates, methadone, valium, and thalidomide. The Pill, mass abortion, and genetic research are other morally significant developments in the medical area.

The military applications of technology have revolutionized our world. Hydrogen bombs and intercontinental ballistic missiles, chemical and biological warfare, and electronic games in the skies are now an accepted part of life.

Finally, the communications industry is based upon public technology. The sight of a man on the moon, live pictures from the Mars Lander, and world weather satellites are only special instances of the vast consumer network constructed on the base of electronics. Computational and sorting devices are inevitably changing our styles of computing, accounting, and doing business.

There are many deliberate applications of public technology. But special, unintentional effects occur when public technology reaches a certain scale. If public technology is by definition applied science on a large scale, then an entirely new set of problems arises when public technology reaches the grand scale. There is a qualitative change in the dimension of the moral problem when our manipulation of the environment becomes comparable to the natural forces at work. Our dumping of organic residues in the ocean off New York

City is now comparable to the natural production of carbon in the area. The flow of water through the sewers into the Hudson River is now comparable to the natural flow of the river. The local weather in the neighborhood of large cities is seriously affected by the presence of the cities. The consumption of oil and water in the United States is now comparable to the natural supply. If the perturbation of public technology in the environment is small, the ecosystem handles it in its own way. When the perturbation is large, the finite capacity of the ecosystem may be overreached. Cumulative deformation of the environment occurs. We progressively pollute, introduce new factors, create an entirely new environment. But it is an environment free of human planning, and free of the control of natural forces. It is, precisely, an uncontrolled environment. Eutrophication of our streams and lakes, pollution of our water and air, heavy metal distribution, oxides of sulfur and nitrogen produced in vast quantities, and damage to the ozone layer are merely some of the phenomena currently observed. The thoughtless generation of such effects as byproducts of our public technology is not one of the more moral aspects of our civilization.

Responsibility for Public Technology. Clearly, in the area of public technology one observes a large supply of irresponsible behavior. The allocation of responsibility is complicated by a number of factors. First, there are a number of different sources of public technology. The professionals, the scientist, the engineer, the inventor, obviously have a large share in the introduction of technology. But the practitioner, the farmer, the builder, the soldier, the artisan, have also generated significant parts of public technology.

Secondly, it is not at all clear that all the distant consequences of their novel invention are the moral responsibility of their initiator. The consequences are largely unforeseeable. It is not reasonable to attribute either the good or the evil effects of the public communications system based upon the radio to Marconi. The phenomenon is too large, too collective, too cumulative, to be under the prior control of any one person.

Third, the motives at work in public technology are not exclusively scientific. Science is power, but power never stays in the hand of those who happen to have some intellectual skill. We are dealing not with pure science, but with consumer science, business science, military science, politicized science. Responsibility requires control. The control of public science is mainly out of the hands of the scientist.

Nevertheless, there are moral dimensions to the practice of public technology which can be mentioned here appropriately. Let us initially mention two delusions about the environmental effects of technology. There is the *romantic* delusion. We are told not to try to dominate nature. Play your part in the ecosystem, let nature direct the course of events. Of course, we must cooperate with natural forces, not stampede them. But nature on its own is not kind. It is full of dangers, poisons, smogs, floods, storms, earthquakes, wild animals, parasites, insects, famines. We cannot avoid large-scale manipulation of nature if we are to eat, if we are to avoid the flood, if we are to survive the winter.

There is also the *utopian* delusion. The scientist–king with his comprehensive knowledge and his comprehensive power will order all things rightly. Systems analysis, a source of inexpensive power and modern technology, will save us all. Unfortunately the leader of Utopia who is intelligent enough, wise enough, and good enough to direct such an enterprise is nowhere to be found.

The realistic solution is something else. It is empirical. We must feel our way with caution and modesty. We must experiment, fail, and try again. We must learn continually, improve continually, but maintain a margin of safety, a buffer for error. We must preserve our resources prudently and keep our options open. In contrast to our behavior in the past, we must be perceptive, and monitor what we are doing. Unless we know what is actually the case, wise and moral behavior is impossible.

Responsible public technology requires that we recognize that much of our technology is really a vast experiment. Since we cannot foresee long-term consequences or the individual side-effects of our technology, we are in effect experimenting on the human race and on the ecosystem. We cannot avoid the experiment, but we can conduct it with scientific integrity. We can avoid hasty, ill-considered, or hazardous technological experiments. We can avoid unmonitored, unreported, and unevaluated experiments. If the scientist has a special role in the responsible control of public technology, it is to insist upon the scientific quality of our public experiment. The scientist must shout loudly when non-scientific forces insist upon practicing technological manslaughter.

In addition to the scientific integrity of the practice of public technology, we need a cost–benefit analysis to guide the responsible introduction of new technology. The direct benefits to be conferred by the innovation must be balanced against the direct costs of the procedure, as well as the indirect costs in terms of long-term consequences, and in terms of the depletion of our limited resources. The calculus of consequences must take into account reasonable pretesting, and sophisticated prediction from past experience. It must provide for the monitoring and evaluation of results. Environmental impact and health impact must be a part of the assessment of technological innovation. We must minimize risks and provide insurance for the unforeseen.

The responsible practice of a mature technology requires us to live with uncertainty. Adults accept and live with it. We must also accept the fact that it is an imperfect world. There are no perfect solutions. There is no zero pollution level. There is no solution without a drawback. The best compromise and reasonable effort are all that is required of anyone. Finally, responsible public technology requires that we be willing to pay the price. It is more costly to provide indoor plumbing, but we accept that as part of the necessary cost of building a house. We must accept equally the cost of sewage treatment, the treatment of industrial effluents, and the cost of waste disposal.

It is not enough to insist that our public technology be scientifically competent and mature. It must also be humane. Ultimately technology is for people. At one level, technology can provide the means of economic liberation for our race. At a higher level it can provide the tools for the good life. It is a moral responsibility of us all that technology not be a tool of repression, an invitation to hedonism, or an enemy of culture.

CONCLUSION

The moral effort of the scientist is developmental and social in character. It is not a set of ready-made rules; it is not free of ambiguity and confusion. Nor is it unrealistic or utopian. The scientific moral effort is a challenge, an evolution, a learning and a growing process. It is an education in which areas of concern are successively isolated, and viable solutions gradually elaborated. It is a process which includes failure and reform.

The moral task of the scientist is, in part, a social task. Professional morality is beyond the control of any one individual. Reform of professional practices demands the cooperation of many persons over long periods. But we can all make the effort to leave the profession in a better state than we found it. We can do what is in our power. We can cooperate in the effort to change structures and procedures. We can enter into a social role in the profession where our influence for a just science and technology may be more widespread. In this way ethical scientists will create a just technology for all mankind.